THE WRITINGS OF
WILL ROGERS
IV-5

SPONSORED BY

The Will Rogers Memorial Commission
and Oklahoma State University

THE WRITINGS OF WILL ROGERS

Will Rogers'
Weekly Articles

STEVEN K. GRAGERT, *Editor*

Volume 5

THE HOOVER YEARS:
1931-1933

OKLAHOMA STATE UNIVERSITY PRESS
Stillwater, Oklahoma
1982

Printed in the United States of America
Library of Congress Catalog Card Number 79-57650
International Standard Book Number 0-914956-19-1

CONTENTS

Unless otherwise noted, illustrations courtesy
Will Rogers Memorial, Claremore, Oklahoma

INTRODUCTION

The 1930s witnessed a plethora of social and political commentators, disparate personalities like Walter Winchell, George Bernard Shaw, H. L. Mencken, and Father Charles E. Coughlin. Unique among them was Will Rogers, a man born and reared as a cowboy in Indian Territory who, through his philosophy and humor, emerged in his adult years as a leading proponent of traditional American values. A keenly insightful individual, Rogers took to the stage, the screen, the broadcasting studio, and the printed page to offer perceptive, humorous comments on politics, world events, the social scene, public figures, economics, and countless other topics. A roper from his youth, Rogers spun his beloved humor as expertly as he did his well-used riata, and seldom in either instance did he miss his target.

Perhaps Rogers' best-known vehicles for his wit and wisdom were his syndicated newspaper columns. A prolific writer, he provided newspaper readers throughout the country with a daily dosage of his popular sayings. His so-called "daily telegrams" appeared almost every day, save Sunday, from 1926 until his death in 1935. Older and lengthier than the daily columns were his weekly newspaper features, which first appeared in December of 1922 and continued until his death. Indeed, the last recorded words of Rogers are contained in a weekly article that he was typing during his ill-fated flight to Point Barrow, Alaska, on August 15, 1935.

The present book, *Weekly Articles: The Hoover Years, 1931-1933*, is the fifth of a six-volume collection of Rogers' weekly newspaper columns. It also comprises the fifteenth volume in a projected comprehensive twenty-one-volume edition of *The Writings of Will Rogers*, a literary and historical project sponsored by Oklahoma State University in conjunction with the Will Rogers Memorial Commission of the state of Oklahoma. Volume five of the *Weekly Articles* continues the series through the final two years of the administration of President Herbert C. Hoover and through some of the bleakest moments of the Great Depression. The length and range of his weekly column allowed Rogers to take an in-depth look at the world around him—and the articles in this volume reveal that he was profoundly touched by what he saw and felt.

Followers of our series will find the format in the present volume familiar. No changes of a substantive nature have been made. New readers may want to refer to the introduction in the first volume of the *Weekly Articles*, wherein we described and explained at length the editorial procedures employed in producing these books. As in our previous efforts, we have limited our editorial remarks and annotations in order that the finished work be as purely Rogers and as uncluttered as possible. We have used his original manuscripts where they have been available. In all other cases we have used copy from the agency that syndicated Rogers' material or have chosen from the *Tulsa Daily World* or other reliable newspapers that carried his columns.

Several individuals have made invaluable contributions to the production of this and other volumes of *The Writings of Will Rogers*. Especially appreciated has been the work of Dr. James M. Smallwood, associate professor of history at Oklahoma State University and immediate past director and editor of the Will Rogers Project. As director he successfully guided the project through a critical stage in its work, during which the entire series of the *Daily Telegrams* and one-half of the *Weekly Articles* volumes were published. On behalf of the staff of the project, I express our sincerest gratitude for his past untiring efforts and his continuing conscientious concern in our work.

Other persons have also played significant roles in the work of the project. Dr. Reba Neighbors Collins, director of the Will Rogers Memorial at Claremore, Oklahoma, greatly facilitated our work by her and her staff's courteous and generous cooperation. From the memorial we obtained manuscripts, photographs, and other materials for inclusion in these volumes. Dr. Collins gave freely of her time to proofread the annotations to this volume and to offer insightful advice on the improvement of the same. I add, however, that neither she nor anyone else, other than the present editor, should be held accountable for any weaknesses found herein.

I am also grateful to the president of Oklahoma State University, Dr. Lawrence L. Boger, and his predecessor, Dr. Robert B. Kamm, who have endorsed and supported the project fully as have Dr. George A. Gries, chairman of the Will Rogers Advisory Committee at Oklahoma State University, and Dr. Smith L. Holt, dean of the College of Arts and Sciences. Dr. W. David Baird, chairman of the Department of History and a member of the advisory board, has been most generous and helpful in his attention to the continued success of the project. The demanding work of typing and retyping countless drafts revised often over several months was performed patiently and efficiently by Ms. Kelli Cottrell, secretary for the project.

Special recognition is also accorded the continued support and assistance of the regents and administration of Oklahoma State University, the Department of History, the Will Rogers Advisory Committee, the Edmon Low Library at the university, the Oklahoma Historical Society, and the Legislature of Oklahoma. Earlier in the history of the project, the Kerr-McGee Foundation, the Phillips Petroleum Corporation, Mrs. T. S. Loffland, Mr. Sylvan Goldman, and the late Mr. and Mrs. Robert W. Love provided valuable assistance. To each I am deeply grateful.

Finally, I am most indebted to Judy Buchholz of Oklahoma State University Press who has, without any desire for personal recognition, worked hard to make these volumes as accurate and useful as possible.

Steven K. Gragert
Editor

WEEKLY ARTICLES
1931-1933

428   ## CONGRESS, REVOLUTION
        ## AND DROUTH

Well all I know is just what I read in the papers. I got back home and am working in the Movies and have a little time in between scenes to kinder see what is going on here and there. You know that King of Spain is quite a fellow.[1] They been trying to oust him these Republicans have for years and just when it looks like he was a goner why he comes up again. They ain't going to get rid of that fellow. In fact I doubt if they could improve on him.

Governments don't have much to do with Nations anyhow, their importance is greatly overrated. The real business of a country is carryied on no matter what King or Emperor, or Dictator or Chief, or President. Even us over here we raise all the fuss and mess around over whether it will be a Republican or a Democrat, and one hundred and twenty million have to make their living under either one of them and it don't matter much. It's the people of a Country that have to change and not the Governments, and they don't change much, so what's the use of worrying. The whole thing is a lot of Apple sauce.

We have lived under over thirty Presidents. They couldent have all been great, in fact if we told the truth about 'em, maby some of 'em was pretty punk. But we drug along in spite of 'em.

Look at the Frenchmen. They look like to us they do everything Cockeyed. Their House of Deputies looks like a Keystone Comedy Company, yet with all their excitement they have made the finest recovery from the war of any of the others. The staid old Britisher that we think does everything just about right, why he is having his toughest sledding right now. Who would think they could ever mishandle their affairs. Yet they will recover, and in five years you won't know 'em. It's conditions that work 'em out, it's not people worrying about 'em.

Paraguay, or Uraguay, or some of those Guys, are having a home talent riot. But their don't seem to be many of their population mixed up in it, most of their people are busy making a living. In Peru some ambitious fellow has got ahold of some amunition, and he is trying to trade it for their White House. But it don't matter much. You take one of those Countries without a Revolution is kinder like us without some hard times to holler about. We just got to have it.

Prince of Wales is prowling around down there now.² He is drumming up some trade for the Empire, and I bet does a fine job of it. There is one prospective Monarch that really makes himself useful to his Country. He is the best add any country has, and he is not too high hat to practically admit that that is why he makes the trips. He knows we are living in a Commercial and synthetic age, and he has to make the most of it. His samples is his personality, backed by the methodical workmanship of the British craftsman. Course he will play a little Golf, but he will pick out some Guy to play with, (and perhaps let him beat him,) some Bird ahead of some Industry that is in the market for an awful lot of things that England make. So he is a mighty sensible and useful young man.

As I write this it's just a day or so before that Congress of ours is supposed to go home. Now whether they will do it or not, the Lord himself only knows. Course they have the prayers of a Nation being offered up in favor of a home coming for the whole mess. But there has been better ones than this that we couldent jarr loose from. I believe the Rascals meant well at this session. They really wanted to help the people, but as usual dident know how.

So it's not really intention on the Government's part that they don't do better, it's ignorance. You see every fellow looks at things from his particular part of the Country. He can't see what might be the condition in some other part.

Now take this Drouth affair down South. Those people were called Farmers. Well they were farmers, they made what little living they ever got out of the soil, so they are certainly entitled to be called Farmers, but they were not the Farmers that the east and the north have been accustomed to look on as they drive by. It's not the big red barns, the cows, the Pigs, the Chickens, the big fat work horses. During all this hardship, its the Renter Farmer, the "Share Cropper." A man that on a cotton Plantation tends ten acres, that is if he uses one Mule. He is called the One mule cropper, or the two mule cropper. He lives in a little box house, generally two rooms and a lean too. They are eternally in debt to the Land owner who generally owns the store or if he don't the local Merchant. That one share of that one little crop has got to keep them for the whole year. They buy everything they eat. They are going too, the Red Cross and the County Agents are, of making each land owner give them about a half acre and put in a garden, that will help a tremendous lot. There is nothing they can work at during the time they are not putting in or tending their cotton.

Those little few bales of cotton that he gets as his share has to pay his whole previous year's Grocery, and other merchandise bills. Now how in the world can he have a cent left. He hasent, he is in debt. Then add a drouth to that, where he don't raise anything, then what happened. The Store man was practically broke along with him. The land owner who also deals just from year to year, he was broke, so picture the condition yourself. No work to be had, no food to be bought, no seed to plant.

Now whose fault is it. It ain't anybody's fault. If it is, it ain't his, he has done the best he knew how. He is tending to his business the same as his Father and Grand Father did before him. Rich men, educated men, on Wall Street and in all big Businesses were perhaps carrying on their Father's business in what they had always thought was a safe and sane way, yet look what happened to them. Look what happened to everybody. The smart the crafty, the schrewd, they all got it, only they had somebody who would help 'em. These people had nobody, their friends were the same as they were. I was raised on a Farm and Ranch combined, was raised where they had Renter Farmers, and I have always conscientiously believed that a poor share crop renter was the poorest and least provided for man in this or any other Country, and the Cotton renter is just half again poorer than this wheat or Corn renter, so you see what shape he is in. The man in the City that has to live in the slums with his family, but he gets something every day for his work, he has something to show for it every week, he knows what he is making, he knows what he is spending. He has his little money, he can buy where he can find it's the cheapest. This poor renter has to stay with the same merchant for the year even if he is overcharged. Then they tell me some of you havent raised your Red Cross Quota. Well all I hope is you are never a Renter farmer.

429   CONGRESS IS THROUGH BUT BUTLER AIN'T

Well all I know is just what I read in the Papers. Of course the most assuring news of the past couple of weeks was the adjourning of Congress. That wasent only news, that was an achievement. It looked for awhile there that the Boys were going to be on our hands from now on. They sure did get rid of a batch of dough, the most money ever appropriated by any Congress, not even excepting war times. All we have to do is make it for 'em and they sure do distribute it.

Of course as usual in the last minutes of congress why they dident pass any of the bills that they should have passed, and did pass all that they shoulent. Now take the Lame Duck Bill, that's the one where they want to do away with electing a man one year and have him seated on his first Grandchild's Birthday. Senator Norris had a mighty good Bill in there to do away with that very Lame Duck term.[1] Well the House voted it, and the Senate voted it, but one made a slight change from what the other had passed, so that meant that it had to go to what is called conference, (that's one of the things that Golf Players are always in when you go to their office). Well do you know as bad as the country wanted this Bill passed so that Congress would meet on the fourth of January, instead of waiting till the fourth of December, and the President was to be innaugarted on January the 14th, just a little over two months after he had been elected, that would have done away with the plan of what to do with our presidents after the time they are elected and before they are seated.

You see it's awful embarrassing the way it is, the President that is in kinder feels like a has been, after they have elected some one else. So that was all remedied, and then they go into this Huddle in Conference and they don't get it threshed out in time to get it passed. There was dozens of 'em like that. But it was such a relief to get 'em away that we all felt mighty grateful.

Everybody says that things are kinder picking up, but you ask the fellow Do you mean that you are doing better, and he will say, "No, personally I am not, but everyone I meet seems to have a little better feeling about everything. But you just can't find the fellow that is doing better. Sometimes I think we are just talking better, we ain't doing any better. But we don't have to do better. We can just keep on doing as well as we can and still be O.K. That's because we are getting used to it. It's knocked some of those big schemes out of us that we all used to bore everybody with."

Well let's see what else has been agitating the Natives here lately. Soldiers are getting their insurance money.[2] Course it is fine to get it, the only thing is, how do you know there won't be a time later on when you will need it worse than you do now. You know we are never as bad off as we are liable to get. Along about 1945 when that would be coming due in full, you would just be that much older, and less able to be working. But every fellow has got to figure his own case out his own way. But I hope none of them are led on by a lot of friends that just want to see 'em have the money now because it is there for 'em. We would all like to take our Insurance money and spend it, and it's mighty hard not to, but we got to figure that later on it will come in handier than even now.

I was glad to see Smedley Butler get out of his case as he did.[3] You know that fellow just belongs in a war all the time. He don't belong in Peace time. He is what I would call a natural born Warrior. He will fight anybody, anytime. But he just can't distinguish Peace from war. He carries every medal we ever gave out. He has two Congressional Medals of Honor, the only man that ever got another one. I don't know him, never met him. But I do admire him. He is a mighty useful man in a war, and as we are always having 'em why I consider him a very valuable man.

We are liable to scare him up something before long. We are looking around now to see where we can get in one worth while someplace. Even our Scouts for the Marines are having trouble locating places for them to go, this is about the first time that they havent been employed. We are even getting tired of continually fighting with Nicaraguans. We always have to take them on when there is no bigger bait. But I see where we are supposed to come out of there.

What other scandal we got? Oh yes Aimee's daughter married the Purser on the boat that they went to the Orient on.[4] I kinder thought Aimee would grab off that Captain, but she dident. Right here under our nose at the Old Soldiers Home, in Sawtelle, they had forty hit by that "Jake" paralysis.[5] That's the disease that originally started in Oklahoma, and was incidentally cured or helped at Claremore, by the Radium Baths. Where is our laws in these Drug Stores that they let 'em sell stuff like that?

We sure do miss Mr Einstein out here.[6] He was supposed to come here for a rest and wanted to be let alone. Why my goodness, he just went out of his way to find something to go to, and Pictures? Why he would go searching for a Camera man if none was around. He sure did make himself a good fellow. He seemed to be a mighty pleasant little fellow.

This writing is going to be mighty tough with no Congress to pick on. I joke about 'em, but you know at heart I really like the Rascals. They are all right. If one wants to do right, our political system is so arranged that he can't do it. The minute one wants to do what no one else has been accustomed to do, why they call him an Anarchist. Some of the old timers stepped out at the close of this one and that was kinder sad in a way. It must be a mighty fascinating game on those old fellows and it's tough to have to bow out of the picture, and mighty few retire rich, so there must be a lot more honesty among them than we give them credit for. Well so long let's see what the new week brings forth.

WILL SEES TROUBLE
OVER PROHIBITION

Well all I know is just what I read in the papers. And I don't mind telling you that since Congress has adjourned, I am not able to pick up much Scandal. Course they left an awful lot of Investigations to be carried on during the summer, for they had to have some place to go. They call it "Junketing." That's getting a trip at Government expense. They investigate everything from Bird life to pre-historic Mamals and radio wave lengths.

Mr. Hoover seems to be doing a little better since he got rid of the Gang.[1] A President just can't make much showing against that Mob. They just lay awake nights thinking up things to be against the President on.

Work all around the Country is kinder "picking up." Los Angeles voted five million the other day to be spent right away putting men to work on street and municipal improvements and most towns have done the same. We are liable to run into some pretty good times this summer just accidentally. Of course the big time is going to be in '32. That's the year of election and as I have always told you the Republicans see that things are fine on election years. Oh I guess in the long run this whole thing has been good for us. I believe we all got a little more common sense than we had before, we are kinder more down to earth.

In the old days we had had good times so long that we dident think anything could happen. Now we know it can, and we will be sorter watching for it in the future. We won't let it sneak up on us again.

Well a couple of weeks ago the Democrats had a preliminary row. This one was just a rehearsal for the big one. It had nothing to do with anything in particular. They just decided to meet, and did, and when they did, Wow. It was a foolish kind of a thing as most rows are. Raskob is supposed to be head of the Gang, and there is a lot of opposition to him that has been held over since last election.[2]

They seem to think that he, on account of his money and personal friendship for Al, is trying to run everything.[3] I don't hardly think it's that way at all. He just wanted to make a suggestion, and did. Well you wouldent think that would cause a row would you? Yes, but look what the suggestion was. It was on prohibition. Well that was the Skunk that they dident want to let out of the bag till they had too. Of course both sides would like to see the whole thing buried till after election, but there is a big gang on both sides that just make life miserable for the ones that don't want it mentioned. Some speaker gets up and says, "Ladies and Gentlemen, I want to speak to you on the economic problems of the day." "Never mind the problems of the day, What about Prohibition?" And they make life miserable for the poor Devil from then on.

Well the Democrats met in Washington to try and dig up ways and means to get enough dough to carry on another Campaign. They had just called the gathering to order, and said, "We will take up the business of the meeting," and somebody blated out, "What about Prohibition?" And oratory, denunciations, threats, and almost mayhem was committed before they could get the house to order. Then to add to the dog-fight, Mr. Raskob got up and delivered himself of a speech that he had been cooking up all winter. He told 'em it was just his idea and that it wasent in the nature of an Amendment, it was made just as a personal suggestion. Well that dident matter what it was made as, it could have been told as a dream, or a fairy story. The minute it was told, Democratic bedlam (by the way what is bedlam anyhow?) well, it broke loose. It always does when anybody is writing about something that comes up quick. My mighty good friend Joe Robinson was on his heels in a jiffy.[4] Joe was for party harmony, and he knew there could be no harmony when the mention of Prohibition had been allowed to perculate. Course Joe was right. It shouldent have been among anything that had anything to do with harmony, cause harmony and Prohibition is two things that just won't jibe. (Say what's that jibe mean, I always hear it used at places like this, so I know it is used right, but what I mean is what is it?) Well there was a lot of support for Joe and his arguments "to not start anything that would be an argument."

Well that was fine till another gentleman arose. You would think that up to now you either had to be on one side or the other. You wouldent have thought there was another side would you? But there was, and that was the one Al Smith was on. He said, "What is Democracy? I thought it was to discuss whatever anyone wanted to bring up. When did we get so that it was a crime for anyone to mention certain subjects?" He just wanted to fix it so they would be arguing there all the rest of the summer. He really dident speak for or against, but he did speak for arguments sake. He wanted to see the whole thing dragged out and start the split in the Democratic Party right away. He couldent see any use in waiting till voting time to split.

But they finally got the thing kinder half way straightened out and then somebody proposed that they raise six million dollars for the coming campaign. Well that flabbergasted not only one side like Prohibition had, but all of 'em. Six million for the Democrats? Why they were becoming Republicansized over night. If they had six million they wouldent want the Presidency. Where was they going to get it? Nobody knew any more about that than they did about where was prohibition coming from. But they decided it was a good fantastic idea, so they are now on the search of it, and the Republicans all laughed and had a lot of fun at the Democrats' plight, cause they are so united on the subject of prohibition.

They can't even find out how Hoover stands, much less the rank and file of the voters. But ain't it wonderful to have something come up in a country where you can find out just how many Political cowards there are?

431   CHINA INVENTED EVERYTHING

Well all I know is just what I read in the papers. But tonight I found out a lot of things without reading 'em. Bill, our eldest White Hope had a friend that had just come back from some expedition over in China with some College Boys, from Pomona College, of Pomona, Cal.[1] And say, by the way that is one of the best Colleges in this whole Country, they are constantly grooming it for "The Oxford of America."

Well these boys had taken a lot of Movies of their trip and he just brought 'em up to the Ranch tonight and run them, and he told us a lot about China. Well China was having some Liquor Pains, and they decided that the trouble with the Country was that the Officials of the Government was doing too much drinking. So they passed 'em an Amendment, just exactly two thousand years before Andy Volstead got his brilliant idea.[2] So they passed it to keep the Officials from drinking, then nobody would be an Official, they would rather have the drink than the job.

So they not having a Democratic and Republican Party that was both afraid to say where they stood, in those days you stood where you stood. So they started in having trouble with Bootleggers. Just think of that, and here we thought we had the original Bootlegger problem.

Well along come the "Progressives" and held a Convention and decided to amend the Constitution, and put Liquor back with Rice as a National Commodity. So China really had all this fuss that we are having away back before Confucious time. That old Confucious must have been quite a fellow, he was so smart they are just now figureing out what he really meant. But he dident get so far in his day, he had to die to make the Boys believe it. It don't do a fellow much good to be too far ahead of his time. It's better that he be a little Dumber and stay along with the times.

He showed us Movies of that great Chinese wall. It was a good deal like the ones the Republicans erected last year by the Architects, Hawley and Reed Smoot.[3] China wanted to keep out her enemies, and Smoot and Hawley wanted to keep out our friends, and also keep our stuff in.

We keep out everything, unless it is owned by some rich Americans that want to bring it in, then the tarriff don't hold. Take oil for instance. You can't bring in wheat, corn, cotton, or any of those in competition with our own, but Oil, you can. You can bring it in from Venzeula, or any other place, and knock ours out. Why? Well that's because it's owned by Americans who are richer and more influential than the ones that have Independant oil Companies over here, but no foreign oil.

Our Alabi is that "It is saving our Oil." That's just like shipping in foreign Autos, saying we want to save the ones we make, they might all wear out. But never mind that. That won't be changed as long as the Republicans stay in there, so we better just let that drop.

This Boy said that China about two or three hundred A. D. (After Democrats) that China had the first League of Nations, that China was a lot of small Nations, and that they formed an exact League of Nations like the one that had the 14 points, and Lodge dident like any of em.[4] Well they decided that that would be a good way to prevent war, they first got the two biggest ones to sign it, saying they wouldent fight each other. But they dident say that they wouldent join together and fight somebody else, so that scared the little ones till they thought they had to join for protection, and they all met and made out a Covenant, and it worked for a little while till they all got back on their feet from the last war and got armed for the next one, then some Lawyer found a flaw in it, and his country, which was one of the original signers, and the big one, they went out and defended their honor against some small ones, till they took 'em over, and the breaking up of the League of Chinese Nations was the start of the Chinese Empire. The League worked fine till they found out that the only way you can annex more territory is not by purchase, but by war.

Now Morrow has gone over to Europe to tell England and France and Italy that the Treaty they made with each other is Null and void, so far as we are concerned.[5] See a lawyer has found a flaw in it. So from what I hear folks say and what I read, it just looks like

China had the original idea of about everything that we had ever done and thought it was new.

Photography was one of theirs, so they are really responsible for Hollywood Printing, Gunpowder, Kimonas, Pajamas in the day time, worn by both men and Women. This Boy says that most all the Revolutionary trouble over there starts in the Colleges among the Students. Well ours over here does too, but one good Cop with a Club can generally quell it.

It's funny how quick a College Boy can find out that the World is wrong. He might go out in the World from High School and live in it, and make a living in it for years and think it wasent such a bad place, but let him go to College and he will be the first one down on the Square on May Day to shout down with the Government. Course not all of 'em, but there is getting more and more, but soon as they grow up and go out and if they happen to make anything why they backslide, and he says it the same over there.

Well one great thing about China they don't bother nobody but themselvs. They sure don't go off hunting trouble like all us "Civilized" Nations Commission some time (that goes all over the world to investigate everybody's business) and go see it.

432   HOOVER, CHAPLIN AND THE PRINCE GO TOURING

Well all I know is just what I read in the papers. Well Mr Hoover got back from a part of the country he had never been in till he was President. It's awful hard for Mr Hoover to find new places to go after election, for he has traveled so much.[1] But he manages to find some. They was going to try a Battleship to see if it would work after they had had it renovated, so he just says, "Here is the time for me to get away from all this mess."

So he picked him out a bunch of congenial friends, mostly standpat Republicans and joined the Navy and started seeing the World. It dident used to be hard to find some place for Coolidge to go where he had never been, all you had to do was just to suggest any one of the forty eight States outside of Vermont and Massachusetts, and he was all set for new territory.[2]

When he set sail for Black knolls of South Dakota, why that compared in importance to him to Hoover leaving for Mary Bird Land in the Anartic. Mr Coolidge did make Cuba one time. I was there at the time, and saw it and he got a great welcome too. But Mr

Hoover went on and found the Virgin Islands. A good many people thought such a place as that was a myth, but he went there and found it really. People nowadays call these "Good will tours." But you can't get people's good will nowadays unless you bring 'em something. He took 'em a speech but no donations. So outside of what fish he got on the trip, it's kinder hard to figure out just the exact benefitiary results. He told 'em that he wanted to give every one of them the same as we had up here. Well that depends on how well posted they are on what is happening to us, how they took that remark. In other words if they took him at his word, and wanted what we got, they would immediately ask for Red Cross relief. But I think it was a mighty fine trip for him to have taken, and it will do a lot of good. Roosevelt went down there when he was President, and everything he did was O K, so I know this must have been.[3]

Well what else we got? Did you ever read such a procession of acclaim as Charley Chaplin is making all over Europe?[4] Why Charley don't any more than land in a Country till the Prime Minister grabs him off to his home, like some Movie fan asking for an Autograph. Charley is pretty foxy though, and mighty well informed on affairs. He can talk and argue with them. He is a pretty rabid Socialist, and has made a pretty serious study of it.

One night a few years ago I was asked to introduce him at the Lambs Club in New York, that's the most exclusive Actor organization. It was his first trip to New York in a good while and he was having some unfavorable Newspaper publicity at the time. Well I told them that in all my little years on the Stage and screen that I had only met one person that I could honestly call an "Artist," every other person I ever saw, some one else could do what he was doing just as good, and that it was all a trick, and not real genius. But that Chaplin was all that these Real so called Artists was supposed to be. And he is, he is the only genius developed in the films since they started. Any of us can get "Artistic" and say we won't work till noon, or won't do this or that. But we are doing it on some firm's money, but Chaplin can come on his set, and turn loose 500 people, tell 'em he will call 'em again some other time, and he is doing it on his dough. Art ain't put on when you are paying for it out of your own pocket. He writes, directs, and acts the whole thing. Any one else making a picture there is at least a dozen people that are directly concerned in its success. Chaplin replaces all of them alone.

No, whether you like him or not, (and how you couldent I don't know) but he is one of the few Geniuses developed during our time in any line. So all this Hooy is not wasted on some Bird that don't deserve it. The Prince of Wales (who is quite a fellow himself, and

11

done some prowling around the world) why a Zulu wouldnt know him from Senator Borah although he is the best known man in the World.⁵ But the old Zulu would sure pick you out Charley in his Derby and big "Dogs."

Say what's going to happen to this wheat thing? The Government bought up a lot of last year's crop, and now they got it, and here is coming along another new crop. Borah wants to give it to China to make rice out of. I would like to see it given to renter farmers in this Country to make bread out of. You'd be surprised if you knew how little those poor people had to live on that was issued by the Red Cross. They did marvelous work as usual the Red Cross, but what I mean is if the same thing come up again, I sure would like to see 'em have enough more money so the issue of rations would be larger. Of course when you are getting Charity you can't be the chooser, but it was barley enough to get along on. Now why can't something be done with some of all this surplus wheat? We are going to have to charge that Farm board's operations off as a loss anyhow it looks like now.⁶ Course I guess they did what they thought was right. But people can raise things faster in this Country than anybody can buy it, even the Government.

Say did you read in the papers about a bunch of Women up in British Columbia as a protest against high taxes, sit out in the open naked, and they wouldent put their clothes on? The authorities finally turned Sprayer that you use on trees, on 'em. That may lead into quite a thing. Woman comes into the tax office nude, saying I won't pay. Well they can't search her and get anything. It sounds great. How far is it to British Columbia?

433 WILL PAYS HIGH TRIBUTE TO ROCKNE

Well all I know is just what I read in the papers. Been so much calamity here the last week or so that it's hard to dig much cheerful nourishment out of the news prints. Poor Knute Rockne so upset everybody that we just can't get over it, especially those of us who had the good fortune to know him.¹ The more you think of him the more remarkable he becomes. I used to go out on one night stand so called Concert Tours, and I always used to play South Bend, and there would be a bunch of the Boys down to my little Lecture. Well the minute I would hit town He would be down to the Hotel and I would be with him most of the day, go out to the school, and if it was anywhere around football time, I would see them work out, and when

I say them, I mean them, there would be literally hundreds of 'em on all the teams togeather.

You know he dident just have the big team and the Scrubs, he had dozens of 'em, Domitory teams, class teams. Every kind of team, all but Fraternity teams, they don't have them there. They have got some kind of a preparatory school there too I guess, for he showed me practicing one time a bunch of little kids, and he would show me how they had all his plays.

He said, "If some Coach was smart enough, he would come here and watch these little kids work out and he would get every play I've got. I have secret practice, to try out my new formations and there won't seem to be a soul in the place, but you come out here the next day and you will see them running through the same ones I had the Varsity working on the day before. They sneak in here away ahead and hide in the most outlandish places, under the stands, the seats, and everywhere and they all try to copy my Stars, they try to walk like 'em, talk like 'em, copy all their little mannerisms. Two of them had a fight over which one was Struldrehr.[2] I will always have pretty good material as long as they study the fine points of the game that early."

Then down at the Theatre that night where I was playing I would get him up on the stage, and also all the team, and it would always be a great night and also day for me. Just to be around him was a treat. He had developed into one of the best after dinner Speakers in this country. He had a great fund of humor, and storys of real happenings and he had so much sincerity in his talks, he really made you believe it. I can easily understand how those Boys played their heads off for him. He sure did inspire confidence.

I think his greatest feat was his last game, that was out here with University of Southern California. Here we thought out here we had the greatest team that ever represented the coast, tremendous Stadium filled, Notre Dame hadent lost a game in two years, and this was their last, it was the last for a lot of their big Stars who were graduating. Rockne was touted to lose. The night before over the radio he admitted that he dident have much of a chance. "Savoldi is out; he was our mainstay.[3] Then on the way out we lost our fullback by illness. We have gone through a tough season, and we just couldent stay on edge so long. The Boys had to have a let down. I have asked too much of them this season with the terrible schedule they had, and it just is not in human beings to keep up their pace till now. We have got to lose, and we want to lose to you in preference to anybody else. It's a long train trip out here. It's much warmer here than back home, and the heat is against the boys, but we will just give you the best we got. But I don't possibly see how we can win, in the shape we are in."

Now what other coach on earth could give such a straightforward talk as that, and not have every word swallowed hook, line and sinker? Then get this last line he gave us that night before, "Now there is going to be a lot of heart-aches tomorrow afternoon after that game. Great big strong young men are coming into the dressing rooms and break down and cry. But my boys can take it a little easier because they don't expect to win, they have steeled themselvs to the defeat."

Well here we are all packed in the stands, really pitying those poor boys from back there, and hoping that the California boys wouldent seriously hurt any of them running over them on the way to the goal posts. Well on the very first play California fumbled. Well from then on it was just too bad. You never saw a team beaten so cool and deliberate like. Notre Dame huddled for a change, and when they come out of it they would walk as slow to their places, and that got poor Cal's goat. They finished by Notre Dame beating them 27-0. It wasent the score, it was the deliberate and mechanical way they did it, it was a machine doing things where the others were trying with their hands.

And here was a great thing he did, as each one of his Stars that would be taken out of the game in the last half and it was their last game for Notre Dame, he would jump up from the bench and go out and meet him and hug him, you could just see the affection that he had for each one, and it was conveyed to that whole audience. I will never forget when little Carideo, (perhaps the greatest field General that every played football) left the field.[4] He had played a whale of a game, handled his team uncanny. There is a lot of drama in a player like that leaving the field for his last time as a College player. I think Rockne pulled him out just to get him that great hand as he left the Stadium. Well when old "Rock" went out and put his arms around that little Carideo and walked him off the field, it wasnt an ovation, it was hurricane.

We dident know then what we was looking at. We thought it was the exit of another great Quarterback. But we was looking at the exit of Knute Rockne. He was hugging his last Player, fine young men all over the U.S. can feel back and cherish the hug they got on their last game from "Rock." But it was little Carideo that got the last hug. Here he was right on the crest. He had beaten the Coast's great team for a two year no defeat record for Notre Dame. But the whole of California loved him, for that night on the radio he apologised for the size of the score and said, "I had to make it big for Coach Jones will make it bigger than that against me next year."[5] He coached Notre Dame Stars in Charity games once or twice after that. But this was his last real Notre Dame scheduled game.

One lone Ranch Hand in Kansas was supposed to have been the sole witness to his passing. But that's not so, eighty thousand of us saw his passing out, his last game, and it will stick with us through life.

434   WILL'S CAREER GETS IN HIS WAY

Well, all I know is just what I read in the papers, or what I see as I prowl from here to there. Everytime I get a new picture finished why I kinder feel the itch to get out to some new place or make some sort of a little trip. Well, away a couple of weeks ago, we had finished, "As Young As You Feel," based on George Ade's old play, "Father And The Boys."[1]

I was going to take a little trip off down in Central America, and then they kept me at home for fear there might be some retakes on it. You know when we get one made we then take them out and show 'em, sometimes at a couple of different towns to see if they are fit to release, and sometimes we have to change something to make some new scenes. So I couldent get away on my trip.

The way I had it planned I would have been in Managua, Nicaragua, on the day after the quake, was going to stop over and see what the Marines was doing down there, and I would have been on the spot for quite a little news, for they sure have had it down there.[2]

Well, we took the thing out and tried it in San Bernardino, California, and the customers giggled quite a bit, so that let me get away. They said, the director and the studio officials that they didn't think we could make it any worse if we tried, so I jumped on the old aerial rattler, and left from there. Honest if people knew how fast and comfortable and safe it is on a Plane they would never travel any other way.

I left Los Angeles from over in San Fernando valley on the American Airways just at daybreak on Easter morning. They were having Easter sunrise service in the Hollywood Bowl. California goes in great for that Gag. Well it was so misty and foggy this morning, they might have got up before daylight and parked two miles away from the place. For I never saw as many cars in one place in my life. But they never had any sunrise service, for no one but an Aerial Magician could have told when the sun did rise on that day. Old

California fell down on 'em. It was so misty and foggy that we dident think we could get away, but these Planes all have radio now, so they got word that there was fine weather all along the line.

You know this radio has made it mighty fine to find out about what's ahead. You see it's never the weather you take off in it's the weather where you have to go through after you take off. I remember one trip on our late tour with Captain Frank Hawkes when we took off one day in a snow storm in New Mexico when you just couldent see a thing, not two hundred feet, and it was that way flying blind for the next hour, but he had heard before that it was clear in Albuquerque where we were going.[3] So it's how is the weather ahead of you than how it is where you are.

Well the Sunrise bunch dident get much started that day I am afraid. You know California can get more people into something free than any place on earth. Course that particular thing was a very meritorious cause, and is a good idea if you live in a country where you can depend on the weather. This thing is just a big boxed-in Canyon, that they call the Bowl, and they have had some mighty fine things there. It's a sort of a Moses on the Mount idea. We out in Hollywood take all the Bible things and improve on 'em, make 'em bigger. Now Moses when he read his Amendments dident have thousands of cars parked around, and he dident advertise how many he could seat on the sage brush on the hillside. But we did out there. We just don't go in for little things.

Now take the Lord's supper that has never interested our Movie producers, for there was not enough Guests there. It was a Stag affair, and that wouldent mean much to the Producers. We did however put on the Prodigal Son's return, course we changed the name on account of that one not being very well known and Hollywood called the Story, "Sonnyboy returns to his first love," and the place they had him return to was bigger than all Judea combined. We just do 'em big out that way, and the eastern Tourist out there expect it. California can't do anything natural, they won't believe it.

But it's a great old place, and we get as much fun out of it as if we believed it all ourselvs. Speaking of services and religious gatherings why we been missing Aimee lately.[4] She is away off prowling around some place and we can't hardly figure her out. Her church is running, but it without Aimee is like the modern girls without her lipstick, it just ain't her at all.

With Aimee away for all this stretch, and Clara Bow on her best behavior and me behaving myself, why there just is not much scandal out there at all.[5] Doug Fairbanks is over in India getting even with some tigers, but anybody that knows Doug knows that he never

16

hunted in his life.[6] He never shot anything, but if he can come back with some pictures with the right foot up on the neck of a dead tiger or elephant why it will be all right.

Mary is kinder ranting around.[7] There is some club out there called the Mayfair, that has some sort of a shindig every week, and they put on fights, I mean impromptu fights, people get mad at each other after they get there, and they always open and close their dance with a fight. Well, we have all been shocked to death to find Mary among (not the fighters) but among the guests. She has a ringside table at every public brawl they have. Doug has got to come home and put her to work, keep her out of devilment.

Chick Sale is out our way.[8] I am figuring with him to put me in one up at the ranch. He is working out the design now. You would be surprised the trade that he has, he has just practically quit acting, and is specializing entirely. It was too bad; he is a fine comedian, too, one of the best that ever left the stage.

But this new work is high class, and not hard. It's mostly just consulting, and working out architectural plans. I wish I could hit on some side line that would stop me having to just keep digging away day after day. It's certainly made a fortune for him. You would be surprised at his prices. He has an office in Hollywood and is doing practically all Beverly Hills work. You just have to have 'em done by Sales or they won't be patronized. Luck guy.

435   HERE'S CHANCE TO SEE CENTRAL AMERICA WITH WILL

Well all I know is just what I read in the papers, or what I see as I prowl hither and thither. And brother believe me I been doing some prowling lately. For a long time I have wanted to go messing around in the Central American countries, and the establishment of an air line all through there give me just what I was looking for. Now in the first place you can leave almost any American place, right by plane and go either to Fort Worth, Texas, Brownsville, Texas, or Atlanta, or anywhere along the line and catch the Pan-American line. It leaves American territory at Brownsville, and goes to Tampico and Mexico City, then from Vera Cruz, Mexico, on down through all Central countries, then around through the north coast of South America, and back up by way of Virgin Islands, Porto Rico, Cuba and all points east.

I had had the idea in my head for a long time. I wanted Mrs. Rogers to go with me.[1] She got one look at the map, counted the countries and reached for a time table to Hollywood, said that was as far as she was traveling right now. Ever since a kid, those countries and names appealed to me. I used to study in geography (not much, but a little) about Guatemala, San Salvador, Costa Rica, Honduras, Nicaragua, Panama, Columbia, Venezuela, British Guiana, and all the mess of 'em. Well, just think of the pleasure of getting up one morning, having breakfast at home in Santa Monica, grabbing the plane and being in El Paso, Texas at one o'clock, going over the Rio Grande River to Juarez to get some beer and see a bull fight, as it was Sunday afternoon, and my plane didnt leave there till Monday morning for Mexico City.

Did you ever visit Juarez, Mexico? Well, don't miss it. I went by the bull ring and bought our tickets as I had about 4 pilots from the line who had brought me in from Los Angeles, American Airways Co., and a great line. Well, the fight was not to start till it got cool, for they won't even kill a bull till the sun is so low that the fighter won't get sunburned. Then as we were driving around the town I saw a fellow with a lot of braided uniform get on an old poor decrepid pony, and just know from his make-up that he was headed for the bull ring, so I got cold feet and dident go. I gave away my tickets to some fellows that hadent been saved as many times by horses as I had.

Well prowled around and saw all the sights of the town, then back and early the next morning out to the airport and then by the C.A.T. line. (Continental Aerial, Transportation), American pilots, powered with Wasps on Lockheed planes. Well, anybody that flies knows that from pretty near any part of our country you can leave and be in Mexico City the next night, and not fly nights either?

Right down over Chicawawa (that's not the way it's spelled but that's sorter like it sounds), that's where the old Mexican Tarasas had the biggest ranch in the world, a whole state, flew right over his old headquarters ranch, lost it all during the various revolutions.[2] Poncho Villa lived off him alone for years.[3]

Well, we must get moving. Got to Mexico City that evening about four thirty. Made my first speech in Spanish for the Spanish movietone. I know few words but none of 'em fit what I want to say, but I just used 'em anyhow. I heard afterwards that in the theatre that it went big. Well it would. I was sorter panning our country and boosting theirs. It dident take much exaggeration to do either one. Met a lot of old friends at the field that I had known there during a previous visit, and then out to Mr Clark's, the American Ambassador there who took Mr Morrow's place.[4] He is a real fellow and is doing a

fine work. He was very familiar with Mexico for years and he is well
liked there now, and it took some guy to follow that little fellow
Morrow, (anywhere). He hasent done much in the Senate, but that's
what makes him great. The more you do in there the more your
constituents suffer.

Well, after I go through with Mexico City, hit out for the real
tropics, down through Vera Cruz, then out of there on the Pan
American Airways, and over the real jungles, and stopped first at a
little Mexican Army Post called San Geronimo. Gassed up, was
thirsty but everybody said, don't drink water in the tropics, and by
golly I havent. But my first mangole, I believe it was to eat. Now we
are on the west coast of Mexico, we have crossed the neck, or
straights and are headed for Guatemala. We make some other one on
the line, and then into Guatemala City, the capitol of that country.
We have seen it on the maps of our old geographys.

It's in the rolling hills, and quite a bit of aviation activity, and is
a pretty little city from the air. They raise coffee, and tell you that it's
the best there is in Central or South America.

But wait a minute, we havent got to Costa Rica yet, and they tell
you that too, and I believe they got it on Guatemala and Honduras,
and all the rest on the quality. It's so good that America won't pay
the price. It's most all shipped to Europe. It grows on a little bush,
and they have high trees planted all among it to shade the coffee
plant, sometimes banana trees but generally big wide looking shade
trees.

You would be surprised at the amount of people that speak
English in all these countries. Almost all the young men of wealthier
families are sent to our schools since the war, in preference to Europe,
and they speak better English than we do. I can't get you all the way
down now, but I will get you to the Canal the next letter. It's quite a
gully.

436   WILL PANS HOOVER AS DIPLOMAT

Well all I know is just what I read in the papers and believe me I
have finally found a paper that's got something in it. It's the "St.
Thomas Mail" of the town of St. Thomas, Virgin Islands, U.S.A.
Now you might have read in the local press various references to Mr.
Hoover's statement about the condition of the Islands after he had
visited them a few weeks ago.[1]

Now in all fairness to our President, I don't think he meant it exactly like it was reported to have been said. He did see that they were in a pretty bad condition financially, and he might have in order to stir up a little interest in them and perhaps be able to get them a federal contribution of some kind, have thought he was doing them a favor by bringing to the public's eye the fact that they were bad off.

But at any rate, it seems to have had the opposite effect and if you ever saw anyone up in arms it's these Virginders. Here is how I happened to know and get in on all this. It was a lovely afternoon, we had flown some several hundred miles from Trinidad, Port of Spain (which is owned by the British), and is a very beautiful island just off the northeast edge of Venezuela.

We were in one of those great big giant Condors, carries about twenty people. It runs from Brazil to Porta Rica. Well we were headed for Porto for that night. We come down in the Bay of St. Thomas for gas and mail. It's a beautiful little harbor, and a lovely picturesque little town, some mighty hospitable folks there.

It was a Navy base, but they are moving it away. In the days before America had gone "Racketeer" it made rum, and good rum. It was a legitimate business, carried on by experts, that had made it for generations. Then during a time when our ambitions were bigger than our judgment, why we thought we should spread out and try and be "A" Nation.

Now if there is one thing we do worse than any other nation, it is try and manage somebody else's affairs. We are very original, nobody else can see things our way (of course they are wrong), but they just won't be broadminded and let us show 'em how they should live. During this expansion we thought we ought to have the Virgin Islands. Denmark, (I believe it was), they owned 'em, and we just bought 'em, give 'em twenty-five million dollars.

But let's get on with the story. Mr. Hoover had just finished a siege with the Senate and he needed a rest so he went to Porto Rico, and also to the Virgin Islands, and then home and made his observations. As we land on this lovely afternoon why I am tickled to death to be able to fly by and see our absent countrymen, and get their reaction on our President's visit.

Well did you ever see a community mad? No, you havent, you only think you have. You havent seen a community mad at all till you see the Virgin Islands. I guess you can get madder at a President than anybody else, because he is bigger and so much more prominent. So as I told you at first, all I know is just what I read in the papers.

Well, they handed me their little paper, and let us read as it is here before me as I pen this: "To the Virgin Islanders. Regardless of how much our feelings have been hurt by the remarks of the President of the U.S., who alludes to us as a 'poorhouse' and expresses regret that the U.S. ever bought us, we must not forget our dignity, and so in the future place ourselves beyond the reach of future insults. We must be loyal to our local government and to the U.S.," signed by the editor.

The editorial goes on: "When Denmark (I thought it was the Sweds, but I guess it was the Danes that sold it to us). When Denmark transferred the Islands to the great U.S. they certainly did not constitute a 'poorhouse.' She made them so by her stupid laws, unsuited to our well being. Any American alluding to us as a poorhouse is devoid of decency, even though he be President of these United States. Our welcome to the President was both loyal and dignified. The St. Thomians were not awed by his presence, for they have become accustomed to meet, BIGGER MEN THAN PRESIDENT HOOVER. THEY HAVE CHATTED AND DINED WITH THE CREAM OF EUROPEAN ROYALTY, NOT FOR A FEW HOURS, BUT FOR DAYS, and these men were appreciative of our hospitality and did not repay it with abuse, but they landed at Kings Wharf (that's the place I went ashore too), they landed there, nicely dressed and NOT IN A GARB AS THOUGH PREPARED FOR A BUCK DANCE IN THE SLUMS, AS MR. HOOVER DID.

"Virgin Islanders have always been strongly in sympathy with America. During the Spanish American War, when we belonged to Denmark, we always welcomed American battleships into our harbor. We did not walk into America's arms for charity. America has no concept of the rights of other people. This narrowness, (although the richest Nation on earth) makes her the most hated nation, even when she is doing a real good. But may the day never dawn when the inhabitants of these Islands look on her in the same manner as do the people of Mexico and Latin America."

Now folks, them is harsh words, talk about the Democrats knocking the President! Well they took me ashore, and they said they wanted my visit to offset his, so I told 'em to go ahead and make their rum, that there was no reason they should take Prohibition seriously just because they belonged to the U.S. So with a bunch of them we all went and had a nip of rum punch, and I don't mind telling you the Islands looked great to me.

I disagree with Mr. Hoover, they dident look near as poor as some parts of our country. Why there was no bread lines, no Red Cross Relief. I asked where most of the people were and they said, "Out at the golf course." That was the only evidence of poverty I saw. For as you know practically all our unemployed are at ours.

I sure liked the place, and wished I could have stayed over a few days. Met some mighty pleasant folks there. It looked like a very happy little community. (Till the President hit it.) Saw a few Marines scattered around, but as it was American territory, they dident have many. Couldent have been so far behind the times, they had two of my pictures there (talkies) and one of them I hadent even seen at home yet myself. I was awful sorry that they had misinterpreted this Prohibition thing, and quit selling their rum, and when I explained to 'em the interpretation that the mainland of the U.S. had put on the amendment, why they were tickled to death, and started right in to get ready to manufacture on a big scale.

I gave them Capone's address, as I wanted to see 'em get started with the best folks over home, where they could get the most for their product.[2] Of course, they will have to start from the bottom in regard to competition, for the U.S. had twelve years of business start on them. But they will be all right now, and the next time a President visits them, their product will be making them rich just like Chicago, or any of their competing centers. I am going to have those Virginders so rich they will be able to have $20,000 funerals, and Presidents won't mean anything to 'em.

437 WILL CHEERS THE 'FOURTH ESTATE'

Well all I know is just what I read in the papers, or what I see as I prowl hither and thither, mostly thither. Was in Washington about ten days ago, and saw quite a few of the boys that was still staying there that wasent up for re-election this year. You can tell the ones that are going to run. They have to rush home and start fixing things up. But the ones that are set for a year or so more they can kinder lay around and sorter mix with the lobbyist, and have a good time without getting blamed for it.

Was up to New York and spoke for the Newspaper Publishers Association. That's a gang that gathers in from all over the country once a year, and belong to an association to help better each others conditions, then go home and write editorials against unionism. Not all of 'em, but some do. But we did have a fine dinner.

You know even the food at dinners is getting better, they don't cook the chicken at these banquets in the afternoon like they used to. We had tender squab. It's mighty rare for a banquet to get tender squab. This was at the Pennsylvania Hotel. It's the eating house for that line. I want to tell you that Mr. Attebury had done a mighty good job with his hotel.[1]

Amon G. Carter from Ft. Worth, owner of the Star Telegram was the Toast Master and he made a mighty good one too.[2] He always was a good talker. But this was the first time they had ever asked him to talk, and they couldent have picked a better one. He knew the newspaper and he knew the shape they were in, and he knew the shape the guests were in, and he just shaped his remarks accordingly.

Pretty near every big publisher in America was there, they had just had a convention, but like most conventions they had done nothing but "resolve." If you take "resolve," out of conventions you are just about naked.

At this convention there was some little animosity against the advertising on the radio, that is it had been a direct confliction with newspaper advertising, and dident have the investment and pay the taxes that the papers are compelled to. So they naturally took that phase up, and come right down to it there is no reason why they should give the radio programs all the free advertising. It should be paid for the same as a theater does. But some of them spoke of the investments they had, and what right did some other thing have to come in and destroy the worth of their investments. Well, they was kinder forgetting when the Prohibition amendment came in and put all the brewerys and distillerys out of business with no recourse to the courts or any claim. Even if you are in favor of the amendment, it was legitimate up to then, and if it was voted out they should have had some claim. So some of these yells kinder made you think of what those fellows stand for.

But its all a lot of "hooey." The radio won't put the papers out of business. We got to have something besides toothpaste, so we will always read the papers, besides if it wasent for the Peanut Vendor song there wouldent be any radio.[3]

Good papers will always last, and tabloids will continue to do a big business for those that can't read. They have learned to know every character in America by their picture alone. They have to read little papers in New York and big cities, they can't unfold a big paper, they havent got room. They like pictures of their favorite murderers just like some others like movie stars. It's getting so a murderer to draw well in the papers must be good looking. It's getting so there is no use of an ugly man committing a crime, no one will look at him. He just can't get in the papers.

Charley Schwab was the principle speaker at the dinner.[4] He had a prepared speech to deliver on "Business Management," but after he saw the shape the crowd was in he switched and told jokes instead, and he told good jokes too. He said some of them were old, but they were sure new to me, and the way he tells 'em, they sound new anyhow. Did you ever hear the one he told about the cow? Well he owns a fine farm up near Bethlehem, Pa., a little city in Judea, and he raises fine stock. Every rich man has some mild form of insanity and being a farmer is Charley's. He has his own fair up there, so he takes all the prizes. Somebody give him a cow and he asked if it was a fine cow? They said no, just a cow. "Is it a milk cow?" The old farmer that was giving her to him said, "I don't know if she's got any milk or not, but she is a good old soul and if she's got any she will certainly give it to you."

Then he went on to tell that he (Schwab) was a good old soul, and if he had anything they wanted he would give it to 'em. He sure did clean up with the gang. You can easily see how he gets work out of his men, he has a great personality, and is terribly likable.

Carnegie gave some of his old time steel mill friends some fine Xmas presents one time, most of them works of art.[5] One old fellow that had risen from Foreman and retired, he gave a large statue. The old fellow called Schwab said, "Charley, the old man (meaning Carnegie) sent me a rock woman, what will I do with her?"

He says he is an optimist even now, and that we are not so bad off. Well maybe we ain't. This hunger may only be an illusion. Met at the dinner this fellow Roy Howard that buys all the newspapers.[6] They bought the New York World, and combined it with the Evening Telegram. Well, he and Scripps are mighty keen birds.[7]

I also met Scripps. He has whiskers, and that with Roy's full dress evening cape, makes a mighty hard combination to beat. They are young, full of progress, and good credit, and it looks like the only way to keep from selling your paper to 'em is to just disband it. Howard took me to his fine office. He asked me what I would have. I told him chop suey. It's furnished like a joss house. He is growing a queue, and signs his name with two pens at once like chops sticks.

The boys were really mighty sober at the dinner, another and mighty good indication of hard times. Some of 'em just had to get what little they could from the other's breath. Some small town editors had to just act soused in order to impress. But it was a fine affair; one of the best I ever attended, made so by Schwab and Carter and a good audience.

All I know is just what I read in the moving picture ads, and say boy what an education it is! I thought the underwear ads in the magazines were about the limit in presenting an eyefull, but these movie ads give you the same thing without the underwear. Even I myself appeared in a nightgown in "The Connecticut Yankee," so on the billboards it would add a touch of romantic glamor, to say nothing of a smattering of sex appeal.[1]

Mind you, you musent let the ad have anything to do with what you see on the insides. You are liable to see the wildest stuff facing you on the billboards, and then go inside and everybody is dressed as esquimos all through the picture. In other words, Will Hays' big trouble is getting pictures that will live up to the pictures on the ads.[2]

You know in all Latin American countries (I am speaking of authority as I flew over them at an altitude of sometimes as low as ten thousand feet), in those countries, if you put a picture on the boards to advertise what you are having inside or if in your wording you say that Miss Mille De Hokum will entirely disrobe on a tight wire, why on the said night Mille better do a mighty good job of stripping or the cash customers will clothe Mille and her management with some seats and chairs, and any other handy article laying around.

Or if it shows a picture of a bull fight and a matador being gored, by an unruly ox, why the day of the fight you better have the man gored or be prepared to be gored yourself. In other words, you got to deliver what you advertise.

So the big problem of the movies now is to deliver up to what the lithograph makers and ad writers have shown on the outside.

In other words, that branch of the industry has "outstripped" the production end. We just can't seem to get 'em as wild as they show 'em on the outside. We got to get wilder people. A lot of these have been out here for years, and they are getting kinder old and tame. There is an awful lot of us out here that just can't arouse the passions in our public like we ought to. And that's why we keep trying to get new blood into the art.

Then in the titles of pictures, there is where it's getting hard. They just can't think up enough suggestive titles to go around. They bring every big writer out here from New York and England and have them in an office just thinking all the time on titles that will lead you to expect you are going to see on the inside about four of the most prominent commandments broken, right before your eyes. But there is just so many of those titles and every company is fighting to get 'em. You take old plays like the "Old Homestead," now they are just

25

Will Rogers as "Sir Boss" in A Connecticut Yankee *(Fox Film Corporation, 1931) from the novel by Mark Twain. In the lower scene Rogers appears with Brandon Hurst as "Merlin" and William Farnum as "King Arthur."*

waiting till they can think up some title for that and then it will go into production.

Few of the best that have been turned in by the highest priced writers up to now is: "The Old Love Nest," "Home In Name Only," "The Birthplace Of Folly," "Devilment Galore Among The Honeysuckles," "What Took Place Under The Old Roof," "The Gal Pays The Mortgage With Body And Soul," "The House Is Old But The Carryings On Is New And Spicy," "The Gangster's Birthplace As Far As We Know."

So you can see that they are right on the edge of getting something that will combine all these, and give you an inkling of what the old roof has seen take place under it, and then they will start in making it.

The word "Hell" while generally frowned upon as conversation in the grammar grades, has been literally pounced upon by the movie title manufacturers, and they have just about "Hell'ed" everything to death. They have pictured the doorway, the stage entrance, and every part of Hell, till Hell has just got so it don't mean nothing anymore but another word in a title. Putting the word "Hell" on the billboards and expecting to scare up any excitement among the prospective victims anymore is just blowed up.

Course my old friend, Will Hays still insists that virtue triumphs, but they keep making you more and more doubtful right up to the end, in fact, most of them hold back till after the final fade out. And I have seen some of 'em here lately where it looked like it was still in doubt, as to whether it triumphed or not.

That's called "Subletry." All the writers try to be what they call "Sophisticated" or "Subtelry." That means nobody knows what you are talking about and don't give a d——. Sophistication means talking all day about nothing. You are both bored but you have to do something till somebody mixes another cocktail. We are getting a lot of these kind of talking plays now. Titles that if printed on the old silent screen would have got the "rasberry" now are considered smart, for they apply to nothing and mean less.

I saw one the other night called "Kiss And Leave Each Other Flat." It was so subtle that it didnt say whether you can leave 'em flat physically, or financially. They call 'em drawing room plays, women with nothing on their minds eat 'em up, kids hiss 'em, and old men sleep right through 'em.

They had 'em on the stage till they ruined it. So between "Subtlery" and gangsters we have run the old cowboy trying to save the Sheriff's daughter, right back to the dairy farm. No modern child would want to learn how to shoot a 45 colt. He wants to know how to mow 'em down with the old Browning machine gun. But we will live through it, and come out with something worse. We always do. So we better make the most of this while it's here.

439   OH, JUST SEE U.S. WITH ROGERS

Well all I know is just what I see, and Say, Brothers, I have seen something right here lately. Couple of weeks ago I was prowling around, My Wife and I, trying to scare up something new to see.[1]

We have bummed around over quite a mess of these United States and fragments of Europe, so just any little thing wouldent make much of a dent on us. But we sure did run into something that knocked us back on our reserve supply of astonishment.

If you was looking for unusual and new things to see you would naturally look up or ahead would you? You wouldent be walking along with your head down around your hoofs would you?

No, you would be looking for Al Smith's Skyscraper, the tallest building in the World, the one he built so he could look down on the Republicans.[2] It's big enough to hold all the Democrats and give 'em each a different room so they can't meet and disagree.

Course if you had never been around America much and started out to see the sights of it, due to past advertising you would perhaps head for Niagara Falls if you could dig up a new wife to take along, or the Grand Canyon or the Yellowstone Park, or the great Virginia Natural Bridge. Now all of these are everything they are cracked up to be, and no one should miss 'em. But we got a new wonder in our Country.

It's sprung up in the last few years, and the most astonishing thing about it, it's not a thing but a hole in the ground. Now off hand that don't seem much to get excited about does it? Well I dident know there was so much underground. We think the ground is just practically filled with dirt. But here is a place where there is a hole in the dirt, the dirt is pushed back and there is the most wonderful sights in this vacuum you ever saw.

It's down in the south eastern part of New Mexico, at Carlsbad, a might pretty little town, a regular oasis on what is sometimes almost a Desert. It's on the Pecos River. I was through the place years ago when they used to call it Eddy, and it was a good Town even named Eddy, but it's got some water there that will cure you of a lot of minor ailments. Course you got to go to Claremore Okla-

Will Rogers and Thomas "Tom" Boles, Superintendent of Carlsbad Caverns. (Courtesy, National Park Service)

homa. That's the place that will keep you right out of the Obituary column. But this old time Eddy will help you a lot. Well it don't look like a place that if a fellow was searching for another wonder to add to the World, he would head for.

There is not much to give you any indication that you are prowling around over some of the most fantastic formations that were ever opened up to the gaze of man. It's just a rocky old hillside, not even too much grass. But it's a cow Country, and many years ago the old-timers used to know it was there as the Bats would fly out of there by the thousands. Well, anywhere a Bat comes fogging out of, no particular fair-minded person is going to go prowling in the hole to see what made the Bat come out.

But finally so many come out they knew there must be a pretty big hole in order to hold all of 'em. It's got a pretty big sized entrance and always did have they say, so really discovering it wasn't any great effort on anyone's part that happened to be riding in that end of the state.

It wasn't the finding of the hole, it was the going inside and seeing why it was there, was the main thing. A Cowpuncher named White with more curiosity than anyone I ever come in contact with (for they are generally mighty leary of any hole in the ground), is supposed to really have been the one to going in there and discover that while there was Bats off in one end, in other parts there was the most unbelievable formations of water turned to stone.[3] You really prowl around in there by well-formed trails for over five miles. There is rooms in there with a ceiling of 400 feet. One tremendous room is almost a mile long. With all these marvelous formations of Stalactites and Stalagmites.

Them's big words, but I know what they mean now. One is like an icicle formed from the top by the water dripping (that's the Tite one), and the Mite one is formed by the water falling on it and building it from the ground up. They hang like Church steeples upside down. They form totem poles and Elephant ears (exactly the shape and thinness of an actual Elephant ear).

Different rooms have different formations. Oh I ain't got room to tell you in here what it's like, I would have to be writing a book to do it properly. The Government has taken it over, and formed it like our other National Parks. It's mighty well handled, and you are splendidly conducted through it by a fine bunch of trained Park Rangers. Tom Boles is the General Superintendant, comes from Arkansaw and knew my wife years ago.[4] She dident see half of it for gossiping about some old "Nestors" back home. You walk down now, but they are putting in Elevators.

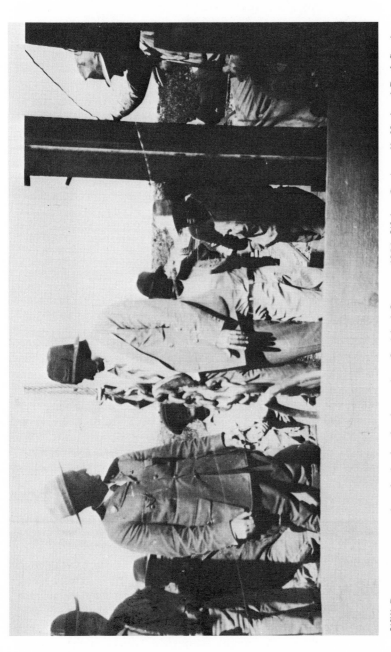

Will Rogers prepares to board a bucket for descent into Carlsbad Caverns, 1931. Walter G. Attwell, National Park Service engineer who designed and built the elevator system at the caverns, is in uniform at left. (Courtesy, Walter G. Attwell)

And I made the first trip down in a Bucket (as they got the hole cut through the day I was there). They bored from the top, and also from the bottom. It's seven hundred feet down, and they met in the middle, and the Engineers' calculation was off a quarter of an inch. A Mr. Atwell, he was practically broken hearted to think he had failed so dismally.[5] He is a fine engineer and if this quarter of an inch don't ruin him some day he might be President.

A Ranger named Carrol Miller does a lot of the exploring, and he was itching to break away from us and go see if he couldent find a part of the cave that would be worthwhile.[6] You have lunch down there in a little ante-room five hours just leisurely time to see it. Every move of a few feet is an entirely different picture. So don't you miss this. You will all be coming to California to get in the Movies, so come by there. Good roads, and if it don't drag some adjectives out of you, why send me the bill.

440   WILL ROGERS URGES
          U.S. SOCIETY LEADER

Well, all I know is just what I read in the papers.

I was just reading in the papers about the Girls who were presented to the King and Queen.[1] Over in London, just a year ago now, when I was over to the Disarmament Conference Ambassador Dawes was telling me about that, they have it I think twice a year, and the King and Queen receive just so many from each Country.[2] Well of all the planning, scheming, conniving, Politics and even blackmailing, they work to get Daughter presented at Court!

And they say over there that we are the worst Nation of all for it. The greatest Democracy will go to the greatest length to get somewhere just for the Ad. They live on it the rest of their lives. It's the congressional Medal of Society. "Lizzie Bean as a Debutante was presented at Court."[3] And the Social home town papers always say: "She was the most beautiful one there." Now maby there was twelve Chinese Girls presented that looked as good.

This time there was 400 received, so you see it's not exactly what you would call exclusive. The King of Spain ought to figured something like that out and then there would have been enough socially ambitious to keep him in office.[4] England is a smart Nation; they know that there is just so much hooey required by people and they very wisely supply it. We ought to have a "Social President" or "King of the Drawing Room" or "Master of the Teacup" or some person that would fill the place of what Royalty supplies over there. Let him give the dinners and stand the gaff of the arguments over who was going to eat next to who, and he could lay the corner stones, touch the buttons to open the new night clubs for the local Chambers of Commerce. There just ain't any end to what he could relieve Mr. Hoover of. I know no one would be more tickled than Mr. Hoover, for I don't think he relishes all that junk. Mr. Coolidge is the only one that ever really seemed to relish 'em.[5] He had 'em doped out, they never worried him. He had the same expression and the same conversation for Queen Marie as he had for Senator Moses.[6]

"Hello," when they come in and "Goodby" when they passed out. He just went about his eating and they went about theirs and nothing dident mean nothing to him.

I can't think off hand who would be a good man for that position. Get a man and his wife with good digestions, good dispositions, good to look on, and Masters of Emily Post.[7] I will look around Hollywood here and see what we got left. Pretty near all the socially prominent that come out for the films have starved out and gone back. It's just practically us riff-raff that are hanging on. We are just drifting from one Gang Picture to another.

Oh yes, say Charley Chaplin would be the one for this new job we are trying to create.[8] He is over in Europe studying the King Business. He has got in to all the more notorious homes and knows what is really required. Course he got in bad with some, but one good picture will square all that. Little Charley would be just the Boy to dedicate the Bridge, or head Dining Table and make merry with the Guests, and he is a smart little Rascal, too, don't make any mistake about that. He is a socialists, but then everybody is becoming that in Society anyhow, so he will have an advanced break where the King was going to be, and he turned it down. He claimed it was just the Manager that asked him, and that it wasent the King at all. So Charley bawled 'em all out and told 'em that over there seventeen years ago none of them wanted him, and wouldent give him a job, so he come over here and made good, and at that time he was just as good an Artist as he is today, so he dident owe them a thing.

So after that we are liable to have to use him over here, so he might be just the fellow for my job. Course he hasent got any Wife (right now), but he can remedy that any minute, and speaking of Washington and our Government, what is going on there during these early hot days?

Mr. Hoover has been going out to his Camp on the Rapidan every week-end and it hasent been all for pleasure either. Every week-end he takes a different gang with him. For instance one

33

weekend he took Pat Hurley, Secretary of the War, and told him "Pat, Mellon has gone and let the Politicians overdraw our Bank balance 950,000,000, that's just 50 million under a Billion, that holds the record for an overdraft.[9] Now we got to all get together and help the old Boy try and make it up some other way. Now how about lopping part of your Army off? Can't you leave some spurs and some Sam Brown belts or something off and help save Andy's record, so that it will stand up with Alexander Hamilton's?[10] So you go back to your office and see who would be the least needed in our next war and give 'em their two weeks' notice. We got to be prepared, but see if we can't be prepared a little cheaper.

"What we want now is cheaper preparation. Course soon as we get used to this overdraft why it won't be so bad, but it's just while it's new that everybody's attention is focussed on it. You know a Billion is getting so it's a lot of dough, even in these hard times. So we all got to pull together and get this thing kinder hushed up before November, '32, comes on us. If we can just stall this all off till after then, why we can get back to normal again, and you can have all the help you want. But right now, You Boys got to help get Andy out of the Red. Take some oats away from those Army Mules or something. I am going to the Navy row out to the Camp here and make them do what they can. Secretary Dave Ingalls quit flying to Cleveland every day to get his mail.[11] Then those Virgin Islands we got to cut down on them, they are living too high. Then we ought to try to catch Sandino for less money this year than we tried to catch him last year.[12] But we all got to pull together like one big happy family and get Andy out of the Red, cause a Billion dollars worth of Red is SOME Red. We got to stop Alexander Hamilton from laughing in his grave."

441   LOS ANGELES MAKES
THE BIG LEAGUE

Los Angeles, which has been in the Bush League as far as Racketeers are concerned is getting right up in fast company. We pulled off a double header of a Murder here a couple of weeks ago that would do credit to a Chicago or any of the Big Timers. The Racketeers are mixed up with phases of the City Government just like a regular Class A City. The Killer walked away as usual.

In the old Wild West days, the Bandit had to back out shooting, and make his horse by the blaze of his guns. But nowadays the Robber or Killer or whatever his day's work might be, why he does it all casually, just in the regular routine of things. If there is a Bank to rob, why he just saunters in, the only way he can possibly be noticed is that he will perhaps be dressed better than the Banker.

Well the young man simply walks up with no mask, no western hat, no big forty five, just a little Automatic, which a Baby can shoot as well as Billy the Kid could, for all you do is point and keep the trigger pulled and you hit everything in the place, there is no possible way you can miss any part of anyone in the building.[1] The more nervous you are the more you hit. If there be one thing that has increased crime it's been the Automatic Pistol. It's made no practice necessary to be an outlaw. Give any young Egotist two shots of dope and an Automatic and he will hold up the Government Mint.

He goes in gets his money quicker than you can get it with a boni fide Check. Out he comes. His Partner has the Car running, and away they go perhaps to their Country home, or their Golf Club. The toughest part of robbing nowadays is to find somebody that has something. The minute a Robber gets a clue why the rest is easy. Now that's about the routine of the modern Robbery, and the Murder is about along the same routine, course it's a little more expensive on account of having to use a little ammunition.

But the fellow that's hiring the fellow to do the job has to pay so much and ammunition. The fellow that kills you nowadays, why he don't have it in for you, he don't even know you. You are not even pointed out to him till just before he bumps you off. That's all a business, done through an Agency, just like any other Agency. They can furnish killers for "Singles" or "Double Murders" or "Group." You get a rate if you want several put out of commission. It's cheaper to have it all done at once. It's very little more trouble to shoot down a group, than it is one.

Oh we are living in progress. All of our boasted inventions, like the Auto and the Automatic, and our increased "Dope" output, terrible liquor, lost confidence in our Justice, Graft from top to bottom, all these have made it possible to commit anything you can think of and in about 80 percent of the cases get away with it. We can get away quick in a Car. He can't miss with the gun he's got. If he is caught he knows it will be accidental. Then if he is caught, his connections with his gang will get him out, so it's not a dangerous business after all, from the looks of it. But there is no use going on with what's happening out here in our Town cause the same thing is happening in yours, so I don't want to be like all these Californians and be accused of bragging.

35

But goodness sake, we get enough crime without writing about it, so let's see what else we got. We sent a bunch of mayors to France, nobody knows for what reason. I think it was at the invitation of France themselves, so they got nobody to blame but themselves.

Our local Mayor from here, of course, you know at that time did himself proud.[2] He won the approval of two of our local pastors, and lost France, his host. That's one thing when we are foolish. We don't stop halfway. We go the whole route.

Right now in Washington, the main thing is Mr. Hoover trimming down the various departments. He did a fine job when he lopped off a lot of these old obsolete army posts. They are a sentimental obituary to the past, but let the states themselves keep them up. But you know I sure did always love the looks of those old posts. They always seemed to be located in such pretty places, most all built around a square, where the soldiers drilled.

And of all the unattractive and out of the way places were these late war encampments. Yaphank, out in an end or part of Long Island, that even an aviator can't find. Nobody had ever been there before or since the war. Another over in Jersey, and all around. No late war soldier ever wishes to go back where he trained, in fact they can't. Nobody knows where it is now.

Say speaking of Jersey, the other day out on our movie lot I was working, and come on the set was Mayor Hague of Jersey City, you all know him, that is anybody that is anybody that knows him, all Democrats.[3] He is a big man, in the ex-organization. I tried to get something out of him for I knew he was well loaded politically. He knows both Smith and Roosevelt mighty well and I was trying to find out what was going to run, or would they draw straws for it, or what, or would they get any little difference they might have settled up.[4] Now he could have told me, but like anybody that knows anything he wouldent tell it. You know it's people that don't know anything that's always telling it. Now I, for instance, will tell you anything you want to know, but if I know anything about anything I wouldent tell you, so that's why I can tell you about everything. Course election is over a year away, but they are commencing to send in their entry blanks. It's going to be a great election, with the twenty million unemployed voting against the twenty million that are. The slogan will be "I believe every man should have a job, but not mine."

442 WILL FINDS OKLAHOMA RIGHT
IN LOS ANGELES

Well, all I know is just what I read in the papers or what I happen to run onto. Run onto a queer mess out here in California the other day. You know California is made up of every ingredient in the World but Californians. Well these various emmigrants from their various sections of the Country have a habit of holding a Picnic. The State of Iowa started it and theirs got so big they had to hold it in Arizona, then the other States got to holding what they called State Picnics and then the Counties and then the various towns, all over the U.S. their Rufugees that were here would hold a Rogers, Ark., Picnic. My Wife would be up at daylight so she wouldent miss that old home town one.

Well, the other day Oklahoma had one and I am sorry to say that it was a success. I had no idea there was that many Renegades had left, but from the looks of things half of Los Angeles come from Oklahoma. Our Governor, "Alfalfa Bill" Murray come all the way out here to speak to us at this gathering and they asked me to introduce him.[1]

Well, it's kinder of a tough job introducing an Oklahoma Governor. You never know before you get through speaking but what he has been impeached while you was singing his praises. But it looks like they are going to get even with Bill and let him serve his time out and maby sentence him again.

So I think I will just jot down a lot of junk that I used at Camp Meeting, held in Sycamore Grove. As well as I can remember it run not to wit, but to length, something like this; "This is Memorial Day, established for two reasons, one to commemorate the passing of our loved ones who have gone before, and the other reason, to try and cheer up in some small way, the misguided Oklahomans, who were misled by a California Chamber of Commerce.

"Our loved ones past, are dead and gone, so we need say no more for them. They were fortunate, they passed away before the last Republican Administration. But it's for the living (or rather, existing) Oklahomans, who are also dead, but living in California, we are gathered here on this beautiful sunshiny day, with a rain coat on every arm, to console with them.

"Our Governor, or that is, he was our Governor when he left, has come to bring us solace from the Homeland. He has come to pray with us, not for divine guidance, but to find in some way means to getting us back home. Here today are twenty-five thousand souls, who thought that Climate was digestable and not a Real Estate Add are here doing Penance today.

"Twenty-five thousand is a lot of folks to escape the Insane Asylum of their native State and reach one place. But forgive 'em Governor, for they knew not what they were doing, and they have found nothing to do since they come.

"You musent, Governor, take this great gathering as a tribute to your drawing power. Los Angeles folks will burn $5 worth of Gas and burn out four bearings to reach anything given free. Anything free here can get a crowd. This enemic looking gathering you see here, just proves you can't live on orange juice and look like anything.

"These are Pioneers, Governor, they are some of the first people to cross the Desert in a Ford. They know what hardships are, you can see punctures and blowouts written on every face. You, Governor, crossed in a beautiful Private Car, belonging to the Rock Island (they want something, and will perhaps get it). But these Poor Devils had to Chevrolet their way across.

"I will give 'em credit though, they left Oklahoma at a time when it looked like a Democrat would never get in. They had no idea the old State would ever return to Christianity. They haven't lost touch with the Home State, they write home and touch everybody they can think of. They are only now waiting till you make the State so prosperous that their kin folks can send out and get 'em. But in talking to 'em, Governor, don't believe all they say, some of them have been here so long they lie like a Native.

"Now, Governor, I wouldent have taken the job of introducing you here today, for it really should be done by some Scholar, some learned person, but I got to thinking over the occasion, and the audience and I figured that it wouldent take a very bright man to talk to a bunch of people who had left a State like Oklahoma (with all its natural resources and oppurtunities) and come clear out here to see a Lemon grow, and get in the Movies. Bill Murray threw down a chance to go to Claremore this same week, they were having their annual 'Take a Bath Week,' and he was invited and come clear to California to keep from going. He wired 'em: 'Will come and speak, but will take no part.' I wired 'em, 'Will come as a Spectator only.'

"Murray sympathises with you exiles, he knows what it is, he started one time in California, took the wrong road at Woodard, and landed in Boliva. He knew what it is to be out of touch with Civilization, even before he got into Oklahoma State Capitol. He has been in a Spanish Country, he knows what it is to live on Frejoiles, like you all do. I am sorry our Mayor of Los Angeles is not here to welcome you Governor, but he is making friends with France.[2] Nothing worth while has passed into his lips since he got there and nothing worth while has passed out of his lips.

"But you would like our Governor, he is a regular guy, but he is from Frisco.[3] Frisco is the place that keeps this end of the State in the Union. It's to California what the Cherokee Nations is to Oklahoma, It's the Aristocracy of Commonwealth. It's the Tulsa of the works. So I take great pleasure, and pain, (for I had a broken leg at the time), I take great pleasure and pain in introducing the only man in this entire twenty-five thousand who is fortunate enough to have a Ticket back to Oklahoma."

443   PICTURE PRODUCERS
        NOW WILL JOIN MOB

Well, all I know is just what I read in the papers, or what I see as I mess around. We was making a Movie here the other week of Booth Tarkington's Book and Play "Plutocrat."[1] That's what it was called. But it's liable to be released under the title, "Riches Traded for Virtue" or "The Gangster's Lost Moll." Well in the Picture my family and I are on one of these Mediterain Cruises and we got to Morroco, or some country down there where it's hot and full of Arabs and Camels and Riffs.

Well, I will say one thing for Hollywood. If you want a couple of hundred real "Arabs" in a scene, you just let the casting Department let it be known that you do and you get that many real Arabs. Anything under the sun you want, it's in Hollwood. I believe you could round up a hundred Esquimos and if you want the Wailing Wall in Jerusalem, you can get that with the original cast, in fact, the Producers of the Pictures will join in with the mob, the way business has been lately.

Now among these Arabs and Turks and Foreign Legions and all we needed a few big "Senagambians," big colored Boys, in their bare skin. Well, out here there is an awful lot of Prize Fighters and "awful" is right and every old time Pug is here and among 'em is a lot of Ex-colored Fighters that work around the Pictures.

Well, we had the greatest gang on this street Scene in Algeirs, or wherever it was. I was raised down south, by and With colored folks. Claremore is full of Colored Rogers, that their folks belonged to our family (they took the name, you know, when they was freed). They got more humor and good nature than any race in the World. Well, there was two or three of these old Boys that hadent been spoiled.

One was Sam Baker, a pretty good fighter three or four years ago.[2] He fought Wills and was a trial sparring Partner for Dempsey.[3] Then there was I think it was Lester Albert Johnson and Vic Alexander.[4]

Well, the Director couldent get me on the set for laughing at these birds kidding each other about fights. I believe Sam Baker talked the best fight of all. They got him to tell about the time he was sent to Portland, Ore., to fight the big (name deleted through friendship) when he was making his famous march through the Buckwheat belt, bowling 'em over in one and two rounds.

Well, listen just a minute to Sam Baker, and you will get an earful of modern fisticuffs. "I was woking down here in Hollywood, wasent bothering a soul. I had me a big part, putty uniform, taking care of de front door at a high hat night club. Dis gentleman had been assainating around all up and down and it seemed like in Oakland, another Colored Boy, or something was to go out in the fourt round and dident, he stayed till the sixth and could a stayed for a week, but his seconds throwed in a towel, when all that had happened to him was that he was jes going against de rules. He jes wouldent lay down. Well I had fit up around Portland and I had been a 'Big Shot' and eat regular up around there, so they sent for me to come to Portland. Well I ain't been training on nothing but close ups, down here in Hollywood, but they tell me they will fix things and they sho had 'em fixed when I got there.

"I is called on by a couple of Gun men, who inform me that there is One Thousand dollars and it's mine to keep, hold or destroy, but, here the Guns come into the scene. That I was to go out in the first round. First round understand. Not to get my dates mixed and dive in the second, but the first. Another Colored Boy crossed us and we been hunting for him for two weeks. But ye ain't going to hunt for you, you are right here where your body will be found. If you carries all this out according to de aforesaid, you gets another thousand and if you don't you is carried out. You ain't to hit this gentleman in de face. He is got a Movie Contract in view and he don't want to jepson his chances. You play for his stomach, but you don't play hard. You make it look like you is going somewhere, but ain't. You jes headed that way, that's all.

"Den they showed me they still had their Guns, and then rubbed 'em under my nose and axed me if I could smell 'em. I told 'em I had a cold, but could get a sort of idea what was around. Well den I got to thinkin to myself after day is gone. Here I am in my old stampin grounds of Portland and I got a lot of folks that think I am still the 'Big Shot,' so dey is liable to get on me and if they sees me taking a nose dive they liable to have some Guns too. So I call 'em back and ask 'em about this, they say, there ain't going to be but two Pistols in that hall that night and these is both of 'em. And you want to have that 6 foot 5 ready for nap not later than the first round, see.

"Well they goes on out and I says to myself, there ain't no sensible arguing against a thing like that. Sammy you is out now. I goes down to the Gymnasium and makes out like I is training, but I is just hopping around eating all I can get, sipping a little Gin on the side. I ain't worrying about him any more than he is about me. He knows I am fixed and I knows I am fixed. But I do wants to make it look like as good as I can. I been acting around here in these Pictures so I figure I can do me some Barrymores, when the time come.[5] Well it sho had come. If I was a Actor, I sho was going to have to start acting.

"When we get in de ring his managers all comes over one at a time, there was a dozen of 'em, and they say 'Remember.' De Gun men is setting in awful good shooting distance, no reason for a man missing at that range. I dashed out and goes like I am rushing like a Bull, he uppercuts me, and I have a terrible time falling. It looks jes about as faky as it was. I ain't acting so good.

"So I gets up quick and make it look like I maybe slipped, and he hits me on top of de head and down I goes again. Dis one I fall a little better cause I am getting some practice. Den he swings and I think he is going to hit me a terrible blow so I start falling early, but he misses me. Well I couldent stop the fall, so I had to keep on. Well, even Portland couldnt swallow that. So I arise amid de Boos.

"But he is standing straddle of me all the time. So they had to laugh at that, and that got their mind off the fall. So I lets him knock me down as I am getting up, but it don't look like a good enough one to stay on, so I ups and lets him hit me into the ropes. I makes out like I am falling back-wards and there I hang with both hands down, he steps in and starts belting me, one after the other. If he could a hit hard he would a killed me for I was just laying on the top rope with both hands down. Den I sunk down easy, glanced over at the Gun-men, and stayed there. I wasent going to make any mistake about the round, and here I is back in Hollywood safe and sound, and still jes as good Actor as Mr. John Barrymore. He acts when he don't have too. I acted when I had to ACT, or else."

41

444 UNVEILING MONUMENT
JUST NONPLUSES WILL

Well all I know is just what I read in the papers. Awful lot in the papers about Mr. Hoover and Mr. Coolidge joint appearance at the Harding Memorial.[1]

Mr. Hoover put over the best speech. He came right out and said something, told how Mr. Harding had been imposed upon by his own friends, which of course was the absolute truth. But Mr. Coolidge, you wouldent get him coming out declaring anything as definite as that.

Course Calvin made a good old straightaway, just what you would expect a politician to say of any of his own Party, touched on Politics of course, and told what the Republican Party had accomplished under Mr. Harding. Even in Death they got to give the Grand Old Party a boost. But Mr. Hoover really touched on his humaness, and then when he brought out so strong about how his friends had imposed why that was a fine and rather a brave thing for a Politician to do.

Course it's exactly what a man in real life would do. But when you are in Politics and depending on somebody to keep you in, why you really ain't able to act like real life. It must have been a mighty nice affair.

Marion is a pretty little City. They say the Aeroplanes was flying over head so much that you couldent hear the speeches, and it annoyed Mr. Hoover and Mr. Coolidge very much. What is it that makes a Guy that can fly wait till a bunch of people gather some place and then start in showing them that he can fly? They look like they just wait till a crowd gather to reherse.

It's generally some advertising scheme. Well if they can read the add, I would think that its ill effects on the crowd would more than offset the good. If they were advertising "Three Strikes You are out Cigarets" over a gathering, I believe people would go right out of there and ask for "Four Tip Cigarets" purposelly, even if they dident smoke, just to get even with the add.

Of course, what this whole trip of Mr. Hoover's was, was the opening chorus of the 1932 Follies. Politicians will use any means to get their cause launched. A Funeral, or a Commeration, or a Christening, any occasion that looks important, why they will decide to launch along with the Chaplin's benedictions, "Some of the promises of what the future holds in store for you, if you are just wise enough to retain the incumbrent."

Then they dug up another monument, or re-painted an old one

or something over in Illinois. This one was to Abraham Lincoln, another Republican.[2] Guess Mr. Hoover just said, "Well let's do all this Monument Circuit at once. Get 'em all dedicated on one trip."

By the way, I was supposed to dedicate a Monument one time. It was down home in Oklahoma; in fact, I think it was on the Capitol Grounds at Oklahoma City. It was a kind of a cowboy affair that some Lady had built and asked in the deed to it to the State that I be the one to present it to Statue Lovers of my own Commonwealth. Well, I was all excited and trying to learn a speech that would fit a good Statue. You see, I was handicapped.

I had no Politics to put over at the occasion. I wasent going to run for a thing, so that naturally dident leave me much leeway in the way of a speech. I had to confine myself almost practically to Art, and Statue, and Oklahoma. None of the three which have anything in common with each other. Well, I was digging and studying and getting ready to fly back and do the honors (secretly hoping that they would have a Barbecue in connection with it, so I could do something natural), and, Lo and behold! What happens? Well, there was a big Tarpoleon spread over it, and it had been there over it ever since it had been there, just waiting for my unveiling.

Well, one of those Oklahoma Cyclones come along. (Chamber of Commerce of Oklahoma kicks on that last statement; kindly send stamped envelope.) Well, this wind hit the Statue, and the old "Tarp" wouldent hold; she was strapped on with a "Squaw Hitch" instead of a "Diamond," and away she blew. The tarp landed in Alfalfa Bill Murray's house down south (before he was Governor) and it come in mighty handy as bed clothes, for Bill was sleeping mighty close to the boards about then.[3] So the wind was really a public benefaction, and they wired me immediately on receipt of the cyclone there:

"Don't come. Another Big Wind has beat you to the unveiling, and did it in one tenth of the time it would have taken you to blow it off." Well, I don't know when I ever felt so nonplused.

445   LIFE IS FULL OF THINGS — BUT THEY DON'T MEAN ANYTHING

I guess I just get the usual amount of mail of anyone that writes junk for the papers, mostly people that sho don't agree with anything you said in the papers, and showing you where you ought to be calling Hogs somewhere. But this week I got some interesting letters.

One I sure was surprised to get was from Will Durant, a man that has studied Philosophy like Mr. Coolidge has Politics, and both have reached the heighth in their chosen professions.[1] I met this Durant one time. He is an awful nice fellow. I don't know much about what his "Racket" is, this Philosophy Gag.

He wanted me to write him and give him my version of "What your Philosophy of life is? I who have lived philosophy for many years turn now from it back to life itself, and ask you, as one who has lived, to give me your version. Perhaps the version of those who have lived is different from those who have merely thought. What keeps you going? What are the sources of your inspiration? and your energy? What is the goal or motive force of your toil? Where do you find your consolation and your happiness? Where is the last resort your treasure lies?"

A copy of this letter is being sent to Hoover, McDonald, Lloyd George, Mussolini, Marconi, Ghandi, Stalin, Trotsky, Tagore, Einstein, Edison, Ford, Eugene O'Neil, and Bernard Shaw, and three or four others that I had never seen in weeklys.[2] Now I don't know if this guy Durant is kidding me or not. If I got this kind of a letter from some body less I would say it's a lot of "Hooey" and wouldent even finish reading it. But putting me in there with that class, why I figured I better start looking into this Philosophy thing. I think what he is trying to get at in plain words, (leaving all the Philosophy out) is just how much better off after all is an highly educated man, than a dumb one? So that's how I figure is the way I got in that list. He knew that I was just as happy and contented as if I knew something, and he wanted to get the "Dumb" angle, as well as the highbrow.

That education is sorter like a growing town. They get all excited when they start to get an increase, and they set a civic Slogan of "Fifty Thousand by the end of next year." Well that's the Guy that sets a College education as his Goal. Then when they get the fifty thousand they want to go on to make it a Hundred, and the Ambitious College graduate wants to go on and make it a Post graduate in some line, figuring he will just be about as smart as anyone if he can just get that under his belt, and the Town thinking that the hundred thousand will just put them by all the other competing towns, not figuring that while they are growing that all the rest are doing likewise and maby faster. When they get to a half million New York will be twenty million, so they are no higher in the ladder comparitively than they were.

And the Educated Guy, he is the same. He finds when he gets his post graduate course that all the other Professors have got one too, and lots of 'em a half dozen. He begins to wonder if he hasent spent all this time wondering if he knows anything or not. He wishes he had took up some other line. He talks with an old broad minded man of the world of experience, and he feels lost. So I guess he gets to wondering what education really is, after all. For there is nothing as stupid as an educated man if you get off the thing that he was educated in.

Now here is a funny co-incidence in the same mail I got a letter from Old Man W. T. Waggoner.[3] I expect the biggest Cattleman in Texas, and the also biggest oil Man. What a pleasure to read it, the real Philosophy of that old Cowman, two pages of life on a ranch. He was just rambling along, but every line full of pleasure and satisfaction. No learning in the world could have made him as smart as his life has made him.

Then right the same week comes one from Bill Hanley, of Oregon.[4] You don't have to tell the Northwest who Hanley is, any more than you do the southwest is who Waggoner is. I had read the most wonderful book of Hanley's called, "Feeling Fine." It's got more real Philosophy in it than any book today. I am going to send one to Will Durant, and I want him to get this old Bird's idea on a few things. It's the story of his life, not as he has lived, but as he has observed. He shows you a lesson of every day life in every little animal or Bird we have. Lord, what a wonder he would be to lecture in a College to Boys. What confidence they would have in his knowledge. They would know that it come from a prairie and not from under a lamp.

An educated man just teaches the things that he has been taught, and it's the same that everyone else has been taught that has read and studied the same books that he has. But if these old fellows like Waggoner know anything, it come direct to them by experience, and not by way of someone else. If I had Hanley's knowledge I wouldent give it for even Secretary Hughes' and Nicholas Murray Butler's combined, (and I like 'em both personally and think they are great men).[5] But I would know I knew something if I knew what one of these old Cattlemen knew, and if I was as smart as Hughes or Butler I would still be in doubt, because I would be educated so high that I would know that I only had a smattering of what I did have.

So I can't tell this doggone Durant anything. What all of us know put together don't mean anything. Nothing don't mean anything. We are just here for a spell and pass on. Any man that thinks that Civilization has advanced is an egotist. Fords and bathtubs have moved you and cleaned you, but you was just as ignorant when you got there. We know lots of things we used to dident know but we don't know any way to prevent 'em happening. Confucius perspired

45

out more knowledge than the U. S. Senate has vocalized out in the last 50 years.

We have got more tooth paste on the market, and more misery in our Courts than at any time in our existence. There ain't nothing to life but satisfaction. If you want to ship off fat beef cattle at the end of their existence, you got to have 'em satisfied on the range. Indians and primitive races were the highest civilized, because they were more satisfied, and they depended less on each other, and took less from each other. We couldent live a day without depending on everybody. So our civilization has given us no Liberty or Independence.

Suppose the other Guy quits feeding us. The whole thing is a "Racket," so get a few laughs, do the best you can, take nothing serious, for nothing is certainly depending on this generation. Each one lives in spite of the previous one and not because of it. And don't start "seeking knowledge" for the more you seek the nearer the "Booby Hatch" you get.

And don't have an ideal to work for. That's like riding towards a Mirage of a lake. When you get there it ain't there. Believe in something for another World, but don't be too set on what it is, and then you won't start out that life with a disappointment. Live your life so that whenever you lose, you are ahead.

446   'TISN'T THE WEATHER! IT'S THE REPARATIONS

Well, all I know is just what I read in the papers. The heat has just about knocked the news right out of everybody. California papers have had nothing in the world on every page and in every column, but the amount of people that were killed in other parts of the Country by the heat. All our deaths out here died from natural causes, but the ones anywhere else it was the heat. But I guess it has been pretty hot back where you folks live.

But Mr. Hoover pulled his debt canceling right in the midst of it.[1] It wasent too hot for him to be thinking of something besides a cold drink. Now that may just be a mighty fine idea. It has already jumped the market up, and everybody got pretty excited over it. We are in such shape anyhow the last year and a half that we will jump at almost anything that is offered in the way of a scheme.

We know that nothing can do us any worse and we figure it might help, so we are liable to jump at things that after more quiet meditation we wouldent even monkey with. I don't see how it could hardly effect anyone so greatly but Germany, for they are the only one that is saving anything. Germany owes France, England, Belgium, and I reckon Italy, (I don't know what for, but I guess just on General principles.)

Well then, in turn each ones takes what Germany pays them and pays it to us, so when the debt is canceled for a year, that don't mean anything to England, France, Belgium, and maybe Italy, for if Germany pays them nothing they pay us nothing. If Germany does pay them, they in turn turn around and pay us, so the money only passes through their hands anyhow. If it does pass they pay it out, and if it don't they don't, so what's the answer? Why nobody is the loser or the winner, but Germany to be in a better position to buy from other Nations. But Germany makes or raises about everything they want anyhow, so they are not going to turn right around and spend all that they have saved. I imagine that the psychology of the thing is what makes it really acceptable than the actual figures in dollars and cents.

We lose 245 million that the Allies owe us, and 15 million that Germany pays us direct for the charge of the Army of occupation. They were to pay any one that wanted to send in an Army to occupy their Country after the war to remind them what an Allied Soldier looked like. Well that makes us lose 260 million. These are the real figures, (I just got them from "Time "). That's where all the authentic news comes from but we can afford to lose that much, for it takes more than that to do us any good, we are so far in the red that 260 million wouldent even stabilize our Liquor market.

But Mr. Hoover is dealing now in International problems, something that he knows something about, much more than the ordinary run of our Public men. He has fed these Nations before. This is not the first time he has fed 'em. That's his business and he must know that the way things are going that Germany just can't keep on paying. So it must have been to save a very delicate situation that he saw fit to do this. Of course it was not a new idea, it has been proposed a hundred times, in this and other ways, but it never was proposed by the man that had the authority to do it, even if it was a good idea.

Now what about the old Boys here on the home grounds? Well maby this thing will eventually reach him in some beneficial way. Lord knows what way but it may trickle down to him some day. Well the whole thing is beyond the understanding of us Dumb Birds anyhow, so just get back in your bead line and let it go.

A week or so ago we had it in our papers that Capone was broke.[2] Well it was just like saying Mellon and Ford had taken two adjoining cots in the county poor farm.[3] Capone broke ! ! !. We knew that depression had hit his Industry, but we had no idea that it had

47

had such far-reaching effect. The Government is sending him to jail for illegally selling Liquor, and collecting a legal income tax on an illegal act.

If they can do that why can't they make Robbers pay an income tax on what they received in loot? If you rob a Bank of 200 thousand, and they nab you, why can't they in addition to sending you to jail make you pay an income tax on what you got away with?

They got records of Capone for all these years. But they dident get any of the Liquor, that is paying for it. I think that "Broke" gag is another Racket. He always did handle his money in cash all the time, so that Old Boy has got dough piled a lot of his different Distilliers and Brewery's. You know what they tell you in Chicago?

The men that know they say that when you get Capone Liquor from some supernumary of his, that if you find any kick with it, that is too poor quality, he is more than glad to take it back and make it good. They say that he is more reliable in his methods than even the great Marshall Field store.[4] He prides himself on a high class organization. Well it would be too bad if it stopped while he was in Jail, for a thing like that ought to be perpetuated.

447   'SLOW POKE' JULES VERNE

Well, all I know is just what I read in the papers. And this hot weather the last few weeks, every paragraph is prostration. Then come the fourth a couple of weeks ago, and that with it's fire cracker, drownings, and auto accidents just about got what the heat had left.

But if things don't pick up it don't make much difference anyhow. But they seem to think this debt thing is going to help some of 'em out — some of 'em. Well, it's kinder lonesome around the Rogers ranch (not really a ranch, but we call it that; it sounds big, and don't really do any harm). Mrs. Rogers and Mary, that's the daughter that just become a young lady right while I was looking at her, she turned eighteen and I swear it don't seem ten.[1]

I was playing in a vaudeville theatre in Houston, Texas. It was the opening matinee, and I got the telegram of her arrival. She was with her mother, and her mother was at her old home at Rogers, Arkansas. A beautiful little town in the edge of the Ozarks, and that wonderful White River, great summer resort all around there. We didn't have any home, we was just living in theater dressing rooms, and raised in trunks. That was before I knew there was such a thing as a Ziegfeld Follies.[2]

The act then was mostly roping, and a good deal of jokes, in fact the same one I am still using. Roosevelt was my best bet in those days.[3] He was the best known public man that ever lived, and they kept up with everything that he did, so when you started in talking about something that he had just said or done, you didn't have to stop to tell what it was before going ahead with your comment. Our public men nowadays haven't got near as much color as the ones then had. People are not interested enough in the ones nowadays to read what they are doing, which generally they ain't. But they are pretty able I guess at that.

But what I started out to say was that Mary and her mother have gone on a little trip over to Honolulu. Mary had heard that the dance orchestras over there were especially good so she wanted to make sure. I was working on a movie and couldn't get away.

I would like to go to that Honolulu some time. I just come by there one time many years ago, on my way from Australia. But I do hate that boat trip. If I could fly over I would go tomorrow. If I could get this Gatty and Post to take me over.[4] Those boys did a great job, didn't they? I wish I could have gone to Oklahoma when they welcomed them there. They asked me to come. I would like to meet them, and the old fellow that backed the trip.[5] It will be a long time before that record is beat. You won't get another combination like that.

Such a navigator, and such a flyer, and they can't get any better ship. Just think! Clear around the world with one motor. Then you find people that are afraid to go up for an hour with three motors. How in the deuce did they do about all that loss of sleep? Lord, if I miss two hours sleep I am dopy for the next day or so. I would have gone to sleep right in some Russian Reception Committee's whiskers, and when it would have come time to get up and take off again, I would have left the record remain with Jules Verne in 80 days and even that was imagination.[6] Poor old Jules, he *must have had* a relapse when he heard them flying over his grave.

We hear a lot now about the world becoming little, but I tell you it's plenty big yet. It will be a long time before we know much more about each other than we do now. And I guess it will be just as well we don't. Just think of those boys flying away up in Siberia. That's where we used to see the pictures of these wolves jumping up at those sleighs, and the horse had something like a high yolk up over his neck.

Well, these old boys got enough altitude that no old wolf couldn't jump at them. You know, too, these Russians were mighty nice to these boys, when you consider that we don't give them much the best of it. We think they are running their country cockeyed, and I guess it's mutual, at least it should be.

Now don't get the idea that a plane is new in Russia, for they have a fine aviation system. I made a little part of this trip that these boys made. That was, I flew from London to Berlin, then to Moscow in 1926. They made practically the same jump, and when I landed in the afternoon in Moscow in a commercial plane, single motor, I was the only passenger, and the air was full of planes training, and we had to circle the field several times before we got the signal to land. Now that was five years ago.

I bet these boys saw many a plane in Russia. They have aviation societies over there that are maintained by the members not the government. They all throw in a small sum each and that goes to buy planes and fields and training flyers. It's a patriotic thing like we donate to our Red Cross or some other charity. You know those rascals along with all their cookee stuff, have got some mighty good ideas. If just part of 'em work they are going to be hard to get along with. Just think of everybody in a country going to work. I don't mean just like the ones that want to work, but I mean everybody.

What they mean by working is to produce something, to be of some benefit to the whole community. Just look at the millions of us here that tonight we haven't done a thing today that helps the country, or that helps anybody. We have just gone along and lived off of it, and we are just "lousy" with satisfaction of ourselves, just think what we could do over here if we ALL worked.

Don't get scared. I am not putting this in as a plan. But we must admit that other things being equal the nation that works and saves and don't let the profits go into the hands of a few thousand or million men, they are going to be dangerous competitors. We can't just laugh it off. We prospered for years on nothing but our natural resources. Well, they have got twice as much of anything as we ever had before we used it up.

It's a terrible way to live, and do, but you can't beat hard work, sacrifice, and unlimited resources. It's liable, if it does just even half way work out, to have us winging on our foreign trade. But that's for Mr. Hoover and Pat Hurley to worry about.[7] I am sleepy, goodnight.

448 ROGERS GIVES CHEER
FOR POST AND GATTY

Well, all I know is just what I read in the papers, and what I run into as I prowl hither to thither. I must tell you about a fine long visit I had with Post and Gatty, the round the World flyers.[1]

I happened to write a little piece one day complimenting the backer of that wonderful flight, Mr. Hall of Chickasha, Okla., speaking of his modesty.[2] Well I got a nice wire thanking me, and saying that in return he would like to bring the Boys to Claremore. Well the only way he could bring the Boys to Claremore was in an Auto, and knowing they were real aviators I knew they wouldent come in an Auto, so I wrote and said that if they got there they would have to land in a Parachute, so the old Town got busy and in five days built one of the dandiest little Airports you ever saw, and sure enough Hall made good.

He was to bring the Boys there. Well I was sitting around our little ranch in Santa Monica and just happened to think, why if I get up early in the morning, catch the east bound plane I can be in Tulsa tomorrow night and be in Claremore for the Big Doings the next morning at ten o'clock. Well that's just about the way I do things.

I don't ever plan ahead for anything. I don't even like to have dates ahead if I can help it. I like to do anything right now. So I grabbed the old aerial rattler the next morning, wired to Tulsa to have a Special Plane meet me in Amarillo Texas and they sent a Dandy, one of these Low wing Lockheads, with the retractable landing gear, (that folds up under the wings when it's in flight) so we really did fly to Tulsa.

Well they were giving them a big welcome there that night, and I got to the Banquet just in time, too late to eat, but of course had to deliver an oration, a real grammatical masterpiece—some of the old Oxford and Eton stuff.

Well you would have been proud of Claremore, even if you dident have any knowledge of it before. The little town had done a fine job. I flew over that morning in the Winnie May, (the ship they broke the record in). I was in the back compartment with Gatty and he was explaining all the different gadgets that he used to tell where he was. He was about eight or ten feet back of the Pilot Pots, and there was gas tanks in between. They talked by a head ear phone tube. They couldent even see each other.

Now a few things they told me of the flight. They had no Parachutes, they would have taken up too much room, and been too hard to sit on, and besides if you had to use 'em, where would you been anyhow. They carried nothing at all of any precautionary nature. Post said, "It was make it or else."

Now all you Radio Nuts get ready for a shock. Their Radio was a flop. Gatty said they didn't expect to use it only on getting the weather at the place they were headed to land at, but that it was a fliv. He says no radio had been made that will fit those particular requirements, so Radio played no part in their Accomplishment.

Now about their sleep. They only got one hour a night for the first five nights, and only fifteen hours in the whole trip. They attribute their staying awake to their lack of food, as they said they always kept hungry. They never allowed themselves to eat but just enough to get them by; in that way it helped to keep them awake. They also trained for it before starting. They tried staying awake a lot.

The most wonderful banquet, the finest food and the greatest assortment of wines, (they dident drink but they said they had eight different kinds served) was in Moscow, so evidently everybody is not as bad off as we hear.

They said they slept in a room that must have belonged to the Czar, and that it was the most gorgeous thing they ever saw. Said the Russians were wonderful to them. Said that the Country of Russia was the most wonderful in natural resources they ever saw, also about a thousand miles of China, where it was beautiful and fertile but not a soul or a house on it. They had to land in one field in Russia where it was entirely covered with water, and they dident know how deep it was, but there was not a place where it wasent covered with water.

Post said it was kinder scary landing; the water was from six inches to a foot and a half deep on the entire field. They only changed their Spark Plugs once, and that was on account of some heavy oil they got in one place. They did not make any miscalculation in landing in Solomon, Alaska, instead of Nome. They had intended landing in Solomon, as there is where their Gas was waiting for them. They had never intended landing in Nome.

They are very unusual Boys. Gatty is the more talkative of the two, (which ain't saying much). They both have absolute confidence in each other ability, they are still the Companions. Generally close association like that brings out all the bad in each other and they wind up wanting to eat each other up. They are mighty likable Boys. That Post is just full of determination. I would hate to tell him he couldent do anything.

Never will there be such a combination again, of ideal Flyer, Navigator, and Backer. This fellow Hall is unusual. Now those Wives, you Women would sure like them.[3] They are like their Husbands, the most modest, quiet, retiring, and both very pretty. You know that takes a lot of nerve to let a Husband make that trip. They are mighty brave little Women.

On leaving Claremore, their husbands took off for New York. They were in another Plane leaving for the west. I went to the Plane to bid the wives goodbye; each had their handkerchiefs to their eyes. They dident want to let me see 'em crying, they were rather ashamed. But darn it, it just give you an idea what they have gone through. Women played a part in that flight, greater than they have ever got credit for.

449   BACK HOME AGAIN

Well, all I know is just what I read in the papers. And I been doing a lot of reading in the papers here lately, for that's all I could do. You know the other day coming home from the big Claremore celebration on the Plane I either eat something that dident agree with me, at lunch in El Paso, where we stopped, or it was the general effects of what I had stacked in while at home in Okla. But anyhow I got home sick.

We always have such good things to eat at my sister's in Chelsea.[1] Beans, and what beans, kinder soupy navy beans cooked with plenty of real fat meat. Well when I can't knock off a whole bowl of those myself, why I am sick before I start. And then the ham, fried ham; they cure their own ham. Tom McSpadden my Brother in Law, he is the prize ham curer of any I ever saw. Smoked 'em with the old hickory log fire, then salts 'em away for all this time. Then the cooking of all this has got a lot to do with it. Sister Sallie has got an Senagambian Soul there, but she is more for arguing purposes. Sallie fixes it all up when I get home.

Then the cream gravy. You know there is an awful lot of folks that don't know much about eating gravy. Why not to be raised on gravy would be like never going swimming in the creek. They got their own cows and real cream. Ham gravy is just about the last word in gravys. Course good beefsteak gravy is good. You know we fry our beefsteak. It's cut in thin pieces, and say let me tell you something. Did you know all this eating raw, bloody, rare meat, like they order in these big hotels, and City people like, well that's just them. That ain't old western folks. Ranch cooks and Farm women fry steak thin and hard. That old raw junk goes for the high collors in Cities, they are kinder cannibalistic anyhow.

Well, you can get some awful good gravy by putting the old milk in the skillet after you fried a lot of good beefsteak. There's an awful lot of good gravy! A good old home cook can mix up a tasty batch of gravy just about out of anything. No sir the old city eaters missed some mighty fine grub when the don't take advantage of making gravy one of their regular dishes at every meal.

Now then comes the corn bread. Not the corn bread like you mean. I mean corn pone, made with nothing but meal, and hot water and salt. My old Daddy always had that at every meal, said it was only the high toned folks that eat biscuits, and light-bread or loaves like you all eat now. He called that "wasp nest," and thought that was just for the heathen. Well this corn pone is mighty hard to go hungry after. You see I am just a telling you My dishes that they have when I come. I am not telling you of what they have cause they know I would rather have it than to go out and kill the fatted calf, or kill a turkey or some Chickens.

Beans, cornbread, country ham, and gravy, and then just raw onions, either the young ones if they are in, or the sliced ones. Sallie had some dandy Bermudas that Tom had raised. He has the best garden in that part of the country. Well these wasent strong, so she was going to send me some to California. But I don't guess they would let them come in. No, that's one thing about California, if you raise anything better than they do, they got a law against it coming in. That's why it's awful hard to get good vegetables and fruits in California. They make you just use home talent.

Then for desert? Don't have room for any desert. Had any more room would eat some more beans.

Now then I go from there over to my old Home place where I was raised at OO-la-gah, and there her Son and his remarkable wife Madeline give you an encore on all this, and maby it tastes better, for this is the house you was born in.[2] So about all I do when I go to Oklahoma is just shake hands and eat.

So the day I left we come by the old ranch place and Madeline did have a fine dinner for us. Now she is out in the country with no ice, electricity or all that and yet she has got things that she can make everything that you would have at a town dinner. Can make ice cream. Yes got some kind of a doodad that makes ice out of a hot water thing, and she can put up and can more things than you ever saw, and this girl learned all this in the last five or six years. She wasent a Rancher; she was from the city of Los Angeles, but, Brother, she made a real Rancher's wife and a good one too. You know that's a funny thing, ranch girls don't stay with it much. Looks like the City ones, when they have to, really come through the best.

54

Well the old home place looked mighty fine. Bout all we got left to farms is their beauty. Lays on the bend of the Verdigris River. My father settled it just after the Civil War, same old log house weatherboarded over. Most of the farmers are all raising 'em a good garden and getting ready to try and offset a tough winter. What they going to do with people this winter anyhow? Conditions can't improve enough to help everybody by then, so Lord knows what it will be and especially if we hit a tough winter.

Oh, yes, I started out to tell you bout being sick. Well, I have been for a week or so, thought I was going to die, something I eat either at El Paso where the plane stopped for lunch, or the night before at Amon G. Carter's "Shady Oak Farm."[3] I had dinner with him and the Gas Sextette and there was an amateur Doctor Walker, that mixed up a batch there laid me low.[4]

The Doctors called it Catarrhal Jaundice. I was the yellowest White man you ever saw. I never have heard who else died from this Carter dinner; the diet was, cove Oysters canned, then canned tomatoes, and raw onions all in one mess. Well, if they was laying for me, they got me. Next week I will write you of all the pleasures of being sick.

450   FARM BOARD KNOWS SOMETHING AFTER ALL

Well all I know is just what I read in the papers. Been under the weather and been doing nothing but reading, and taking some pills, and trying to talk the Doctor out of some more grub. Good deal of debts have gone under the Auctioneer's hammer since I last communed with you, both private and National and International. Germany got a Moratorium, the Big International Bankers got theirs guaranteed, Taxpayers got another assessment, and the Farmers got exactly what everybody had been predicting they would get—two bits for their wheat.[1] But we are told that indirectly this good that we did Germany, will trickle to get through the weeks and mortgages.

Course here is one thing where the Farm Board is right; (I havent heard that in so long that it scared me when I wrote it down).[2] They told the Farmers NOT to plant so much wheat, they said there was going to be a big supply this fall, and you knew yourself that they hadent sold last year's crop. So I kinder string with the Farm Board in that. You know the Farmers don't use their own heads a whole lot. Some of 'em don't even use anybodys.

Now it was last year that the Farm Board bought up all this wheat, and had nothing to do with it. From the day they started buying the first bushel it started going down, and no matter how fast they bought, it went down faster. Well there you was. You hadent put in this year's wheat yet. Now Russia had an awful big mess of it, and if you read, you knew that they would lose money on it in order to take away some one else's market, especially us. You knew that they would perhaps under the five year plan put in more wheat than ever before, because they ain't supposed to know how to raise anything else.

Now the Argentine had a bumper crop. They had their last year's crop still to sell. Then you got to take this consideration that every country both big and little that havent heretofore raised wheat, knowing they were at the mercy of those few big powers, have encouraged raising all that their folks could. Italy and England raise a lot more than they used too, not near enough but it all counts up.

Now then here is the Farm Board with their millions of bushels. Granaries full of private wheat. The worst depression in years. Now I just want to ask one question. What in the World made any Farmer think that things could possibly be any better than they was when he planted the wheat? Had he been listening to Chamber of Commerce speeches? How did anyone think that just over night we was going like we used too? What was there to look forward to that was going to raise everyone out of the dumps any more than there is something to look forward to that is going to lift us out overnight now—not even overnight but over a year? So why would a man, knowing the amount of wheat that was going to be on the market the next year, knowing that nobody was going to have anything to buy it with if they did want it, why would he go and gamble everything he had in more wheat?

We used to think that a wheat Farmer was smarter than a Cotton Farmer, and the Wheat one thinks so yet, (Well maby not now). But, by golly, it looks like there ain't no way to get any people to cut down on anything as long as they think the other fellow ought to do the cutting down first. There is some excuse for the Cotton Planter, especially the renter one, for he has to put in what he is told too or else, and he hasent enough machinery and stock to put in anything else. But with the wheat Farmer it's most generally a man that is his own boss. He generally owns the land, or had it rented to do with what he likes.

So it looks like he is going to do the same as the south has with its cotton, just go broke with it and be buried right in the patch, but he is going to plant plenty of cotton. You know there is few things that even the Government can't protect you against, even if they wanted too, unless they send you to an asylum. Now here is where the Government made their mistake; they said "Don't raise so much wheat," so you raised it, and they can't say they "told you not to." But they dident tell you NOT to raise anything, and everything else has been as low as wheat. See? That's what they should have done. They should have said, "Don't raise a thing only what you can eat yourself." You would have let your land gain a year, you would have saved all your seed wheat, or corn, or Oats, and while you wouldent have made anything you wouldent have lost anything.

But the Gag now is not to raise anything only that fits your appetite. Then the price don't worry you. The Republicans don't fret you. The Democrats don't preach at you. Just raise all you can eat and let the low prices go by.

451   ALFALFA BILL KNOWS HIS OIL

All I know is just what I read in the papers, and I havent had much time to peruse the prints here lately. Being a Col. on Alfalfa Bill's staff means action.[1] These Wars of his were coming so fast there for awhile that they were over-lapping. We finished licking Texas over the Free Bridge late one afternoon and before dark that same night, why Bill had one matched with the Big Oil People. And he told me that that was nothing to what he had in view for the future.

You know not only in Oklahoma or anybody else's State we havent had a fighting Governor for years. Most of 'em have just been plain old every day Politicians that dident look for any more excitement than the next election. But with Bill it's different. He knows Oil ain't what it ought to be, and so he just loaded up his old Musket and started out to put it on a paying basis.

The Standard Oil and all those big fellows ain't monkeying now with injunctions, and Habus Corpuses, and all that old hooey, they are up against bullets now. Us Hoklamonians don't mess with all the ordinary procedures; we just go shoot it out till we get our price.

If Bill gets away with this, why it will be the road to a lot of industries loading up and trying to get $1 a Bottle for Pepsident, or 75 cents per gill for Sloan's anticeptic mouth wash. I would like to see the old Butter and Egg men go out for a higher revenue on the output of the Heifer and Pullet. Trouble is there ain't any of them that have got another Bill Murray. You got to have Leaders, and Bill ain't enough to go round. Just Our own industries alone is going to keep us Boys in the trenches till Xmas.

Bernard Shaw and Nancy Astor, two of my old London friends, been to Russia and got back a couple of weeks ago.[2] Shaw was so impressed that he couldent tell the reporters a thing. (Free), he was waiting till he could get home and write it himself. (I have done that same thing many a time.) Bernard and I and Calvin got to live on our "Cracks," wise and otherwise, and we can't be handing out a lot of information on where we had been and what we have seen.

Shaw seems to have got over mighty big up there. He has always kinder pulled for 'em, and it was a great thing for their Country when they landed him to come up. And taking Lady Astor and her husband, who have a lot of money, and favorabley impressing them, why that was a big job, cause if Nancy don't think it's working, why she will sure blat it out.[3] There is none of the forflusher in her; she is the plainest spoken Woman you ever saw.

Bernard told 'em if he was a young man he would stick with 'em. That was a mighty pretty compliment; it dident bind him to anything. He was already old, so he dident have to stick by it, so he can go back to London to all his luxury and don't have to worry about the five year plan only from a distance. I been reading a lot of books on that thing and it sounds so big it almost scares you, a whole nation of 150 million people all working, no profit, no board of Directors, No Dividends, No Wall Street to Support.

Just think for a minute what would be the profits on products in this Country, if there was no Grain or Produce Exchanges or Wall Street to provide for. Look what a Farmer would get if he got all that the Consumer paid. Then all the Big Industries being run with no profit, turning everything out at cost. Their own Steel mills, their own Ore Mines, own water power and an unlimited supply of coal, Wood, the greatest forests in the World, all productive. No Deserts. You see they are playing with the biggest natural resource fountain in the World.

If Italy started the same thing it wouldent mean so much, for they could work as hard, but they would have to buy raw materials from other Countries. But these folks have everything that any other Nation has only more of it.

Now they are buying brains, people to show 'em how to get all this organized. We have thousands of trained men over there, working to show them how to work with different machines. Now when they learn that they won't leave us any corner on it, for no nation has a monopoly on brains. The thing sure is worth watching for just the idea of everybody working and producing something is going to have collosal effects.

Look at what we produce, and there is only about one third of us producing anything. The two thirds are living off the one third, and then we got more than we can sell. So just imagine what price they will be able to sell stuff for. No, you can't laugh 'em off, they sure got some weird ideas, and things that a people like ours would never in the world tolerate. But they have got some ideas that if carried out properly is bound to make the world do some changing in this unequal division of wealth.

For that's what's the matter with us. No Country ever had more, and no Country ever had less. Ten men in our Country could buy the World, and ten million can't buy enough to eat. So the salvation of all that might come out of these Cuckoo Russians. If it does, it will have paid for itself whether the whole five year plan works or not. So we ain't going to get nowhere cussing 'em. We better watch 'em, and if they got anything any good, why cop onto it, and maby we can feed everybody.

452   IF THE FARMER QUITS

Well all I know is just what I read in the papers. Let me state you all some figures! 3 bushels of wheat buys 1 bushel of Potatoes. It takes 5 bu. of Oats to buy one bu. of Potatoes, 2 barrels of oil buys one bu. of Potatoes, and mind you potatoes ain't high either, they are only worth about 80 cents a bushel.

2 bushels of wheat to get a frying chicken, and the old Pullette ain't high either. She is only retailing at about 50 cents on the hoof. It takes ten bushels of wheat to get a 50 pound sack of flour. Think of that, ten bushels of wheat to each sack of flour. You would think the thing wasent made out of wheat wouldent you? It takes 20 bushels of wheat to buy one pair of shoes, and then you only got five dollar shoes.

A pair of good Cowboy shop made Boots would just cause you to raise three whole acres of wheat at about 33 bushels to the acre, and that ain't counting on the rust. It takes a bushel of wheat to get a mess of roasting ears. You know what that is, you City Slickers? Well it's that stuff you eat off the cobb, and get it all in your ears, and if you got a front tooth missing you miss one row. 3 bushels of wheat to get you two pounds of bacon.

It takes two whole bushels of Oats to get you one pound of steak, and that won't be so tender either. 2 bu. of wheat buys you one pound of coffee. You have to trade two bushels of oats for one quart of Motor Oil, and three barrels of oil for one quart of Motor Oil. You see, it's like the wheat and the Flour, what a thing is made out of has nothing to do with the finished product. The price of a Cow has nothing to do with a steak, wheat to flour, or Oil to Motor Oil. A Bushel of wheat will get you a dozen eggs to go with your three bushels worth of bacon. So, for about a quarter of an acre's growing of wheat, you can have bacon and eggs in the ONE morning.

It takes a bu. of wheat to get a package of Post Bran. Now what's it made out of? I dident think it was wheat, and I guess it is not. If you want some butter on your bread that will cost you another bushel of wheat, and it takes a whole bushel of wheat to get one package of Cigarettes. Up to now you have blowed in 159 bushels of wheat and all you got is some bacon and eggs, one chicken, some fried potatoes, and a pair of Cowboy boots, on three full wagon loads of wheat. Oh yes, you had some motor oil and some roasting ears and a package of Cigarettes. Now you got you some smokes you got to go to town and show the boys you can inhale. It will just cost you 2400 bushels of wheat to plant yourself in a Ford Sedan. At forty bushels to the acre, the Ford will just set you back 60 acres of wheat. Course you can go seventy acres and get a Chevrolet, that's if you got plenty of acres.

By now you need some more Cigarettes so you got to shell out another bushel of oats. Takes another five acres to get you a Radio so you can keep track of the Market, and see how many bushels of wheat a Package of Cigarettes are running that day. With a radio you can tell how bad you are off every minute of the day. 2 pair of silk hose will knock your old grainery loose from 8 bu. of wheat, or twelve of Oats. Just one lone Golf Club bumps you off for another ten bu. of wheat. Now the wife and children are smoking, we got to have more cigarettes. "Lets get 24 boxes?" Well, haul twenty four bushels of oats to town and make the trade.

Need a hair cut but I forgot to bring a bushel and a half of wheat with me. A shave is a bushel of oats. "Here, Rastus, is a bushel of oats; give me a shine." 200 bushel of wheat gets you one set of new harness to start raising some more high priced wheat. A new work team will cost you 600 bushels. A bushel of oats will get you three packs of chewing gum. Now we need ten gallons of oil for the car, so we got to sack off 15 bushels of wheat.

What you say about a Permanent? Cost you twelve bushels of wheat. If we had just put in another acre of wheat we could have got that pair of silk pajamas. Well take in another truck load of wheat and bring out another day's rations of meat and bread and bran and Cigarettes.

"Pa, if you got ten bushels of wheat the family can all go to the Movies and see the gangsters kill each other and talk about Millions. What do you say we get a Tuxedo and turn Gangster, Pa? This farming is the bunk. All we got to do is see two more pictures and we can do it as good as the Gangsters." Send in the truck with another load of wheat, we got to have some Gasoline, Radio Batteries some new Rube records, and Cigarettes. Minnie is going to High School but it takes 20 bushels of wheat to get her a Bathing suit.

And Lord rest my Soul if there ain't the tax man. This land is taxed at $60 an acre — was taxed when wheat was $2.50 a Bushel. Now wheat is two bits and it's still taxed at $60. When they going to do like the City folks do, pay on your income. If you don't earn anything you don't pay anything. And if there ain't the old Banker who had a mortgage on my crop and Teams and Tools. Paid him 8% and a bonus to get the loan. Reading where money was loaning in the City for as low as 1%. Well that's what you get for living in the Country I guess. Wish all the Farmers would move to town one year that's the only way I know to clear the thing up.

453 WHY NEWS IS SLACK

Well, all I know is just what I read in the papers. News is awful slack. Depression is on in the news world. We had quite a run of news up till a year or so ago. But everything seemed to fail us at once. Good many lay it to Coolidge getting out. He was always news. Every new picture he had made, every different hat he wore, every pan cake for breakfast, every sausage, all was news. Mr. Hoover does just as much, maby more, eats just as much, maby more. But when depression is on, it's just on and you can't do nothing about it. You can't make news out of nothing, no more than you can make work out of no jobs.

There just ain't no news and now some of our big men predict that there will be a turn for the better, that there will be news coming our way any day now. They claim that News is just around the corner, and that it will be on us before we know it. They claim that there has been times like this before, and the Press has come out of it, and that it will do it again. But never has there been as general a shortage of news all over the World as there is now. Now in the old days when there might not be anything doing in the United States, why over in England there would be some big news in parliment, or an argument with Ireland, or the Prince of Wales would be doing something. Or they would be ruling the Sea somewhere, or over in France, they would be argueing with some Tourists, or down in Italy Mussolini would be either making a speech or getting shot at or something, or both.[1] But Lord we can't even depend on him any more. He has fell down on us like Sister Aimee.[2]

Since the King left Spain it was just like a little Circus having their only Elephant leave.[3] The Show just don't do no more business. Argentine and Brazil, and Chili all used to be good for some news, but now the Tango is as dead as the Charlestown, and the Gigilos they furnish this country ain't much improvement on the home grown. Australia not only can't afford any Adds, but they can't even send us in any "Personal Items." They are as dead as Austria, who havent made the front page since the Merry Widow Waltz. Germany here a few weeks ago made a little spurt for news, then died right back out again.

Russia has been a sort of a partial life saver. They put on a Five-year plan that sounded front pagey at first, but then we don't understand it and the more we have it explained the less interesting it becomes. It will take us five years to even fathom it, so it's not news any more.

Had a series of Aeroplane flights, but they all come so thick that we got 'em mixed up and we couldent tell who was flying which Ocean, or what was the names of the ones that did. Post and Gatty helped us out mighty nice for a week or so there.[4] Lindy and Anne sorter stirring things up now.[5] Then some other Boys started to go round the World and traded their compass for a Camera away off over there and started in taking Pictures for a sideline.[6] Was just getting a focus on a Japanese Fort, when the Japs developed their plates for 'em, and only charged 'em a thousand Bucks apiece for it.

Bernard Shaw and Lady Astor eloped together to Russia, but their ages kinder acted against the news value of the story.[7] Mexico never was as uninteresting. Depression has knocked the Revolution business back where it just don't pay to loot. The Earthquake was the last news we had from Nicaragua.[8] Since Smedley Butler left the Marines you can't hear much from them.[9] Navy is resting on its Oars. The Army Fliers the other day was given a Boat to sink, and they dropped every thing on it but their Parachutes but they couldent sink it. Finally it rotted.

Mayor Walker is over in Germany looking for the Child Slayer Bandits.[10] Mr. Hoover wouldent take a vacation this summer, so that knocked us out of all that news. Remember what a lively summer we had when Mr. Coolidge went to the Black Hills? So it's just been one bad break after another. Congress is out of session, so that means the old laughs is missing from your morning papers every day.

What the Republicans are doing, and what the Democrats are doing is of no interest to anybody any more, for no one knows one from the other. There is no fighters on either side. They both want a Tariff on what their part of the Country raises, and free trade on what is raised in other parts. But the depressing part of it is that I don't see much hope of any news coming anyways soon. Out of these other news depressions something big has happened to get 'em some news. It's generally been a war. Nothing revives interest in the Press like a good war. It don't necessarily have to be local, it can be foreign if it's a good one.

You see the trouble nowadays is that no one can think of anything new to do. Everything that is done has been done before, so there is no news in it.

Murders have just been done to death. You got to have a mighty good murder to get on the front page. People just lost interest in 'em. Automobile accidents they just list them over in the personal column. We just in a big slump and we gradually got to read ourselves out of it. We got to make less news do us. We got to get back to the old times when we was satisfied with reading just what had actually happened, and not just laying for the Big things to read. Everybody has just got to buckle down and say, "Here, there is no news, but we are going to stick to the ship and keep reading and be satisfied with what little there is that happens." That's the only spirit that will bring back the news.

We just had an Orgy of news, and now when it's not coming why we are yelling. Those times never will come back. We got to just reconcile ourselves to that, so buckle down and be satisfied with less. It may be years before there is much news. It's going to take a new generation of people to make new News. For there just ain't any interest in the old bunch here now.

454   TOUGH ON THE LEADERS

Well, all I know is just what I read in the papers. Lot of Prime Ministers have passed under the bridge since I last broke news with you.

Poor Mr. Ramsay MacDonald he is still in there, but under another uniform.[1] He was a very able conscientious man. But just like all the leaders everywhere the victims of the slump. Being President or leader of any country during the last two years was just like arriving at the crossing just as the stop signal was against you. There is nothing you can do but just stand and watch your predecessor get through a-flying, and you wait till somebody switches something over which you have no control.

I don't suppose there is a leader today who, if he had known what was in store for him, wouldent have thrown the job right back in your face when offered it. It's just an off season for leaders.

The labor government come in when things looked bad over in England, and the people thought that they could do something for labor. Well, Mr. MacDonald and Mr. Hoover can't get you a job if nobody wants to hire you. They havent any personal positions to put you in. So when things went fluey, why they were the goats.

You see, over in England when you and your cabinet can't agree on some major issue and everything is all cockeyed, why the Prime Minister is supposed to have lost control of his party and he resigns and sends his resignation to the King. In fact, I think he takes it. Well, then that generally means another election to put in some other party, but a general election costs a lot of money, and besides it is sometimes unwise on account of conditions to leave a thing to the people. They might not be in the mood to receive it like you would like to have them receive it.

They can't have an election now in England for there is so many unemployed, and so many dissatisfied that they are liable to even vote further than for labor and go almost Bolsheviki. A hungry man is looking for immediate results and not caring for future conditions.

You see the whole thing come about over the amount of the "Dole." They were running short of money, and wanted to cut down on the amount given to the unemployed. Well, these have been getting that so long that it's like saying "Now here, you been eating three meals a day but we got to cut you to two." The unemployed are NOT working, but they are in a position to dictate. Well, Ramsay wanted to cut the Dole in half. So instead they just cut his authority in half. Then they said in order to give him a kind of a dignified exit, "You go form a colition cabinet, and see what you can do with it." That means that he can take in a few from each party. So he got him three conservatives, three labor and a couple of liberals. The liberals are the old Lloyd George party, and they are the smallest party, but neither of the others have a majority so that leaves them like the Progressives in our Senate.[2] They are the ones you have to deal with before you put anything over.

Well, the co-lition got together and they knew that their only hope was to cut some of the Dole, but they knew what had happened to Ramsay when he wanted to nip off half of it. So they kinder studied and figured if they proposed to slash off a third would they still be able to retain their positions? Then they held another huddle and decided that about ten percent ought not to make 'em so mad that they would throw them (the co-lition) out on their ear. So co-lition really means careful.

Now they are going to pull through. They are that kind of people. They feel their loss of banking prestige worse than they do anything else. When you have been the world's money headquarters, why it's sorter hard to see it slip away. But they got great what do you call it re-cuperative powers, or stick-to-it-iveness. They will juggle around and fit their business to present conditions.

You know Mr. Hoover is sorter right about that "Dole." He has seen what it has done for England, and he knows what it would do for this country. Of course, no country in it's right mind would ever adopt the method that England did. That is just give people money that couldent work, and not make them do something for it — just let them sit and draw enough pay to live on. It's got to be done by giving them something to do for that money. That's what ruined the whole plan over there.

I will never forget in one of the Arkansaw towns that I visited with Frank Hawkes last year on our tour.[3] They had been feeding something over three hundred in their soup kitchen, and one night they announced that they had arranged so that everyone would be given work the next morning at about (I think it was $1.50 a day). You could get a real meal in town for 25 cents, and after three meals that would have left you 75 cents. Well, the next morning there was less than seventy-five out of the three hundred showed up. So you see that is where England pulled their boner.

You can't just give people something for nothing, you got to do something for what you get. Now they got big committees working in all the big cities getting money for the coming fall and winter. Mr. Hoover is going to insist on the people taking care of each other as long as it is possible to do so, and that will be a long time, for never was there as much money in the hands of the few as now. So you see England's problem is our problem. Germany, Italy, Australia, everywhere you look or read about it's the same unemployment.

Well, we been twenty years honoring and celebrating the inventor who could save a dollar by knocking somebody out of work, now we are paying for it. Machines are a great thing, but if one replaces a hundred men, it don't buy anything, it don't eat anything, while the hundred men spend theirs back for food, shelter, and hundred of various commodities for them and their families. So they can have all the theories and plans they want but till you get rid of something and put people back to work, you ain't going to be able to fix it. You can call it co-lition, Republican, Democrat or Bolsheviki. But folks got to have work.

455   ROYALTY IN THE MOVIES

We had a kinder funny experience the other day over at the Studio. I was working on a Picture that is supposed to take place over in Europe. I am Ambassador to some mythical Kingdom.[1] It's kinder the story of Roumania, with the young King and Queen seperated, and a Kid who is King, and I drop in as Ambassador A la Aleck Moore, who incidentally made us a dandy Ambassador to Spain.[2]

Well, we was shooting the big Reception scene, where the young King and the Queen was receiving all the Diplomats and we had the real Nationalities. You know that is one thing about Hollywood, you don't have to fake any Nationality, just issue a call and there will be dozens of any breed under the Sun. In our last Picture before this we wanted some Arabs on the desert. We had over a hundred that come right from Arabia. All lived here in Hollywood, Greeks, Armenians, Indians from India, and everything. Well this day we had a great many Russians, Russians that really were somebody before the Country went Bernard Shaw.[3] Every one of them spoke four or five languages, Germans, Poles, Checko-Slovakians. Well all these different races were in full court dress, with all the decorations. Well who should come out on the set but the Siamese Party. Not the King and his wife that are visiting over here, they went home through Canada, but it was his own Uncle, Prince, (he said you spelled it just like our Indian word for the Indian cross, "Swastica," only with the C out.)[4] He and his wife and his two sons.

One of the Sons goes to Georgetown University, and the other to Yale. They are a couple of mighty fine Boys, little in statue like all the Siamese, but pleasant and a good sense of humor. But it's of this King's Uncle that I got to tell you about. He is a Bear, you would be crazy about him. He speaks English with no trace of an accent. He is an Oxford Man. Of course we went over old times when he and I and Brisbane were there.[5] Well it seemed kinder odd to be making a picture of a Royal Court, and here was some real Royalty sitting there watching us. We wanted him to replace Mr. Sam Taylor who was directing the scene, and let the Prince direct it himself as that scene

Will Rogers in the title role of Ambassador Bill (Fox Film Corporation, 1931).
Arnold Korff portrayed the commanding general of the imaginary kingdom of Sylvania.

should be right up his alley.[6] He had served his Country on every important mission to every important Country on the Globe. A Russian was standing near us with all the old Czar decorations on. The old Gentleman called him over and said, "I have all five of those decorations. That's the White Eagle, That's the St Andrews," and he reeled off each one and then he pointed to one that the imitation decoration was not just correct. "That Insigna is not that way, it's this way."

He had made five trips to Russia on important missions, and making of new Treaties. So we kiddingly wanted him to direct the scene. He said no we wouldent pay him the big money that Movie Directors got, and he wouldent be a cheap Director. So we started taking the scene. I was announced and come in, walked the length of this great room with all the beautiful Ladies in sparkling Gowns, and men in bright colored Uniforms. When I reached the Queen and was announced as the new Ambassador from the U. S. the Queen put out her hand, and instead of me kissing it I just grabbed it and shook it. Well the old Prince let out a snort and said "No, No." He liked to have had a fit. He dident know that we purposely took it that way for the comedy effect.

Then when I told the Queen that I was a single man and had no children but would like to adopt her Boy (the King) why the royal party did like to have a fit sure enough. But he soon got on that we were playing it for comedy, (about the only way to take a Court). He had the most pleasant little wife, and the jewels she had on, these Movie folks that were there had on a lot of fake jewelry in the scene with their Court costumes, but she made a sucker even out of their Junk. She was dressed awful plain, but the bracelets and rings mostly of Rubies, they had us all gapping so we couldent act. He was on his way up to Vancouver to join the King and Queen of Siam and go back home with them. I told him I was coming over there in about a year and visit his country as I was going to make a trip around the World. I asked him how I could find out who or where he was over there. He dident get me for a minute and said, "Oh you can find me, I am chief Justice of the supreme Court of Siam, I am Royal Prince of . . . ," and then he got it that I was kidding when I asked him.

But he asked me to come see him. Course that's what everybody does when they are away from home, then you go and try and get in. But you know they must have a mighty fine little Country over there, and their Royalty seem to get on fine with their subjects. But a kind of a sad part of the scene was that here were a lot of Russians in the Picture, playing just extras and small parts, yet they had all occupied more or less important positions in their home Country.

Whether you were for the Czar or not, they were born and raised under them, and it wasent their fault. One had been a great Actor in Russia, played at the royal Theatre in leading parts. Several High Military officers, and the stories they all can tell of how they got out of there, and the struggles they have had since, each one is a novel in itself. There is no more interesting place in the world to meet characters than a Movie set. If you have lost anybody anywhere in the World and don't know where they are, they are in Hollywood trying to get in the Movies.

456 CROSSING THE SHOALS

Well all I know is just what I read in the newsprints. England has been the most consistent headliner of the last couple of weeks. We do love to read about some other Nation's difficulties, it kinder gets our mind off our own.

Well now I tell you you better do your gloating pretty soon over her hard times if that's the way you are geared up, for she won't be that way long. Always remember she never looks good till it looks bad, then she comes through. A Nation is built on Character the same as a person is and no matter what their financial difficulties are that old Character shows up.

They got many long headed old men over there, and when they get in trouble they just drop the Politics and start getting together regardless of Party. The fellow Ramsay MacDonald must be quite a fellow.[1] I don't think the labor party did themselves any good by throwing him out. He is either mighty sincere or the best Actor in public life.

Then there is old man Lloyd George.[2] There is a smart old hombre. He is kinder the Borah of the islands over there.[3] I heard him make the best speech I ever heard in any Congressional Hall when we were over there to the Dissarmament Conference last year.

Chili broke out a couple of weeks ago. Their Navy revolted and took to sea with the ships. The Aviation end stuck to the Government and went out and started in dropping various articles on 'em, mostly lead and the revolters give up so quick it looked almost like a frame up.

Our Army Aviators had some trouble hitting a ship of ours. But these old Chilianians sho was poking 'em down the smokestacks of those old battle wagons down there.

Did you hear what Dave Ingalls, Secretary of the Navy for

Aviation, told the Army fliers when they couldent hit that old tub?[4] Well he sure kidded 'em plenty. But one side is about as good as the other. There would be no reason why one branch of our air forces would be superior to the other. They are all flyers and good ones. I would hate to be in even a row boat and have 'em dribbling things from the air at me.

Now we got England and Chili fixed and Aviation, we will take Mayor Walker.[5] He has kicked up a Revolution of his own. Everybody in New York was either shooting at somebody or getting shot, so he grabs a Boat and goes on a tour of Europe for his health. Last spring he was out here with us in California while they was going through his record back there. He is always on the jump while the Boys are looking over the minutes of the last meeting.

France give him the Legion of Honor, England the Knight of the Garter, and Germany the Watch on the Rhine. He has gone through Europe like Aimee through a Revival.[6] He has met people that the Republicans investigating him at home couldent get in apple throwing distance of. Last summer we sent twenty Mayors over there to offset the good our Soldiers had done. Now Jim has to go over to offset the Mayors. If the Rupublicans get out enough Inditements against him he will be met when he comes home by Democratic New York like a Channel Swimmer. He can pick his own job to run for. When he returned from California the Town raised his salary fifteen thousand a year in answer to the Republicans' charges.

The kid is just too swift for 'em. He hasent much against him however, for the Republicans have used the poorest judgement in fighting Tammany.[7] They have never guessed right yet. It seems funny that the dumbest Republicans must be located in the State of New York. Smith used to whip 'em every time they peeped.

Now Walker has made a sucker out of 'em. He may be the best Mayor in the World or he may be the worst but the opposition can't tell you right now. They have accused him of everything from Bigamy to mayhem, but they can't convict him of a traffic ordinance.

Now let's get back home and see what is doing here. Is things going to pick up? Yes, and No. Yes for the rich, and No for the poor. Now what is our problem? Why it's to take care of those that havent. How? Well how can it be done only by taking from those that have and giving to those that havent?

The question is how are you going to take it? First you are going to ask 'em to give it to you. Try and get it by voluntary subscriptions. That puts a tax on genorisity, for the liberal will do all the giving and the skinflints will do all the talking about it as usual.

So that at best will only be a temporary way, and can't last through a long hard winter, so it ought to be done by taxation. What kind of taxation? Why on those able to pay it. Off incomes in the higher brackets. England did it the other day, they had a tremendous high income tax, but they boosted it still higher.

They don't monkey with playing Politics when something is needed. Five percent on incomes of over $100,000 would be fair, for the rate stops at $100,000 for some reason or other, it don't keep on going up like it does up to the $100,000.

A man making a million don't pay any more on his last $100,000 than the fellow on his first. Why stop it up there where a man is just getting in shape to pay? That five percent would do the whole thing.

Will it pass? Not unless you poison all the Republicans. They take care of big money for big money takes care of them.

A Sales tax will also do it, with practically no tax on necessities and a big one on luxuries, and a big Inheritance tax to get the fellow that don't spend. Well that practically settles that, so by next week everybody ought to be doing fine.

457   GANDHI AND AIMEE

Well all I know is just what I read in the papers. With Aimee marrying out here a couple of weeks ago, there just dident leave much else to be said.[1] They hadent any more than finished saying "I Do" till the breach of promise suits commenced pouring in. Poor Ma Kennedy she hadent got the bridal veil off till old wives commenced showing up all over the country. It looked like she had married a professional marrier.

Well her and old "Whataman" was just kinder getting their License straightened out when Aimee grabs a Baritone, one of those old Choir loves. Well then everybody that had ever slept through Church started in saying he had deceived 'em in some part of the country or other. One was a Nurse and she claimed that she was an old flame of his when she wasent nursing. Why don't they let the Woman alone? She does a lot of good with her Church. She is what every Preacher in America wants to and is trying to be, and that's a good showman. She has got some kind of a musical show on at her church now, based on the Bible, and this old Boy she married is Paraoh, and they got the stage or pulpit all litered up with Bull rushes, and Girls. But it's good clean wholesome entertainment, if you don't get any religion out of it it keeps you out of some other devilment.

Next to Aimee the biggest headliner lately has been this little fellow Gandi.[2] He just blew into London with nothing on but a Diaper and he has had the whole British Empire bringing sticks out of the water for him. They look on him over in India as almost a second God, and I guess he does come nearer living and acting like our Saviour than any one else ever did. He is different from Aimee, she believes in the Lord but she believes in some luxuries along with it. She don't deny herself anything. While this Gandi he actually lives like our Saviour. He couldent figure out England being so hard up, and yet spending so much money.

You know there hasent been a case like that little fellow in our lifetime. If he is not sincere then he is the World's best Actor, and say old England as big as he is is sho paying some attention to him. Everybody thinks he is a great man but Jimmy Walker and Jimmy had never heard of him.[3] Gandi is not what you would call a Tammany man. Jimmy got home from his investigation cure, and those dumb Republicans in New York are no nearer getting anything on him than they ever were. They always talk in generalities and not in any specific case where they can prove something.

World Series will be on pretty soon and that's when depression will end for about sixty thousand every day. Philadelphia plays St. Louis as usual. St. Louis dident win for years then they accidentally won one year, and saw what a cinch it was, they have practically kept it up since then. Most teams when they found out they had to play the Athletics in the World Series dident try to win. But St. Louis is a glutton for punishment, they are getting ready for another sock in the jaw.

I want to make that if I can. I havent seen one of the World Series games in three or four years. I used to have some great friends playing ball in the good old days, Speaker, Walter Johnston, Cobb, Duffy Lewis, Harry Hooper, and a host of others.[3]

I never have seen one of these night games. I just can't imagine how they can get it light enough to see how to play ball but they say it's great, and is drawing a lot of people out here. Los Angeles and Hollywood are fighting it out for the Pennant. They call the Hollywood team the "Sheiks" out here, and Oscar Vitt another old friend and ex-Detroit Player is their Manager.[4] Football is coming so fast that it's not leaving much news for depression. The Four Horsemen of the great Notre Dame fame have been out here donating their time to the making of a great picture called the Spirit of Notre Dame, including all the famous Stars of past and present, and afternoon they did me the great favor of coming up to my little ranch and playing around, riding horses just like a backfield can.[6] They are fine Boys, and everyone of them are making good as Coaches.

That must be a great school. I sometimes wish I had gone there instead of stringing along with Brisbane and going to Oxford.[7] Course I made the Cricket team and knocked a couple of hundred runs in one game one series. But after all Tea and Cricket don't do you much good when you got to get out and battle Republican made depression. It's all right as long as Democratic Prosperity is with us why an Oxford diploma will get you by, but when steel hits a new low, and Radio quits splitting up four for one, why you got to have some real learning.

Going to Claremore this week end. We're going to have big blow out. Did you know Claremore has Polo now? You bet your life she has. We got one of the best Military Schools in the west, and they have Government Horses, and a fine bunch of young boys there that can really ride. We will be giving Roswell, New Mexico a tough go pretty soon. In a few years Polo will be as big a sport in schools as football, and it's a great thing for the Horse raisers, ranchers, feed raisers, everything. Well will see you at the World Series. So long.

458   FROM CHINA TO TEXAS

Well all I know is just what I read in the Papers. Japan pounced on China.[1] She has had China cut off from her hole for a long time, like a cat does a rat and just says, "I'll nab you when you make a run for it."

China is in pretty bad shape fighting amongst herself at home, and this Manchuria is a mighty valuable piece of territory and will make mighty nice reperations after the thing is over. You know you often hear it said that nobody got anything after the war. But what about the German Colonies? You don't see England or France or any of those giving any up do you? Germany I imagine would mortgage quite a lot to pay for them back. That's one of the reasons that she is up against it, she hasent got those Colonies to transfer trade and raw material with.

China is so big and the names are so much alike that it's hard to tell where she is fighting at. Texas and Louisiana had war. The Legislature of Texas called the Gov. of Louisiana a Liar by vote.[2] Just show you that anything can pass a Legislature. It's going to take about two years to prove that the old Boy in Louisiana is right. He says they shouldent plant any cotton at all this year anywhere. Well they havent sold last year's, or the year's before crops, so who looks like they are right? It certainly won't hurt that land in the south to not plant anything on it for a year, for it has had a Negro and a mule walking over it since 65.

There is so many things they can raise down there that they don't even know exists. There is feed and fertilizing crops that grown in other parts of the country that would be wonderful for their land but it could never get in the country on account of the Cotton which had a monopoly and wouldent let anything in. But if your Father and Grand Father raised wheat, or if he raised Cotton, why Cotton is the only thing. Stick to your raising.

But those little arguments that look big at the time, by next week's paper they are all forgotten. Texas has got a pretty good bunch in their infirmary there at Austin. It was just one spell binder that got 'em all worked up, over their honor. You can always get a body of folks riled if you drag in that their honor has been attacked. Collectively we havent much more honor than we have individually, so it's never enough to fight over.

Then England kicked up a mess a couple of weeks ago when they did somthing about their Gold. I don't know what it was, but it created a lot of ink at the time. It looks like the world is on a Gold Standard but only two have got any gold, Us and France, and if things keep on like they have there won't be any Us in there.

You see France is getting everything, for they went to work the day they got back from the War, and the rest of the Nations went on a spree, so France got back to normal when the Guns stopped shooting, and we are just getting back, but we havent been normal in so long that we don't recognize it since we got there.

This finance business has got the big Boys worried as much as the little ones that havent got any of it. Here we talk about high taxes. Say England can show you some taxes, they are getting what we will get if this unemployment keeps up, and it should be that way, there is lots of people able to pay yet over here before the Government starts in to do it itself. That was what Mr. Hoover was doing out in Detroit telling the American Legion not to start asking for aid again. You see, he believes in the people helping themselves right up to the time that's not possible, then the Government will help.

Now there is a lot to be said for his plan. There is certainly enough wealth to do it. But getting it away from the ones that have it is another thing. When you rely on just voluntary giving you put quite a hardship on the free giver. He will give till it hurts, while a man of perhaps much larger resources will give very little. So it looks

74

like they got to get at this relief thing through taxation on large incomes. But that will all be fixed at the next session of Congress, as five hundred Congressmen and 100 Senators will all have schemes to remedy everything from depression to protruding Adams Apples. It will take two years to just read all the bills that will be introduced when the Legislative Capones meet.

Well I don't know if I told you or not about Ma Kennedy going and playing a return date with "What-A-Man."[3] We was all in the midst of a lot of excitement out here, when Ma climbs right up on the most protruding rock over Boulder Dam and just took What-A-Man for better or for worse till another wife do them part. I never did get down to Sister Aimee's show I was telling you about, but they all told me it was mighty fine.[4]

We are dragging along about as usual out here, raise lots to eat, and it's cheap, and it's warm, we don't need much heat, and it looks like if the worst comes to the worst we could go through almost another Republican Administration.

By the way, they tell me Al Smith is making quite a stir in the east. They had a million Al Smith Buttons made and sold em right out. Course you can get your name on a button easier than you can get it on the letter box in front of the White House. But Al will surprise you with his strength, so we will have lots of Angles and predictions to work on between now and next June. Cause Roosevelt will be a tough man to beat for that nomination.[5] Then Calvin is coming out of the bushes I hear. There's a great Quartette, Hoover, Smith, Coolidge, Roosevelt. There will be a lot of signing done before next November.

459   COLONEL ZACH MULHALL

We lost a mighty fine old Western Character a few weeks ago. I know you all read in the papers about Col. Zack Mulhall dying, in Mulhall, Oklahoma, a town named for him, and in which he had been the leading citizen for many years.[1]

My show career kinder dates from the time I first run into the Col. It was in 1899 at the St. Louis fair, (not the World's fair) just the big St. Louis fair they held every year. They had decided as an attraction that they would put on a Roping and Riding Contest. They were not called Rodeo's, or Stampedes, in those days they were just what they are, a "Roping and Riding Contest." Well I was pretty much of a Kid, but had just happened to have won the first and about my only Contest at home in Claremore, Okla., and then we read about them wanting entries for this big Contest at St. Louis.

Well some one sent in my name, and the first thing I knew I was getting transportation for myself and pony to the affair. Well I went and Col. Zack Mulhall had charge of it. He was then, and had been for years the General Live Stock Agent for the Frisco Railroad System. That was a very important job in those days, for it took in all the live stock shipments on their whole line. He knew every big cattleman in the Southwest, and almost everybody else. I dident get very far in this St. Louis Contest. I made the serious mistake of catching my steer and he immediately jerked me and my Pony down for our trouble.

But that gave me a touch of "Show business" in a way, so that meant I was ruined for life as far as actual employment was concerned. He had a couple of Daughters, Miss "Bossy" and Lucille.[2] Bossy was quite a good rider but she never took it up in the proffessional way that little Lucille did. Lucille was just a little kid when we were in St. Louis that year, but she was riding and running her Pony all over the place, and that was incidentally her start too. It was not only her start, but it was the direct start of what has since come to be known as the Cowgirl. There was no such a thing or no such a word up to then as Cowgirl. But as Col. Mulhall from that date drifted into the proffessional end of the Contest and show business, why Lucille gradually come to the front, and you can go tell the world that his youngest Daughter Lucille Mulhall was the first well known Cowgirl.

She become a very expert roper, and was the first girl that could rope and tie a Steer, not only do it but do it in such time that it would make a good roper hustle to beat her. He also had a younger son Charley that was afterwards a very good Bucking Horse rider.[3] Charley is now out around Hollywood and works in the Movies. After that Contest and a few others around the Country that he promoted, why I drifted off to South America and around the rest of the universe awhile, and when I got back it was the fall before the start of the World's fair in St. Louis, in 1904.

Well I went out to Mulhall from Claremore a lot that fall and winter rehersing and practicing for the big show which he was to have at the fair for the whole year. I lived with the family at Mulhall. The Col. had always kinder seemed to like me, and I thought a lot of the family. His wife Mrs. Mulhall will always be remembered by me as just about as fine a character as I have ever known.[4] She was a grand old Lady. She had many trials and hardships, but she stood up under them like a Saint. It was a family of great devotion. The Col. thought a lot of these Children, and they of their parents. Lucille never dressed like the Cowgirl you know today, no loud colors, no short leather skirts, and great big hat, no sir, her skirt was divided, but long, away down over her pattent leather boot tops, a whip cord grey, or grey broadcloth, small stiff brim hat, and always white silk shirt waist.

They were received by the best people in every place. The Girls could have had a Society career if they had preferred. She received more Publicity than has fallen to the lot of any one you have today, perhaps as much as Sister "Aimee" and all favorable.[5] We were in St. Louis during the whole summer of the fair, with the "Cummings and Mulhall Wild West Show on the Pike." The following year he took a small picked bunch of us to the Madison Square Garden, to work as an added attraction with the Horse Show. Lucille his Daughter was the big attraction. New York had read of her but never seen a Cowgirl. Our show was a big success in connection with the Horse show. With my little Roping act I was lucky enough to get on the stage with it direct from the Garden.

He always kept in touch with me, and was very interested in my little carryings on. He was a natural showman, loved the spectacular, but never had any fakes. Every boy was a real one. His Shows were of the very best. Neatness was one of his hobbys. His life was miserable trying to keep me persentable. "Look at the Injun, (he always called me Injun) he won't wear a silk shirt and I have bought him a dozen!" He was generous to a fault. When Col. Mulhall had money, we were all nigger rich. When he dident, well you wouldent hardly know it. He never hollered; he never squealed; he took the misfortune with a smile.

Being such a liberal spender, and in his older years naturally not able to earn so well, why he had hard luck, but he dident broadcast it to the World. He always maintained his dignity. There was a lot of class to the Mulhall outfit, none of your cheap show stuff, they were always the Mulhall family, the family of southern distinction NOT the Mulhall Family of Show business. He did many a favor for many person. When he had it you had it. The business of making amusement for the world which he adopted was not kind in the long run to him and his. They deserved a happier finish, for no one of them ever harmed a soul, they dealt fair, but dident always receive their breaks themselvs.

We have no one to replace the old fellow. He is of the rugged old Cowman type that is passing out. Lucille is left alone on the old Ranch place at Mulhall. Lucille Mulhall who's name has blazed across more paper than most public men attain in a long lifetime. The first Cowgirl, one that could do something, not pose, but ride and rope, the only Girl that ever rode a horse exactly like a man, (I mean a real Hand). She is left alone with her memories, and they should be happy, for she has given more than she has received. It's not a bad legacy to leave, the Best Horsewoman in America. The old Col. has gone to book another Contest, and I can hear him holler, "Come on Boys let's give 'em a real show, a Mulhall Show! Lucille now Baby, rope like you never roped before! Injun wake up and get in there!"

460   ZIEGFELD AND THE LION

Well Sir every man that has ever done anything out of the ordinary is a Character, and I would call Flo Zeigfeld a man that had done something out of the ordinary, plum out of the ordinary.[1] He has given to the American Public for Lord knows how many years, an entertainment that must have given them more pleasure and happiness than any other for they have paid more to see it than to any other man in the World. A Circus with all its tremendous aggregation of assorted animals from the four corners of all the earths. Yet Mr. Florentz Zeigfeld can take just one breed, in fact just one half the breed, the she of the specie, and can assemble such a round up of beauty that combined with the best there is to offer at that time in the amusement line, and he can concoct an evening's entertainment that you remember it till the next year.

A funny thing about the "Follies" all the years I was with it, in hearing people speak of the show that year, they never spoke of it in comparison to any other show. It was always "It's better than last year's, or it's not so good as last years." It always stood alone for there was no other show that they could remember for a year. His hardest opposition has been himself. If he had been new every year, and that particular show was his first, why each one would have been heralded as a masterpiece. But naturally they had to compete with each other. But it's not of his shows, or his hundred and one other things that anyone could write on by the hour about that he has accomplished in the theatrical world, it's just of him that I want to tell you something.

The reason is it's fresh in my mind. He was out on the coast a few weeks ago to visit his charming wife who was playing out there in one of the Coast's most successful shows, and as myself and my family are tremendously fond of him and his family why he was up to our little Igllo some.[2] One evening for dinner, we got him started in on old times, and we had a great evening. Here was the peer of all Revue

Producers of all time telling about his barnstorming about the country in his early career. His real start was with Sandow the strong man, I guess the first strong man.[3] That is the first strong man that was strong enough to make people pay to see how strong he was. Well Mr. Zeigfeld dug him up over in Europe, and brought him over here. But let him tell it.

"I remember the first time I was out here on the coast. It was on Sandow's first trip. We had a kind of a vaudeville show built around him sorter like Harry Lauder carried, only a better show.[4] One time in Frisco we had him billed to fight a Lion. Just barehanded. It created a lot of excitement and we had a packed house. We were bringing Rome to Frisco. It was not a part of our programme, it was a special stunt that was arranged there. It wasent framed either. This fellow Sandow really thought he was better than a Lion, so we got him a big old Lion. He entered the temporary Colosium with more bravo than any Christian in the early days ever faced one. The Women kinder half hid their eyes, appearing like they dident want it to be seen that they were looking at such a sight, but secretly hoping that something would happen. Instead of the Lion making for him, he had to make for the Lion. Well the old Lion took to outer edges. Sandow had to follow him, in fact chase him.

"The Lion dident pay any more attention to him than a house cat would. Well there wasent much fight. Everybody hollered that the Lion was doped, but he wasent. I wouldent even think of such a thing. I love Lions, especially after I Counted up the house. Well Sandow kept at him, at least he kept at him till I could get the money from the Box Office to a fast moving conveyance. It was a terrible shock to me to hear the Lion was not the King of Beasts for I had read it all my life. Sandow dressed for his performances in a Tiger skin, in fact he brought that style of raiment over here. He was years ahead of Elinor Glynn, who used it as a mattress.[5] Well Sandow left the Arena De Lions not ahead of the Lions but ahead of the Populace. He wore his tiger skin for pajamas during the rest of that night ride. He was as downhearted about the Lion as I was. I never went to Frisco till the year of their big fair out there, when I took the Follies out. I thought the odor of the Lion had vanished, but some of the newspapers had a memory and said, 'The man that arranged for a man to whip a Lion one time is in our midst again. We will watch him this time. If his Follies are doped then give us some of the dope!' Did I tell you what happened when we were on our way to the Coast? Well the train broke down and a wheel come off a car. When they got a new one fixed I got about 10 men to carry the old broke one into our stateroom. When we arrived at Oakland the Press Boys met us and I had them come in. They saw the wheel in the drawing room. 'What in the world is this?' 'Oh, that's a wheel we broke off and the Proffessor just picked it up and brought it in here.' They photographed it, and it made a great story, when as a matter of fact Sandow couldent even have rolled it downhill.

"He was a great fellow, this Sandow, a very high class man, a fine man, and perhaps the strongest of any of them, the most beautiful body. The Women fell for him hard. An imatator was right ahead of us claiming that he was the real Sandow. We finally had him brought to court, and as the case was progressing and all was argument as to who was which and what, I suggested to our Lawyer to tell the Judge to test them and see which was the real one. I had Sandow's big Iron Dumb Bell brought in, and the Judge asked the other fellow to lift it. He pulled a Kidney loose and couldent even get it out of the box. Sandow reached down picked it up with one hand and was ready to make forward pass with it out of the back window. We won the case. I wish I had some way of testing all my imitators."

He has had a great experience has Mr. Zeigfeld. He looks and is just the same as the days I went with him on his Midnight Frolic Roof, (the first show) in 1914. A many one of us got out start, our real start with him. Those were great old days those Folly days, packed houses, wonderful audiences, never bothered me as to what I was to do or say, never suggested or never cut out. And to think after 30 years of giving them the best in town he still has the best show in New York. That shows it wasent the performers that made Zeigfeld shows, (for hundreds have come and gone). It was just Zeigfeld. I think he holds the record for being Champion. He knew colors, and he knew beauty. He knew how to keep nudeness from being vulgar. His was a gift, and not an accomplishment. Long live the old Master.

461   BACK FROM MEXICO

Well all I know is just what I read in the papers. You know you don't know what a relief it is to get away from the papers a little while, and then sorter make a guess as to what has happened while you didENT get to see 'em. Here two or three weeks ago I was down on Mr. W. R. Hearst's big ranch in Old Mexico and we didEnt get a whole lot of news while I was out there and when I finally did why you sorter wondered if it was what you was expecting.[1]

Of course the World Series was on all the time I was there, and that I had figured about right, with the exception of thinking that

Philadelphia would win, and I had it that Grove and Ernshaw would be the Heroes.² Well it was two pitchers but not them. I had just made a mistake in the names.

I had the number right, and the position that they played right. But it was just Grimes and Hallihan.³ Then this Pepper Martin, I had a fellow figured out to be the Hero, but it wasent just exactly Martin, it was two other fellows.⁴ But I did get part of it right, they played the games in St. Louis and Philadelphia, and they traveled in between. I had all that figured just about as it happened. Then they wanted to kill an Umpire there one day. I had that figured just that way, only I had it every day instead of just one day.

You know you would be surprised at the Mexicans down there that when I finally drifted out into civilization that knew about the games. They are playing a lot of baseball in the cities, and they are getting pretty expert at it too. Of course the other news that traveled so that it reached us away in the interior was the death of Dwight Morrow.⁵ I don't know when I had ever come to like and admire a man more than I did him. I had first met him in Mexico, lived at his home there, traveled around that country with him, and he was the finest and most human man I ever saw.

I was in Mexico with him when he first went down, he was just sizing up the situation, he used to say, "I don't know anything about Diplomacy, but these people are our Neighbors, and we have to live by each other, so their problems can't be any different from those of any other Neighbors."

And that's how he solved everything, he brought it all down from what at first looked like something big, well he just reduced it to its natural size and then sit down across a table and talked it over with the other side. He fixed it so nothing was a "Big Problem." He said nothing was as big as it seems. He put humaness into his so called Diplomatic job. I knew from the first day that I met him that he was going to make good on that job, and it was considered to be the toughest post of any in the service. More public men have been buried in Mexico than in Washington.

But Mr. Coolidge knew his man, and he trusted him, and he come through for him. He was a loyal fellow, he stuck by Mr. Hoover from start to finish, and in doing it he always retained the friendship and respect of the opposition party. Morrow dident have any enemy on the other side. Gosh, he was a great little fellow. Darn it, why is it the good ones are the ones that go, that's one thing about an onery Guy, you never hear of him dying. He is into everything else but a Coffin.

Course too while I was gone, Mr. Hoover rounded up the Bankers and told 'em if they wanted to continue getting six and eight percent out of the Yokels, they better start limbering up and let out some dough without the security of a right eye and a left arm. He told 'em to melt some frozen assets. Nobody knows what he told 'em but he sure did send 'em home renewing notes. You know there is nothing as scary as a Banker, he don't wait till he passes a graveyard to whistle he will do it passing a Hearse. But Mr. Hoover did a good day's work while things havent been exactly picking up, they havent been falling apart so we are holding our own. They havent been turning loose of it so I guess they are holding their own, and everybody elses that they can get their hands on.

We used to call depression a State of mind, now it's a state of health, it's moved from the mind to the stomach. So it's really with us in spite of all the After Dinner Speakers who have barked for a free meal. It's really not depression, it's just a return to normalcy. It's just getting back to two bit meals and cotton underwear, and off those 150 steaks and silk Rompers. America has been just muscle bound from holding a steering wheel. The only callus place we got on our body is the bottom of the driving toe.

We are getting back to earth and it don't look good to us after being away so long.

We have watched the parade but we got no money to go to the show on, and we can't make up our minds to go home and start saving till next year.

If people could get that darn wall street off their minds.

Half our people starving and the other half standing around a roulette wheel.

They going to get some easy money if they have to go broke to do it.

If Russia succeeds it will be because they got no stock market.

Before I decided to appear I asked them to submit me the list that would appear, they submitted the eligible ones, and I Picked out Mr. Hoover, I thought that would be about right. Mr. Coolidge is gabbing away somewhere but his is for Insurance. He says just before you starve take out a nice Policy. Mr. Hoover and I are settling the affairs by Suggestion, not Auto Suggestion but Radio suggestion, we suggest that everyone give as much as they can.

462   FEEDING BALONEY TO THE LITTLE
BROWN BROTHERS

Well all I know is just what I read in the papers, or what I hear
between times that I am not Gabbing myself, (which ain't often).
Couble of Weeks ago Pat Hurley, Secretary of War in these Peace
times in Mr. Hoover's Cabinet, well, Pat had been away over in the
Philippines.[1] Rumors had reached the President that the "Little
Brown Brothers" was just about ready to leave our Bed and Board
and take up citizenship elsewhere. They had heard of the advantages
of Independence, but evidently very little of its drawbacks. So Mr.
Hoover looked over his eight or nine hired men in the Cabinet, and he
chose Pat. He knew that Pat was a man that no matter what argument the "little Brunette Brothers" put up, why Pat would have an
answer to 'em. So he says to Pat:

"Pat along with 876 other difficulties I am having, why the
Philippines are perspiring to Independence. Will you go over there
and see if it's Bolsheviki propaganda, or just Democratic influence.
You know it's hard to tell nowadays which causes me the most
devilment, the Russians or the Democrats. Now go on over there. You
got nothing to do. We havent got a war booked at this time. I don't
know what's the matter with Stimpson, he is backward, but I got him
working on the Jap-China one, and if everything turns out all right
why we ought to have a real job for a Secretary of war before long.[2]
But you havent much on your mind. Your oil is such a good price,
and Oklahoma under Bill Murray is sailing along fine, so you havent
got a thing to worry about.[3]

"Now listen; here is some instructions. If they really want their
Independence, why about the best way I know to get even with 'em
would be to give it to 'em. But don't do it too quick, for that would
make 'em think maby we dident want 'em, and they are a very
sensitive people. You know every people you deal with are always
sensitive, so you musent hurt their feelings. In Diplomacy, the way
they work it they always are careful to not hurt anybody's feelings but
their own people, but you go over there and kinder nose around, and
see what's eating on our Insular Possession. Bring me back a report,
for one more report added to the 623 that arrive back to me daily
from my Commissions, won't be much more, but you can give me
yours verbally. Don't come dragging in here with it like Wickersham
in a Truck.[4] I like you Pat, and your kinder my Head Man, so if you
can't give 'em their freedom, why at least refuse in such a way that
you arrive back here with the report. Kinder look China and Japan

over while you are there, and see if you can find out who's baiting that trap every morning.

"One of our Senators from Missouri has been in the Philippines this summer and set 'em free, so you go explain to 'em just what a Senator is and get 'em all laughing again.[5] Explain to 'em that when a Senator sets you free, that it's kind of a Near Beer Freedom, and they don't want to expect too much results from it. Explain that we have 96 of these that go out every summer, freeing somebody, and we have yet to find one of their cures that was permanent. Now don't stop in Utah on your way out and let Reed Smoot get ahold of you.[6] You must remember that Utah raises sugar beets, and the Philippines raises sugar cane, and both of 'em make sugar. Well you just wave a Philippine sugar cane at Smoot and you got what might be known in the classics as a hostile Senator on your hands. He'll trade you the whole Islands for a package of Cubebs. So he is not just exactly what you would call a disinterested bystander. He is a mighty able man so don't let him get you in argueing distance."

Well Pat went and he saw, and I met him when he come back, he was just oozing Philippine Islands. He flew from one end of 'em to another, he talked with everybody that could talk, and those that couldent why he talked to them. He told 'em that the Great White Father had sent him over to see if they was as bad off as we were. They all nodded and said "Uh, Uh, Yes." He says, "Well I doubt it." He says, "We want to give you your Independence."

McKinley said, "We lost to Spain and had to take you."[7] Roosevelt said, "Aguinaldo, we are here, and I think you should have freedom, but not under my Administration."[8] Taft said, "Ha! Ha! let's all have a good laugh, and we will set you free, soon as the Democrats get in."[9] Wilson said, "We promised 'em their Independence, and I will see that the next President gives it to 'em."[10] Harding said, "It wont be long now."[11] Coolidge said, "Let Hoover do it." Hoover says, "If the other Presidents have stalled for 30 years, (as a good Republican of six long years standing), I don't see why I should not continue likewise."

So it's one of those things that each fellow is going to hand down to the other, and the question will eventually be brought to Young Theodore Roosevelt the 8th. Who will pass it on to President Maurice Cohen.[12]

It's like Prohibition as a problem, it will always be with us. I asked Pat, "Pat are they really ready for Independence?" He says, "No." I says how can you tell when a Nation is ready for Independence? He says, "I don't know. I never saw a Nation that was." I says, wouldent Japan pounce on 'em and take 'em over the very day

84

we got out? He says, "No! Not till maby the following morning." I asked, is there much Russian Propaganda in the far east. He says, "Much more than there is food."

"Will the five year Plan succeed?"

"If it does the Republicans will adopt it."

"Who will the Republicans run?"

"When, in 36?"

"Who will the Democrats run in 32?"

"I dont think they will enter a man, Will."

I says, "Do you know any other things?" He says, "Yes, but I am not going to tell 'em till I get back to the Boss."

463   MURDER IN THE NEWS

Well, all I know is just what I read in the papers. Well the last few weeks there's been a good deal of blathering in the paper. Ever since away back when the Frenchman Laval come over and wen back there just don't seem to be any way finding out what he came after, what he got, what was done or anything.[1]

About all we do know about him is that his daughter danced with Mayor Walker.[2] Now if that was worth the trip why then everything must have been OK. He and Mr. Hoover issued a kind of a joint statement, but the same fellow wrote it that wrote the Wickersham Report.[3] We couldn't tell if they had even met or not.

I think that is the hardest thing in the world to do is tell the press what you and somebody have been doing, when you have been doing anything at all. Laval run into Borah while here and we had no trouble telling what they talked about. He don't seem to have got far with Borah, but that's no novelty. Neither did anybody else that wanted anything. Borah is the best "Refuser" we got.

They talked about a corridor in Poland. That's an alley in Poland that they wanted to get to the sea. Mr. Wilson give it to 'em for he really thought they wanted to see the sea, but a Pole knows no more about the sea than a Cherokee.[4] So Borah says it ought to go back to Germany. Well when you talk to France about giving anything back to Germany why you haven't got a very sympathetic listener. So you can see how far Borah got with his hospitality.

France ain't going to give Germany back even an alley. Well that's their business. They live by 'em, they know what to give 'em and what not to give 'em. France dident send Laval over here to suggest giving back California to Mexico.

We are always handing somebody else's stuff around. Poland is in a mess and always will be, for they just carved the country out of about three other ones. About a fourth of the population is Germans that want to get back under their own country. About a fourth is Checks. Sounds like money, but it's folks that belong to Czechoslovakia. Well a fourth are them.

Then a fourth are Russians. Now let's see that's three fourths. That only leaves one-fourth real Polish. But then the Jews have to be subtracted from that fourth, so there just ain't a few dozen real Poles.

But they are an old time country and they want to get along. But you can't get along with somebody else's land. But that ain't our business. We got all we can do to capture Sandino.[5] Maybe he is in that "Corridor." We can't find him in Nicaragua, but he finds us.

Well anyhow they say that J.P. Morgan was pleased with this Laval's trip and after all he is about the only man in America that everybody seems anxious to please.[6] So the trip bore some fruit. Germany has got some fellow coming over now. We get all excited and each one of these pilgrimages or conferences we think and read of it at the time as though it was the last word, and that it would settle everything. Then two weeks after it's over, we can't for the life of us remember what happened. If we could get half as excited over what to put in the plate to make it look like soup and taste like soup and act like soup in our bread line, as we do over some international event that ain't going to ever come off anyway, why we could be better off.

Six months from now we can't remember whether Laval came from France or Siam. Our minds just flit from hither to thither and all we want is something to occupy 'em till we get to the asylum. And other nations are just as bad off as we are. Look at England, they was all excited over Ghandi coming there to get freedom for India.

Poor old fellow has just hung around and wore pretty near all his clothes out. Been there three months and India hasent got any more freedom than Pat Hurley give the Philippines.[7]

These big babies ain't going to give anybody anything. That's why they are big. Everything in the world that is done nowadays received about ten times as much publicity as it deserves. Publicity should be written after a thing and not before. Then that would save us of having to read. Right now we know more about Mrs. Ruth Judd's life than we do about Lincoln's, Washington's, Napoleon's, or Greta Garbo's.[8]

You can kill all the people you want in this country and not attract any attention, but if you kill 'em and put 'em in a trunk why you become famous. It's how you dispose of a dead body that makes you sensational in this country and how many dead bodies did you create.

Don't figure out who you are going to kill, figure out how you are going to kill 'em. But we are all plodding along just as though we were in our right minds. So what's the answer? If we knew any better country we would go to it. Long as we can go to our radio every hour of the twenty four and be advised what toothpaste to use and what Cigaretts will be fairly kind to our madulla oblong gotta, why we are happy.

464   SOME VIVAS FOR MEXICO

Well all I know is just what I read in the papers, or what I see as I flit from limb to limb. Couple of weeks ago I had a great trip down to Mexico City. That is a Town. I like Mexican Towns, and Mexican people, they move just about fast enough to suit me. But I don't know, they are likeable anyhow, they all got humor, and as for hospitality, well you havent seen any till you see them.

Hal Roach the great Comedy movie Director, who makes all the really funny Pictures, and is responsible for the best team of Comedians, Laurel and Hardy, you know they are the favorites with all us movie folks, as well as the audiences — well Hal, and Eric Pedley the great Polo Player, who played on our international team against England the last time, and he made more goals single handed than all of England combined, well he is a wonderful Athlete, was the champion Boxer of his Division during the war, great Tennis Player, Golf, anything, and a fine fellow with it.[1] We were in Hal's private Plane, piloted by Captain Jimmy Dickson, who has covered this country from more different angles than anybody.[2]

Well the four of us lit out. We bid our wives good bye at the Airport at five in the morning, thats before daylight. Now that's what I call a dutiful wife, that will crawl out at that hour and go to the field to see your Husband off for Mexico.

I had kinder promised to take the Women on this trip. But we got out of it in some way. Oh yes I think we kinder hinted that there was a revolution brewing. You see they would have had to have gone on the train.

I was the fellow that was to take them down and then the other fellows fly down and meet us. It was a Dandy idea and I may have to do it yet, and I will be glad to do it, for any excuse that gets me down there is a good one. But I want to compliment these wives. Now Mrs. Pedley knew her Husband hadent flown so much, and it was fine of her to let Eric go. You know Wives have kinder got to get used to this flying business for their husbands.

Mine is pretty well broke in. In fact the last time I went to Oklahoma I took my Mary and Bill Jr. there and back by Hal's Plane.[3] My wife makes short trips, but not any Transcontinental ones. We hit the line and crossed into Mexico at Douglas, Ariz., and if you want to see courtesy why their Authorities sure showed it to us in getting permission to cross. You know this taking a Plane into another Country is not like driving a Ford in, there is more to it.

We hit Torreon about 1100 miles from Los Angeles that night, hit the field after dark and had to throw out a flare. (It's a kind of a lamp of a thing, fastened onto a silk parachute and goes down and lights up the field.) It only cost $40 so it pays to get in by daylight. That's a pretty, and clean, prosperous little City, then the next day over the Mountains to Mexico City.

Oh yes I like to forgot we on the first day circled over the great Hearst Ranch, (I had been down there a couple of weeks before).[4] It's a wonderful place. One Million Acres, sixty Thousand Cattle. We would have liked to landed there but the ground looked wet from a lot of rains.

But the one great view of Aviation is the sight of the valley of Mexico City. It's eight thousand feet high, and still a Valley, with the old Volcano of Popocatepetl, smoking nearby. It was good to see old friends who I had met on previous visits, mostly when I was there with Ambassador Morrow.[5] Things are fine there, of course the usual hard times of all Nations but no more than us, or the rest.

We were asked that night to go out and call on ex-Pres. Calles (called Ki-ess).[6] Now there is a remarkable man, a really big man, one of the few able men during our generation. That sounds pretty windy don't it? Well it's true, if ever a single man kept a Country in check it's this man Calles. No Dictator. Don't want to be President again. He simply wants his country to have peace, and they know he is a real Patriot, and not one these idealists.

Mexico has had plenty of men that meant well had a certain ability, but lacked the real spark and the downright nerve. I mean Political nerve, and physical nerve. Well that fellow has it.

Both Roach and Pedley said they had never in their lives met a public man that any more impressed them than he did. Now Mexico don't want any trouble, and the few that do want to make it are held in check by this man. I was pleased with I went in that he gave me the "Embrasso" or embrace, where each of you put your arms over

Will Rogers (fifth from right) *in a bullring in Mexico City in October of 1931 with Eric Pedley* (third from left), *champion California polo player, and Hal E. Roach* (center, hatless), *director of silent screen comedies.*

the other's shoulders into a kind of pat of embrace, and it's only among particular friends. Well, I swelled up till he couldent hardly embrace me.

We talked mostly of Morrow. He was tremendously fond of him. We also had a very fine man as Ambassador there, a great international Lawyer from Salt Lake, Mr. Clark, he is doing a fine job there, in fact he helped make Morrow's term there such a success. Morrow asked in going there, "Who is the best man on International Law there is?" They all said this man Clark if he could get him.[7] Morrow got him, and he worked with Morrow all the time he was there, then when Morrow left he had him take his place.

He has a great personality, and there will never be any trouble with Mexico while he is there. In fact I don't think there ever will be. We are neighbors and we both see it to our advantages that we are friends, Roads, Aeroplanes, Sports, Schools, Exchanges of Newspapers, a hundred things that are bringing them closer to each other all the time. Quaintness, hospitality, and beer, and of course the cost is about a fourth or fifth. And don't fail to read Stuart Chase's wonderful book, "Mexico a Study."[8] It's the greatest thing you ever read, on any Country.

465   ALL WESTERN TEAMS

Well, all I know is just what I read in the papers, and the birds I run onto as I prowl hither and thither. Well guess who we had out here a couple of weeks ago. Not a soul but my good friend (and yours), Vice President Charley Curtis.[1] Yes Sir, the newspaper men were holding one of the periodicals and Charley was the gold fish. You know he is a mighty human kind of a cuss. He is a Kaw Indian. There ain't many of 'em. It's just a little tribe in Kansas and northern Oklahoma. But they are good Indians. Not as good as us Cherokees, but good enough.

Charley is mighty well liked among all injuns. You know it's a mighty fine thing to have a little old western boy, of part Indian parentage become Vice President of these ex-great United States. He has held about everything worth holding in the way of jobs in the gift of his state and country. He was a Senator for years, and became Republican leader and a good one. He knew trades, he was raised as a jockey and rode on all the little half-mile western tracks, and today he loves racing and never misses going to a meet at any of the tracks over the line from Washington in Maryland. He would rather have a little bet on an old plug, than to hear Borah speak on "The League of Nations and Why." He sets up there studying the dope sheet, while Jim Watson delivers a tirade against Pat Harrison.[2] Then Pat bumps him off with one remark, just as the Vice President has found what he thinks will arrive first in the third race at Pimilco.

I go see him every time I go to Washington. He has always been a good friend of mine. Last time I was there I had lunch with him in the Senate restaurant, and by the way he had Pat Harrison and some other hungry Democrats there with us. You know that's a funny thing about that Senate, they get up there and bellow and rave against each other, and at heart they are all good friends. They know there is a certain amount of "hooey" to be gone through, and they kinder tolerate each other carryings on. They kinder got Vice President Curtis going now though. He is not right sure if he wants to run for the office again or go back home and come out for the Senate again. You know you take an old football player and he never feels the same refereeing a game that he did when he was down there playing in it. Well, that's how Charley feels. He sets up there with a hammer, but none of them are close enough that he can really do much good with it. It's a terrible job, and why they ever wished it on as important a person as the Vice President, Lord only knows.

There ought to be just some clerk or somebody that is drafted for the job. Just a good parliamentarian that knows the rules and he hollers, "Order!" I tried to find out from Charley which job he was out for but you can't get much out of these politicians. But he is "on the fence."

Well, the Senate lost a great character lately, that was Senator Caraway of Arkansas, my wife's old home state.[3] I had known him for years too. He lived at Jonesboro, Ark., and I played at his home town on my little tour last year. He has a world of humor, and it had a real kick to it. He did delight in walking up and down the aisles with his hands in his pockets and when the debate got at its hottest he would just inject "one remark," and that knocked 'em over, and he proceeded with his daily walk.

They were arguing drouth relief one day last spring when I was in the gallery. Senator Gillette of Mass. was against government going into it.[4] But some Democrat had dug up some old records (that's something, too, you got to look out or some fellow will show you how you voted in '69 on the same kind of a question) well, they dug up where one time when Gillette was in the lower House, some town in Massachusetts had had a calamity and the Governor had voted some fifty thousand for their relief. "Did you vote fot it?" asked Caraway. "No I don't believe I did," said Gillette. "A town in your own state in ruins and want and you didn't vote for their relief? What a Statesman!" said Caraway. He had lots of good common sense along with all his sarcasm. It will be a long time before there is ever just such a man in there.

I told you dident I about being down awhile back to John Garner's home?[5] He is the next Speaker of the House. It was an awful homey place. He has about seven acres right in this beautiful little town of Uvalde, Texas, and he has got his own cows, and lots of chickens which he feeds himself every day. Quite a hunter and fisher, he had just killed some deer out of season. He was shooting at some quail when he hit the deer. Course the quail was out of season too, but he dident hit them. I dident want to eat the deer that night for dinner on account of it being against the law to kill it, but it was all the meat they had and I was hungry. He has a lot of pecans too. He said they vas soft shelled. Ain't it funny how a fellow in politics will just lie, when there is really no reason for it? He could see me clamping down on these pecans with one of the best set of tusks ever swabbed in Pepsident, yet I couldn't even make a dent in 'em. Here I had cracked hickory nuts and old black walnuts with these molars, but they met their waterloo that day when I tried to sink 'em into Jack Garner's SOFT shelled pecans.

He raises his own grapes too — and — but as I was saying, it's a mighty livable life he lives there. His son and daughter-in-law, and a mighty pretty little granddaughter lives right next door.[6] It was a place I would have liked to stayed longer, but I would have sure wanted a hammer on those SOFT shelled pecans. I am going to Washington to watch him in the speaker's chair, cracking 'em with his gavel.

466 BACK TO THE SADDLE

Well all I know is just what I read in the papers, or what I see from hither to yon. A few weeks ago I was coming out of Mexico, and stopped over at San Antonio to Broadcast on the Rockne Memorial Programme, and the next day I went out to the King Ranch and Kingsville, Texas.[1] Of course you could write whole magazine Stories, in fact Books, on the King Ranch, in fact it has been done. But I am going to leave that for awhile, till I am able to get over more of it. It's just about the biggest Ranch we have in our land. Been in this same family for years, and they are real Ranch folks. Their hospitality is as big as the ranch, and it's a million and half acres. But what I am going to tell you about now is the "Roping" that's the thing I wanted to see was the Ropers.

Old Paddy Mayes, the old Cherokee Boy from Pryor Creek, Okla., he had been sent up to the Big League, he had been up there a few weeks when I run onto him in Chicago, he was with the Philly Nationals.[2] I met him and asked him how it was going with him in the Big League, he said, "Well all my life I have always heard of the Big Leagues, and heard so much about how they played ball, and how good they were. Well I have been up here just two weeks. Well they wasent overestimated any." Well that's the way with the Ropers on the King Ranch, they hadent been overestimated any.

Now I had just seen some mighty good roping. I had just come out of Mexico where they had given me a special exhibition. They have a great thing there it's called the Charro Club. Charro means Cowpunchers. Well they have a regular place, like a big Corrall, and smaller ones, and all, and some good wild cattle, and all the fellows in the City of Mexico that used to be cowboys, and lots of them that are yet, why they all belong, and on Sundays they go there and have these Mexican Cowboy sports, like "Trailing the Bull," that one we don't do up here. Well the old timers here they say used to. You run up on a fast Pony, grab the Steer by the tail, get a good hold then throw your leg, (which is still in the stirrup) throw it over the tail. Then that gives you a good brace. Then turn your horse to the left, and if you do it right you turn the old Critter tail in front of head. You don't tip him an exact somersault, it's a kind of a side twister, but he slides along looking back where he come from. Well they had some fine roping there, mostly fancy, as the Mexicans are the real originators, and the best in the world as Ropers.

But it's of the actual work that I want to tell you of on the King Ranch. We flew down there from San Antonio, me with Mr. Jack Lapham, a good flyer himself.[3] A big Oil man, Polo Player, and Aviator. His wife also flys. She took Billy Post, Son of Fred Post, the big Polo man from Long Island.[4] Frank Hawkes was down there and he flew his own Plane, the fast one.[5] He just played with us, flying all around, yet over, and under us to kill his speed down to ours going down. We landed right at the ranch, met all the folks who I will have to tell you about later, for I got to get to those calf Ropers.

Well, Sarah, that's the daughter, and Alice, that's another one, and Bob's wife, that's the one that's got charge of the cattle, they took us to the "Wagon" where one of their Round-ups were working.[6] They was dragging out calves for the branding, and when I say calves I mean little fellows, kinder scrawny, weight about seven fifty to eight hundred, just about the size of a horse.

It's brushy down there, and they can't miss. They have practiced all their lives. (They are all Mexican Boys that not only them but their Fathers and Grand Fathers were raised on this same ranch). They are a real bunch of cowhands. They can follow a steer through that thick brush so fast and so close to him that they havent got a chance to throw at his head for the brush, but they put their horse right on his heels, then throw and get his hind feet without swinging, and do it too.

They brand right out on the range. Bob Kleberg wanted me to try it, and I did, but Lord I was in there swinging around and messing the thing all up. I would hit where the calf had been just previously. They had Boys that would rope 'em out all day, and NOT swing just pitch away out to the end, and get veal out on the end.

Head, Hind feet, "Mongano" (Front feet) and they got good horses, they had two or three hundred saddle horses in this "Remuther" and good beans. That's what makes a good Cow outfit, is good beans. Just give me some beans and I will follow you off. I sure wish I was on a ranch. I would like to stay a year on that outfit. But I got to get back and see what Mr. Hoover is doing, and kinder keep my eye on Calvin, and encourage the Democrats. But I like roping the best.

467   HERE COMES CONGRESS

Well all I know is just what I read in the papers, and what I see as I prowl about. This is going to be a mighty noisy session of Congress for every man coming in will have a scheme to relieve the unemployed and it's going to take months just to read all the Bills that will be introduced. Of course they have to go to the Committee first, but it will take the entire Congress and Senate Members to make up enough Committees just to read all of 'em.

There is going to be many a way to save the Country. In fact there will be six hundred ways. There is about five hundred Congressmen and 100 Senators. There is going to be an awful lot of other things too to argue about. This cancellation of the debt for a year that Mr. Hoover did, that's going to start a lot of yapping. They will say he dident ask them about it. Of course as a matter of fact he did ask them, that is the main ones. But that is what will make 'em sore because he dident ask the others. Just knowing that they wasent the main ones will make 'em sorer than ever.

Then it's going to come up as to a Continuation of the Nations not paying. There is going to be great pressure brought to bear from the big financial interests to get a total cancellation. Course that's what they want. Europe owes them big gobs of money, so if we cancelled what they owe us, why that would leave their loans in better shape. You see what they would lose as a taxpayer in cancelling would be nothing to what they would gain by having the first mortgage on Europe instead of the second as they have now.

Well all that will be dragged out and aired daily and by the hour in this next session of Congress. Then up will pop the old League of Nations argument again. You see we have done a few things in the last few months that have been right on the verge of being in the League, so off that Gang will go again, claiming we should be in.

Then of course the fight over the Speakership. It looks like the Democrats have got the edge as I write this. But even Congressmen die, and when they die at the right time why that always brings on complication. Now take for instance down in Texas, right when and where was recently the only Republican Congressman in Texas out of about 18, well he died. Well they may not have time for an election, so the Governor appoints someone in his place. Now you know that Governor is not going to appoint another Republican. He will naturally put in a Democrat. Well you see what that death does when it comes at a time like this. Well they will have all kinds of arguments and shenannigans over the Speakership. Those Republicans will hate to give that up.

Of course if they should win it will perhaps fall to Tilson, and a fine fellow too.[1] He visited me when he was out in California last summer. He was a great friend of Nick's.[2] But it looks like the old Prairie Dog of Uvalde will go dragging into his hole with the swag.[3] If the Democrats can keep their health, or life rather till the first Monday in December why they ought to be the Head Men next time.

Poor Mr. Hoover with a foreign Congress on his hands, that looks like it's too much to add to all his other troubles. Then will come also the argument over how to raise some more money. "What to Tax?" "How to raise it?" I can't see where the argument against the Sales tax can stand up. It looks to be, (Leaving out essentials) that it would be a mighty fair tax. If you bought high priced things, everyone would know that you had paid your tax, or you couldent have them.

As it is now you can't look and tell if a man is paying a tax or not. He may be avoiding it in some way or the other. But with the old sales tax, if he is driving a Rolls Royce, why you know the Government got a big cut out of him, or he couldent drive it away. We don't miss the gasoline tax, it's paid in such a way that it is painless. Mr.

95

Hearst sent a bunch of Congressmen up to Canada to study it, as it's used in Canada, and they all claimed that it was "Great."[4] Well, anyhow we will have some excitement in Congress this fall anyhow. If they can't be instructive and beneficial they can at least be amusing, and they will be too this fall.

468   PEARS TO BE NO PEARS

A few weeks ago I was flying from Los Angeles to Seattle, and incidentally a beautiful trip, especially from Frisco north, up along the Sacramento River for a long long way. They had just had their first snow, and the Mountain tops were covered, and the Railroad and Highway was winding along down there like a couple of black snakes. Then we begin to hit bad weather, snow and a drizzling rain, and clouds begin to close in on us. It looked like we wasn't going to get any further than Redding, a little town in the edge of the mountains. But this Pilot had been on this route for five years and he without taking any chances, kept low below the clouds and wound his way right with the big Canyon and Railroad, and we got through as far as Medford (just over the line into Oregon).

Good field and a beautiful little City of twelve thousand. Well the Radio weather report said we couldn't go, so we decided to take the train in about three hours and arrive in Portland in the morning. Well I was kinder glad. I had never been to this Town before, and I don't know I kinder like to hit these strange towns. I always run onto a few old Birds or young Kids that recognize the old map from the movies and I never lack for company. The Pilot took us into town in his Car as that was the end of his run anyhow. We went to the Depot first, and got our Tickets. (I keep saying We, what I mean was another passenger and I, who I had just met on the Plane his name was Kennedy, and funny thing he had years ago when he was working for the Frigid Air Co., and they had a big Convention in Akron, he had booked me to appear before the Convention.[1] Now he and some other had started in the same business only they called theirs some kind of Ice Box, and they was a great big Company, they catered to the people who dident know what Frigid Air meant but wanted a Ice Box that was cold all the time.)

Well he was on there, and then they had a Stewardess, that's a very charming Girl, she is a qualified Nurse, and she makes things comfortable for the Passengers, and is a great comfort to Ladies on there, especially if they don't feel well. Well this one could have been a comfort to a lot men that was even feeling well too.

Did you ever see this Oregon Country? Well say I want to tell you it's beautiful, lovely streams running all along, big Pine trees, then a long stretch of beautiful Valley. We passed right by Mount Shasta, the clouds and snow was so low that we couldent see the top. A beautiful Stock Farm at the foot of it, where they used to raise those Shasta bred Race Horses. Shasta, Nut, Shasta Daisy, and all named Shasta something. It used to belong to Curley Brown, since dead.[2]

But this is about Medford and the home folks, the Editor called me, or one of them. There is two just dandy papers. This one said he run my Junk. So when I went down town and after checking our Baggage at the Deport I went across the street over to his Newspaper Office. I was a kind of a Traveling man calling on his Trade. Well there was a great Gang in there, as there always is hanging around a Newspaper Office. Out came an old Boy said he used to work on a Paper in Claremore, in '93. There you are, you thought Claremore was just one of these jumped up towns in the last few years. We was a Real Town when Tulsa and Oklahoma City both was just two section Houses.

I dident know what this Town had, but the Pilot told me all the way in that it specialized in raising Pears, (Not Pairs) Pears. The Depot Agent informed me that they shipped the most Pears ever shipped from one place. The Newspaper Owner told me I should stay and see the Pears, (that meant in eight months from then). The Girls that worked in the Office there all told me of what wonderful Pears they had. Newsboys come in and shook hands and informed me that Pears was right up this town's alley. Over at the Train a couple of hours later in come a lot of fine wholesome people all telling me that Pears from there was Mellons from Rocky Ford. The Owner and two Reporters from the other paper come to the Depot and they asked me if I knew that Medford was noted for its wonderful Pears. Now I am not criticising this. It was all done in such a proud way, that it made you know these folks had a town, but most of all they had Pears. And the thing that made it all the more enjoyable is that it was done by just everybody you would meet and not by the Chamber of Commerce.

I dident even see the Secretary of the Chamber. So you see it wasent any organized effort to poke Pears down a Visitor's throat by the better business element. These folks just wanted you to know they raised Pears.

I hadent eaten any lunch on the Plane, and it was then late in the afternoon. I had had two and a half hours of steady Pears, But NO

Pears. Just One lone Pear distributed in the right spot would have done the Medford Pear Industry more good than Lip Service from the total population. But not a soul dug up a Pear. Some School Boys and Girls that knew me from the movies come to the train to tell of Pears, but brought no evidence. It's a beautiful little City, fine folks, but I don't think there is a Pear in the Country.

469   LET'S GOSSIP AWHILE

Some great Columnist on days when they have no Gossip, why they tell you things that "Perhaps you dident know before." Well I never did do that for I never was in any shape to tell you anything you didn't know. In other words I always had to write UP to my Readers and not down. But I am going to have a crack at that kind of thing.

Now for instance, just the other day Harold Lloyd was up to my little Ranch and he offered me a Great Dane Dog.[1] Now did you know that he raises the finest great Danes there is, 40 or 50 of 'em? I dident take him, for the Brutes eat more than I can earn.

And did you know that they (The Lloyds) have the cutest little baby Boy, and two of the sweetest little Girls?[2] One theirs, and the other adopted. And did you know, but perhaps you did, that he is a darn great Comedian and one of the finest and best liked men in the Picture Business?

Did you know that Hal Roach is one of our Best Aviation Enthusiasts?[3] Has his own Plane, and a great flyer, Captain Dickson, Ex-Army Flyer, as his Pilot, and thinks no more of flying any week end to New York than you would of going to the corner Grocery.[4]

Hoot Gibson is a good Pilot and flies his own Plane.[5] So does Ken Maynard, and Wallace Berry has been flying for years.[6] Frank Borzage, just about one of the greatest Directors we have, has just taken up flying and his Instructors said it was uncanny the way he learned.[7] He has his own Plane now, also his wife learned to fly. Clarence Brown the Metro Crack Director is a good Flyer.[8] I think he got his originally in the war. Henry King who directed "Lightnin' " and who has just turned out "Over the Hills," which they all say is just about the best Picture ever made, he is an old time flyer, and Hosts of others.[9]

By the way, in this "Over the Hills," Mae Marsh, who was a big star in the early silent days and did some great things for D.W.

Will Rogers and Patrick J. Hurley, Tulsa oilman who served as United States secretary of war in the cabinet of President Herbert Hoover.

Griffith, they say her performance in this "Over the Hills" is simply marvelous.[10] You know there is many an old timer that can really troop when they get the chance.

Had dinner recently away down in Texas with John Garner, the new Speaker of the House.[11] His wife has been his Secretary for 25 years will continue. She is at the office every morning at 7 o'clock to open up the mail. Alice Longworth always in her home sits in a big easy Chair or on a couch with both feet under her, no matter if it's just a Congressman there or Hoover.[12]

Pat Hurley likes to "Whoop and Gobble."[13] That's an Indian trait. The loud whoop is followed by the Gobble, or imitation of the Turkey Gobbling. If it's done directly at anyone else down in Oklahoma, it means you are crowing over him and it means a challenge to fight. Pat does it in his private capacity, and not as Secretary of War. Incidentally he is making a good job of it, and wouldent be frightened to death if we did match one, which is not beyond the bounds of possibility.

Did you know that President Hoover had surrounded himself with a great and very promising bunch of young men as Assistant Secretaries of very high Cabinet Jobs? Three of which I will name, and there is lots of others. Dave Ingalls, Assistant Secretary of the Navy for Aviation.[14] I'll bet it's not ten years before he is a Presidential Possibility. Not just mention. I mean voted on. Then there is Trubee Davison.[15] Assistant for Aviation in the Army, another great future. Then Clarence Young, Aviation head for the Department of Commerce.[16] Three Young fellows who are real and "have everything" that a Public man to get far should be equipped with.

Did you know Chick Sale had Twins (not lately), but he has 'em, a great pair and a great family.[17] I got the nicest brightest letters in answer to ones that I had written their Fathers, and they were acting as their Dad's Secretarys. One from one of Eddie Cantor's five Girls, and one from Will Durant, the Philosopher's twelve year old girl.[18] I am so glad the Fathers dident write, they couldent touch these Kids.

Amon G. Carter the Ft. Worth Pecan, Turkey and Watermellon grower, knows and keeps in touch with more prominent men personally than any man in America.[19]

Did you know that Marie Dressler was not only the Fans' favorite, but the best liked Person in the Movies, among movie people?[20]

Did you know that Bill Hanley an old cattleman of Oregon, wrote a book, "Feeling Fine," that is the best bit of horse sense published this year?[21] That Calles of Mexico is THE STRONGEST AND MOST DOMINATING CHARACTER IN NORTH OR SOUTH AMERICA? That's all I know.[22]

100

470   WHEAT AND COMBINES

Well all I know is just what I read in the papers, or what I hear as I keep the old long ears to the ground. Here the other week before I started out on this Chinese Roundup, why out to my house one night to pay us a visit and break corn bread with us was a mighty interesting couple, Mr. Tom Campbell and wife.[1]

Now right off-hand if you are not a Farmer, or a buyer of farm products, you might say, "What Tom Campbell?" for it's a rather common name. But to anyone that is up on his Onions and wheat, why he will know in a minute. It's the man we have in the past read so much about.

Don't you remember a big wheat man up in Montana that was drafted by the Soviet Government of Russia to go over there and show them how to put their big wheat farms on a big mechanical farming basis? Well he is the man. He now lives over in Pasadena.

He don't belong to the Hoover Commission, but he advises them after they are appointed, that is if they have anything to do about Farming. He had in, up there in Montana, 90 thousand acres of plowed ground. He would rotate the crops, and have about half that in wheat each year. I remember seeing pictures of it, where there would be eight and ten combines running one right behind the other.

You town waddies know what a Combine is? Well to tell the truth I don't either. When I was the best farmer on the west bank of the Verdigris River, Binders was just coming in, and we was lucky to get to see one of them. As a Kid I used to ride the lead horse, when we used five head, three behind and two leaders.

Then those Combines come along and they just rounded up a whole "remuther" full and hitched on all they had harness for. I think from some of those Pictures I have seen of 'em up in those Northern States they had a whole Cavvy of horses, thirty or forty head. Now they got these Tractors, great big ones that pull the thing. But yet I havent told you Radiator folks what a Combine is.

Well here is all it does—just one machine and in one trip over the ground. On the front end of it is an arrangement that makes a deal to take over the ground (from the bank that is holding the present mortgage). Then right behind that gadget on this big machine is a thing that grubs up the Roots and Herbs. Another thing right behind grinds up the Roots and Herbs into "Sagwa" Indian Medicine, which is sold by a White man who says he was adopted into the Indian tribe. Then just a few feet behind that, all connected with the same machine, are the plows that plow the ground. Then right in the furrow is the seeder, then another plow that plows the furrow back

101

where it was in the first place. Then comes the fertilizer, and then the sickle that cuts the grain. Then it's carried along a little platform into the Threshing Machine where it's threshed, then out and into sacks, and into the big Grain Elevator that is fastened onto the thing.

Then on near the back end is a stock market board where a bunch of men that don't own the farm, the wheat, or the Combine, buy it back and forth from each other. That is if you have threshed a thousand Bushels why they sell each other a million bushels of this thousand bushels which was actually threshed, then they announce to the farmer that on account of supply and demand, the wheat is only worth two bits, (25¢). That's what you call a Combine.

Well this Campbell fellow is mighty interesting. He thinks that the Farm Board is a mighty good thing. But he does also think that they have had a pretty raw deal from the whole grain trade, and the banks. You see it looked like the Farm Board with its Co-operatives and various other things to do away with the middleman just turned them against the whole scheme. The banks knew that the Farmer would start borrowing from the Government at low interest instead of them at 10 and 12 per cent.

He says that Mr. Hoover knows that it's been a scheme on all their parts to discredit the Farm Board, so we wondered, he and I, (him furnishing the idea and me doing the wondering) why Mr. Hoover dident just come right out and tell the people what had happened. We figured that if Mr. Hoover went direct to the people and told them the real Lowdown that he would have them with him. But of course neither one of us holds office, or ever was elected to anything. I guess the truth can hurt you worse in an election than about anything that could happen to you.

Mr. Campbell told me a lot about Russia. He says they are farming 90 million, (that's millions, Brother, Not Thousands) acres of wheat. Most of it is owned and operated by the Government direct. That's the farms he had charge of.

He says there is no such thing as "Dumping." You sell a thing because you need the ready money that that product will bring in. You might say that Cattle men are Dumping the Cattle now, because they are at such low prices. But you got to sell 'em at some price. He thinks we make a big mistake by not selling to Russia. He says they are sure pay, and can use more of our material and products than any Nation. He thinks buying Nations of the future will be (in the order of their importance) Russia, India, then Africa.

He told Stalin when they had their first conference, that he dident believe in Communism, and a dozen other things that Russia was practicing.[2] Well Stalin got up and shook hands with him very

warmly, and told him: "Well, we will get on fine; we at least understand each other. It's wheat we want to agree on and not politics or
religion."

He says he never saw a people so eager to learn, and that their
ideal is always America. He thinks they are a great people trying to
work out a way of helping their condition. He and his wife and
Children had been in there twice, and they all liked it. Course he says
they are going through some tough times, and there is a lot of poverty
and hardship, but he thinks they will work out of it. It was a mighty
interesting visit, and well worth what little Spare Ribs and sour
Kraut that I fed 'em.

471 PROWLING THE PACIFIC

Well all I know is just what I read in the papers, and what I see as I prowl hither and thither, and believe me brother I have been prowling hither for the last few weeks. It would take me a week to tell you all about it. But this one will just have to kinder start me off.

I left the American shores when my plane crossed the Canadian border up above a town called Bellingham, Washington, on my way to beautiful Vancouver, and say, by the way, that is undoubtedly the prettiest aeroplane trip I ever made, that is from Seattle to Vancouver. You fly over all those islands and inlets and straits, and the mainland is in places low and level and a wonderful dairying country. It looked to me exactly like Holland.

There is a lot of rivers and canals, and lots of old milking cows out chewing on the green, and it was green. And here ten miles back was Mount Baker that is some fifteen thousand feet up, and covered with snow. But it is beautiful all up in that country; they say one of the prettiest trips is the inland trip to Alaska by boat, or plane for there is islands off shore and you can keep inside them. But the whole northwest is beautiful from Frisco north, its mountains and pines, and rivers and lakes.

Seattle is a great aeroplane center on account of the great Boeing plane being made there. They supply the government a lot of them and to lots of commercial and private parties. They have a fine field, well equipped, and Vancouver has one out on an island or a point of land, I was so busy looking at the beautiful scenery that I couldent tell. But Canada is going somewhere with aviation, and they should, for they are a country of long distances. Just think the time a plane will save in Canada.

Well, we went to the beautiful and big C.P.R. Hotel there, a well-appointed and really elaborate affair and was to sail on the Empress of Russia, a boat of their line in the morning. I had heard along the line that Floyd Gibbons, the world's champion reporter and radio announcer, was to be on his way to Manchuria too, but I wasent sure.[1] But when I finally got to Vancouver and they told me it was so I was tickled to death.

Just think of the privilege of traveling and being with him. Here is a man that has been in every nook and corner of the world, knows everybody, everything. I got acquainted with him in Warsaw, Poland, in the summer of 1926, and have been good friends with him since. Well, he was coming in on the C.P.R. at eight-thirty that night from N.Y. All the press boys was down to see him in and I joined out with 'em. He had 22 Chinamen on the train with him that was catching the boat too.

They were going back home, BUT NOT TO FIGHT. They said they dident want any war. Well, we all went up to the hotel and the newspaper men had a nice party that night, with all their wives and friends present and of course Floyd and I had to gab. He is just as good as he used to be on the radio, only slower. He gives you time to take it all in when he is talking to you. We had a fine time, met lots of fine folks, and up in the morning and saw Vancouver. It's the coming city of all west Canada, and well laid out and very pretty.

We shoved off the next morning about eleven thirty. It looked like a long trip, eleven days to Yokohama. I am the world's worst sailor anyhow. I get sick before the boat unties from the dock, but you know I says, "I am going to lick this, I am going to eat everything they got, drink ___ __ ___." Well, anyhow I stayed with 'em, and do you know I kept waiting to get sick, and kinder looking forward to it, and days went by and nothing showed up, and by golly I begin to believe that maybe the old Oklahoma kid was a sailor after all. Then we hit rough weather, and when you hit rough weather on the Pacific, brother you are encountering some weather.

The Atlantic is only a fish bowl. The Captain, and a very fine capable man, Captain Hosken, really did a great job of handling that boat in that hurricane.[2] He practically had to stop, then he turned south off our course, as we were not so far off the Aleutian Islands. That's the one these aviators try to sail along coming from Japan. Well, we was trying to keep off of 'em. The waves got so high we lost a lifeboat, washed off one of the top decks.

But I was still riding it, and retaining beautiful. Why any other trip I was ever on I would have died. This foolishness kept up with this ocean for over two days. It was a Chinese typhoon, that had run into a monsoon, that was crossed with just plain hurricane, and Oklahoma norther combined. But I kept eating, and HOW! They gave me good food on that line, and they are always passing something, and I was always not letting anything pass me. We had a fine little bunch on board, as travel like all other commodities has been curtailed by Hoover, I suppose, and there is not a whole lot of world travel. Now is the time to go, you are not run over by what one

105

traveler always called "The other objectionable people." You see everybody is doing the wrong thing when you travel but you.

Read a lot of books. I never was much of a book reader. I am kinder like Al Smith. I never read one through. But I knocked off some on this trip. That old Genghis Khan, that flourished around in all this country around 12 hundred. If you enjoy Jesse James, Al Capone, and the Younger boys, you want to read about this baby.[3] Oh Lord, the world was his oyster. He ruled everything from all of China clear to the gates of Vienna, and from the North Pole to Africa, and he did it all horseback. There was a real buckaroo for you.

Then I read a book by General Graves about our adventure in Siberia with our soldiers.[4] He tells you he was in charge of 'em and he don't know yet what we sent 'em over for. Now that it's all over and he has been looking up till now, he still don't know what they were doing there. I guess it will go down as one of the prize boners of all our foreign invasions.

I want to drop up there to Vladivostok on this trip if I can. You know we have all heard of that place, and I want to get a crack at it. I am anxious to see this Japan and China and all this, and I will write you more about it when we land, which is right now. Oh Lord, here is what they call a rickshaw, a thing where a man pulls you in a chair. What a traffic jam I am going to get into in one of those.

472   IT'S A LONG WAY TO OSAKA!

Osaka, Japan:—Well all I know is just what I read in the papers, and what I see as I prowl. I think the last time I wrote you a long letter we were in the middle of the Pacific Ocean. You know I am the Champion of the World getting seasick, and I know that it is just lack of nerve. If you will just keep up there and battle with it, and keep going why you are O.K. But I am kinder yellow anyhow, and when I feel a little squirmish why I start hitting for the Hay, and when once I get down in the old Bunk why I am a dead Dog from then on, no matter if we are out for a week or a month. So knowing this in advance I was all set for about eleven days fun and amusement right in the old bunk with one of these little tin Bread Baskets fastened onto the side of it. Everybody said, Ah' keep going, eat all the time, Drink!

Well we shoved off in the morning about eleven thirty from Vancouver on the Empress of Russia, a fine boat, a fine crew, and fine Captain, and they sure did do everything in their power to make everything pleasant. I dident want to get sick for I dident want to leave this good Gang. Floyd Gibbons of course was a good Sailor, for he had done nothing but sail somewhere all his life.[1] He was a kidding me and telling me to come on and eat a lot, and have another little glass of beer.

Well it's a beautiful trip from Vancouver over to Victoria, that's the Capitol of British Columbia. So I dident have much excuse to keel over going through all those beautiful wooded Islands and straits. We got over there just about dark, and there was a lot of folks come down to the Boat. The American Consul there wanted to take me ashore and show me the Town. Course it was dark, but we drove by all the big Government buildings and we got a mighty good idea of the City. There is beautiful homes there and gardens and grounds. It's about the most British City of any in Canada, there is an awful lot of Britishers there. I mean the real ones that come direct from England, and are not Canadians, but British. There seems to be a kind of a pack of 'em out there.

Well then we pulled out and hit the real Ocean, and course I went to bed. But even in the morning I surprised myself by getting up and going down to breakfast, and then stuck it out till Lunch, and then dinner, and mind you all this time I was packing in the Fodder. They had awful good eats on the boat and I just went the limit, and then about the middle of Mister Balboa's Ocean we hit a Typhoon, and that's when the Lifeboat washed away and like to got some more.

But do you know those little Chinese Crew, all the head officers were British but the crew are Chinese, and they are real Sailors. Those little Rascals stood out on that deck and hung onto ropes and did work around there when the waves were breaking all over this deck and it was the top one. I like to fell overboard from just looking at it from the inside, and we just had another glass of beer, and they were always passing all kinds of Hors Duervs, (I can't spell it but I can eat it). Well I was cramming that in all the time. And three big meals a day in addition. I bet by the time I landed I was as fat as C. B. Irwin of Cheyenne.[2] (You don't know Charley. Well that's your loss, you ought too.)

Then by that time I was figuring that I was a real Sailor. This thing of a Typhoon, crossed with a Monsoon, and sired by a Hurricane lasted with all that was following it, about two days in all. But what I started to tell you was one time, away out in New Zealand, that's right near Australia, I was working with a Circus, (Wirth Brothers) May Worth the great Bareback Rider was a little Kid with it then.[3] Well I left it to come to America, or rather the United States, for we are not ALL of American. Well I was supposed to make a one night trip by a small boat from down the coast where I left the show, after being it for over six months, and finally made enough to get home on. (But not first class.)

Well the train I was on pulled up beside the Boat, and I knowing that I was going to be sick, rushed aboard right away, and I says to myself I will get in the bunk and maby that will help me from being too sick. Well it's the paint, and that smell of varnish that does it. Well I got a whiff of it going down, and I crawled right into my bunk, (which was in among a lot of other men's bunks). Now I was under the impression that the Boat was going to pull right out. But this old sniff of paint had got me, and sure enough I started in being sick. I had the old Lunch Basket tied right on to the edge of the bed. (They have lovely little Cuspidors of a thing for Birds like me.) Well I sure was going strong. I thought well I havent got long to be sick, for we will be in there before long, and finally some fellow come in and asked another fellow, "What's the matter with this Boat, ain't it ever going to pull out?" Here I was practically dying and the boat tied to the dock, we hadent moved a peg. But the old Imagination had done some working along with the old Stomacher, and here I was dying and still tied to the dock. So when I crossed to Pacific this time with no casualties, why I sure did think I was a Sailor. I was for shipping on as a regular.

473   AMONG THE HEATHERN

Well all I know is just what I read in the papers, and what I see as I prowl among the Heathern (so-called). Say these Heathern are pretty foxy guys. Us Methodist, and Baptist, and Holy Rollers, and Sister Aimee's Four Square, have got to go some to put over anything on these babies.[1]

Now you take Japan for instance. That's where we first hit the dirt. Of course, there was the Aleutian Islands off to our North. There is nothing on 'em, they are barren. Being in that state, of course we won 'em. If they had anything on 'em why some other nation would have taken them over and at least hold the mandate over 'em.

You know what a mandate is? It's a thing you take over a Country, when you haven't quite got the Gaul to take over the Country. It's a kind of a fashionable way of glomming it, and still have a speck of pride left.

Well the Captain kept telling us that we were "off the Aleutians." This kept on for days. "We are off the Aleutians," till I thought he was off his Aleutian. But he was right, we were. They string out and they go pretty near over to Japan (not too close or they would cop 'em) but they sure do look like they were headed for the other side of the ocean. They are the ones that the aviators try to follow on their way from Japan over here. But it's always so rough and foggy that you just as well try to follow a dry Republican into a speakeasy.

It got so rough once we turned south to keep from bumping into these possessions of ours. I was just wondering if Mellon knows we got 'em, and has he figured out any way to put an additional tax on 'em for being there during these times of a misplaced budget.[2] I am going to escape to one of 'em some day and if I see a Revenue man coming I will flee to the other one, and I will keep him following me till after March the Fifteenth. That is the date you got to look out for is March the Fifteenth, that is if you have made anything during the past year. Of course, if you haven't you got to look out for every day. And you know that the trouble over here among these dusky friends of ours, we don't get any news.

Since I crossed into Canada from Bellingham, Washington to catch the Boat at Vancouver, I don't know a thing that's happened. Canada was so tickled that England payed her some attention that she was still writing about them, and they wasent paying any attention to their little innocent Sister to the south. It kinder feels good not to know what is happening at home. In fact it does feel good, for none of it is any good, so it's better to stay in ignorance. Whether Congress ever met or not I don't know. I hope they didnet, but it would be just about like 'em to do it, they got no more regard for the people's welfare than to.

Politics, I guess, is pretty cold for the Boys now, and we won't hear much till they thaw out in the spring, and what an odor that will be after a year's hibernation! Newt Baker was kinder smelling around the old Salt Lick when I left.[3] I don't know if some of the big Bucks horned him out or not. Newt did some good work during the war. Now as to whether we can remember that far or not is the problem.

This Japan has been kicking up a mess politically since I got here (not of course all on account of that) but they had a Budget that wouldent balance, and they had nothing to use for money, just like we did, so they changed Cabinets. Mellon has never thought of that idea. Now as to whether these new ones can find any more money laying around is doubtful. A Cockeyed Budget is the downfall of more Prime Ministers nowadays than was used to be.

Japan has got two Parties too. I don't remember their names any more than they could remember ours. But they keep things in a turmoil just like ours. You see if we dident have two Parties we would all settle on the best men in the country, and things would run fine. But as it is now we settle on the worst ones and then fight over 'em.

But outside of Politics and Tea, this is a great little country. Everybody is mighty nice to you. It looks just like America outside of the kimonas. Course under the kimonas in either place I am not an authority. But the most of them here dress about like we do. Subways, elevated trains, Electric trains, Street cars, and Bycicles. Did I say Bycicles? Well I underestimated. It wasent just Bycicles. It is millions of 'em. Did you ever see a Kimona on a bycicle? Say that's standard equipment here, and they are all carrying something on the Bycicles, generally an automobile, or a Piano, or some little trifle, a tray of dishes is the most common cargo. They will lope off on their wheel from one end of Tokyo to the other with a pot of tea for a friend, and then spend more time bowing before drinking it than it would have taken them to cook up some real coffee.

But they are mighty polite and nice, and they want you to see and like their Country, which you can't help doing. They got everything we got, and if they havent you show it to 'em and they will make it. They are a great race.

474   FLYING OVER JAPAN

Tokyo (By Mail). Well, all I know is just what I read in the papers, and what I see as I listen to the chatter of folks that I don't understand. Well, got away off over here in Japan for no reason whatever. There is no inkling of it around here anywhere. But I was determined to locate it if there was one on foot, so I set out.

Naturally I was looking for a plane if there was one. I wanted to see what aviation was like in the Nippon empire. All us old timers that know Japan intimately call it Nippon. Nippon means Sun (it's awfully embarrassing to have to explain these things to the prolectariat), so I says Nip, what have you got in the way of commercial aeroplanes, and Nip right up and answered me, "Where you want to go?"

So I says offhand like, "I want to go where the war is, or was or is going to be. Where is this Manchuria I been hearing so much about? Lead me to it!"

Now as a matter of fact, and geographically, Manchuria is away over on the mainland from Japan. You not only got to go the length of Japan, which for a nation with as many battleships as she has got, ain't as long physically as you would expect. But it's quite a prowl at that, then you have to take to the drink. You got to fly over some open ocean. Oh, not long, maybe only a hundred and fifty or two hundred miles, but that's quite invigorating when you are doing it in a land plane, that has no skiffs on the bottom of it.

They say they have a regular daily line from Tokyo, that's their local Washington. Got embassys there where you can get a drink just like Washington (I don't mean ours) I mean the Portuguese. Oh yes, and the Greeks.

Well, this Tokyo is quite a capitol. Got everything but Senators, which really may be responsible for their tremendous advancement. Well, they say they have a regular commercial line from there to Dairen. Dairen is the old Port of Dalny (I think it was Dalny) that was originally built and fortified by the Russians, that's the white Russians. They called 'em white before they turned red.

Well, this Darien is the big port of the Japanese that takes out all the products of Manchuria, and it's the real starting place of the Manchurian railway, that you have read and heard so much about in the newsprints.

Well, old man Gibbons, the decrepit old Penman, says he would relish a flight by air, so we take flight simultaneously, or practically both together, on a lively December morning. Gibbons has a fur coat that he claims he bought in Tibet (that's not the singer), and he cherishes it highly.[1] He claims that it was not only a bargain but warm.

Well, he has nursed this dog bed all the way across the Pacific, wearing it into even the dining room on the boat, and in the men's bar it was a continual source of another round. He has in addition to that a polo coat, although he has never mastered even as strenuous a game as checkers yet. So on this day that we went to the field he had on his polo coat, although there wasn't a horse in that end of Tokyo. But he had an assistant that guarded and mothered the giant fur.

He really made this trip to Manchuria just to give these skins a chance to see their native land once more. The poor old pelts had no idea they would ever reach the homeland again. They wasn't the usual sealskin or Kolinsky, or Hudson Bay Fox. Their native habitat was Siberia, Manchuria, and of course, some of the inner hides had been slumming over into Mongolia. But the whole thing had been assembled by some of old Genghis Khan's old henchmen, and this particular garment had been smuggled down into Tibet.

It had, so Gibbons related, once belonged to Marco Polo, but it was too hot to take to Venice, or Naples, or Rome, (or wherever it was he come from before he started in on this lying expedition). But at any rate Gibbons was proud of this collection of varmit hides. To me it was not only ill fitting but ill smelling. But he is a tough bird anyhow and seemed to have become accustomed to its shape as well as its odor. So he has this Bellboy from the hotel accompany us to the flying field, just as an accompaniest to this peltorium.

Well, of course a lot of American friends come out to see us off. And there was hilarity and glee all over the place, and for once in his life, Gibbon's attention was distracted away from the winter housing problem. We went to the plane, had pictures taken of course those always seem to be as evidence in case there is doubt as to the recognition of the remains. Well, then we had tea. No matter what you do in Japan you must first have tea, then after you do what you was going to do you have tea again.

So before the pictures and after the picture we had tea. Then we got on the plane and a boy come with pot and cups, and we just happened to think we hadn't had tea since stepping in the plane, so we asked if all the baggage had been loaded on, including Rogers' two shirts and a typewriter, and Gibbons' twelve pieces. Everyone assured us that they had. So we took off, splendid takeoff (otherwise I couldn't be telling of it) and we had quite a flight.

Japan is a beautiful country to fly over. Any country is a great country to fly over. And then we got to Osaka. It's an Osage Indian word, meaning (I forgot now what it does mean).

Well, anyway, it was cold and raining, and the pilot had been hedgehopping to get in there, so in unloading all of Gibbons' various treasures that he had assembled from covering every war from Grant's down, he missed the coat.[2] Well, there is no way of describing it. He accused the pilot of carrying an assistant that had jumped overboard with a parachute to get away with the coat.

When as a matter of fact, if anyone had put it on and jumped, they would have been well protected without a parachute. But anyhow he had lost the coat. He was for not going on to Manchuria. I offered him my mackintosh instead. But he was inconsolable. He wanted even Russia to win the war. Finally I just took him to the bar room of the hotel and left him with his grief. His coat had been left in Tokyo.

From the Far East, by Mail: Well all I know is just what I read in the papers, and what I see as I prowl hither and thither. You know I kinder like people to talk and write about more than I do places, and Temples and Churches. Well, Sir, there was on our Boat coming out here quite an interesting bunch. We dident have many passengers outside of the steerage, but we had a might interesting little bunch.

Two Germans who had been home from Japan on a visit, prominent business men, spoke good English, that is about like me. Said things were very bad in the old Country, even worse they thought than most of the other places. But seemed might cheerful and optomistic about it. Great race those folks. When they do come back they will do it with a Bang, for they are built of fine stock.

These were great Readers, well informed on everything, and told us more of Japan than even a Japanese Scientist that was with us. He was might pleasant, but he wouldent tell us exactly what we asked him. He was smart though, he had been down to Pasadena, and studying with Prof. Millikan and all those fellows that Einstein was with.[1]

You know, funny thing, it was just a Japanese gardner that had a Truck patch away out in the Desert toward Arizona that had a sort of an amateur globe of some kind and he found a Star, a new one that none of the Scientists had ever found. There was a big fuss made over it, I remember at the time, and they gave him a new set of tools, or Spy Glasses, or whatever it is you find odd things with, just for his contribution to Science, so he went right on picking Radishes, and I bet in about another year he will bob up with another Star, or Planet. Hope he finds one that hasent been hit by depression.

By the way I wonder if they are hit like all the rest of the World anyway. If they are it just shows you how far Hoover's influence reaches. Then, of course, we had Floyd Gibbons on there, and he knows about everything, and has been everywhere, and read everything. A Scotch Golf Player from Canada that was as liberal as any one you ever saw, I don't know where they get that scotch stuff. Then a Standard Oil man from Jersey Company, Mr. Walton.[2] He was headed for Batavia, where they have Big holdings.

But the fellow that I want to tell you about was the "Bee Man." His name was Riddell.[3] He had lately come from up in Alberta, Canada, and he was just about as odd and human a Fish as you will find in a year's trooping. He had on board 500 hives of Bees, taking them out to China. Well up to the time I met him I dident know any more about a Bee than I do about Shakespeare. But the Bee man told me a lot. He had 'em all stored on deck, right out in the cold. He first had 'em down below, but he was afraid of the heat, so they brought 'em up, and they was roped down for believe me you Brother those Bees did some rocking if they was with the Boat.

He would send all over the Country just to buy Queen Bees, that's the Head Bee. There is some Guys called Drones that don't do anything as long as they live, but they Bump those Babies off mighty soon, so the life of a Drone while it's restful, it's rather curtailed. He says they are all organized and that each one has his certain work to do, some bring it in, some store it away, some stand guard. I am going to get that Book of Materlink's on Bees and read it.[4] He says that's what drove him in the Bee business.

I remember Materlink when he was brought out years ago to Hollywood with the Sam Goldywn Company that I was with at the time.[5] I dident know he knew anything about Bees then or I would have asked him. He was a mighty pleasant old fellow, and had a plum pretty little French Wife. I knew he had written a Play about I think it was Blue Bird, but I dident know a thing about this Bee business.

But it was the other qualities that made this Bee man stand out. He at first was kinder a "Windy." But as we kept trying to pin him down, why we found out he had really been there, or he had read it. By Golly those fellows on the Boat that had really read a lot couldent find anything to stick old Bees on. I finally horned in with my reportoire of books consisting of Ibanez "The Cabin," Sandberg's "Lincoln," McGuffy's Fourth Reader, "The Life and Exploits of Jesse James," "When the Daltons Rode!" and on the way over Lamb's "Genghis Khan," and "Marco Polo."[6] Now that's my life's work digging through that mess, and here this Bee Guy not only had read all of 'em but memorized most of 'em, and then would tell me companion books that I should read following these up. But the Rascal was just book smart and he dident have much real horse sense knowledge. He has read a little beyond his limit.

He was what you call a kind of a well read Nut. He thought the three greatest men in the World was, well I can't even remember either one of them. I believe one was Thore, or some name like that, a poet or something like that, and Whitman, and another Writer, he really thought these men had contributed more than a man like Lincoln or Edison.[7] You see they ought to be a law to stop a man reading when he gets too far. Imagine a Poet, don't care what kind of a Poet he was (even a good one) being worth more to the World than Edison. How could you read the Poetry if it wasent for Edison? You would have to do it in the day time.

But Old Bees was pretty tough to down in all argument, and you

114

would about have to buy him a drink to beat him. He was a young fellow too, about forty-two, but he was high on old Thoreau or whatever his name was, he lived up around Boston, Harvard man I guess. I never could find out from Bees just what type of stuff he turned out. Maby was a Collumnist, he had also read a lot of Chinese stuff. He and the Japanese would argue over that, I tell you this old Bee man was a freak.

He knew an awful lot about ants too. That's something he got me interested in, and soon as I can get my mind off Movies I am going into the Ants. This old Boy just put more ambition into me. He has just got me all excited to learn, so no more Hoover and the Senate and Boarah and all that, I am going to devote my time from now on to Ants. They do something.

476   WHAT'S THE NEWS, ANYHOW?

Somewhere East of Suez, by mail: Well all I know is just what I read in the papers, and what I see as I go thither and thither. The thing that makes it tough out here in all these Countries is that you don't get any News, that is I mean OUR news.

My goodness, I was out here a month before I found out that Notre Dame had lost a game. Imagine newspapers being printed in any language and in every Country and not having that in it. Now that I have heard it, I can't find out how it happened, so that makes you madder than ever. Well they made a great record, and I bet they give a great account of themselvs at that. You see these papers have just a few lines of some events that happened back home. But whoever picks 'em out to print must be someone that was never over home, or if so it was just after the Boxer uprising. Now Congress was to meet at home just a week after I left, now as far as we in the Far East are concerned they never did. Of course as far as you all at home are concerned they never did either, but they did meet, I am afraid. What have they done? We can't hear a thing, and I guess you all there can't either, so in lots of respects we are equal.

But darn it, I miss my paper. I used always to sit a long time over breakfast and read my papers, and just think, over here I sit, but that's all. A breakfast don't taste good to me without a good paper.

Japan has one awfully good English speaking paper, it's the Tokio Advertiser. It's about the best in the far east, unless it is Manilla. Course this little one-sided war out here has so upset the news, you don't get anything but it. There is so much Propaganda mixed up in it, on both sides, that they just fill the papers up with a lot of junk put out by whichever Country the paper happens to be in.

The funniest thing in all the war is that up in Mukden there is about twenty Co-Respondents gathered from all over, and they have been in the one Hotel for over four months, just waiting for the one little Battle that they knew must come, but they dident know when. That is the Battle of Chinchow. They all wanted to go to their various Posts like Shanghai and Peking and back home to spend Xmas, but they couldent leave for fear the Japanese would pull the thing off while they was gone. They sure are a fine bunch of fellows. I was around there with 'em for about a week. This Mukden that you read all these war dispatches out of used to be quite a City. It's the Capitol of Manchuria, and was some place in the very old days. But since the Japanese took it over, and there is martial law, why there is not even a Movie in Town. Over at some other Hotel they have one a week, they of course are all silent. Not only silent but absent.

There is a pretty nice Hotel there, with good food and rooms and Baths, and a Bar. But over in this Country everybody sits down at a Table, and have the drinks brought to 'em. They sure do like to holler, "Boy-san." I think that's it and it means boy. They just put the San on to make it harder. Well a Foreigner does like to holler at the Boys, so you have the boy do everything but actually take the drink for you. The American and English, well in fact all the foreign Colony in these towns like Darien, Mukden, and Harbin, all have a Club, which will stand comparison with any of our Clubs over home, and most of their social activities are held there, and their dances and gatherings. There is always the Consuls, of the different Nations, The Standard Oil is in all these, and the Texas Co., Ford's, and General Motors have men, then up that way you run onto a lot of Fur Men that go to Harbin to get their Furs for you Women. Their headquarters are in Tiensein, China. There is twenty or thirty of those that are American Buyers. Kolinsky is the main fur, and then the Mongolian Dog, it's a sort of a half wild dog, well they render that up into pretty near any fur you call for, but it's orginally Mutt.

The trains on the South Manchurian Railway are very nice up to date Trains, that's the line that the war is over, as the Japanese say they are doing all this to protect that line. Course they have gone out three or four hundred miles on each side to do it, but it's supposed to be all just to protect their line. They do run anything in first class shape. Their trains are always clean and right on time, sleepers are some of them like ours, but most of them are the European style, Wagon Lits (like France's). They are the best kind; they beat ours.

Course some of those lines there is a lot of robberies on. The

Chinese lines are not so well protected now. For the Japanese have kinder got 'em all dissorganized and the Chinese don't know whether to run 'em or leave 'em. But the Japanese say they are not safe on account of the Bandits. Course there is naturally lots of Bandits, for the Chinese Army has been kinder let go, so they got nothing to do but Banditry. There is no work and nothing to eat, and they got guns, so they ain't going to starve.

But it's a rich Country in resources, and they will be fighting over it for years, for Russia is in the Northern end and Japan in the Southern, now they ain't going to live in the same kennell, and when Russia gets ready, if this scheme of theirs even just half way works, they are building up a big Army, and a great air force, and they haven't forgot the Russo-Japanese war yet. So that will be a real war, for don't you let anyone tell you these little Japanese are not Soldiers. They fight, and will be hard to lick, so don't put all your money on peace. War to end wars was a bust.

477   MOVIES IN TOKYO

Tokyo, by mail: Well, all I know is just what I read in the papers, and what is see as I prowl, and this is the prowlingest Country there is to prowl in. These Japanese they sure do try to do things up in real European or western style.

Got to tell you about the Hotel we (when I say we, I mean Floyd Gibbons and I, he come over on the same boat with me), well, it's called the Imperial. It's built of bricks, but it's low and rambling. It's freaky looking, but you kinder like it after awhile. It of course was built by an American Architect, but it was the only thing that stood up during the Earthquake.[1]

These Japanese have a real City here, about two and a half million, and it almost connects with Yokohama, another big City and their principal seaport. They are, of course excited over the war in China. These Japanese take their wars serious, they go in 'em to win 'em. Of course, all the Propaganda you get here is on their side, naturally. They feel they got a lot of money invested in that Country and they want to be in charge of things so they can supervise the things their way.

Course the whole thing is so mixed up with treatys, and secret agreements and understandings, that nobody knows head or tail to who's claim is any good.

Well, this is a great Movie Country. They make more Movies

here than they do at home. And naturally I wanted to see some of the Studios. You know the Gag. When a Motorman is off he visits another Motorman and rides with him.

Well being off from the Studio for a couple of months before I was to start another Picture why naturally I must go see somebody else make 'em. But they have a lot of Studios over here, so Mr. Dwight Davis, the Governor General of the Philippines, and his very lovely Daughter, who were on their way back home, were here at the time and they wanted to see a Japanese Studio too, so we got our Company's representative, in charge of Fox Pictures out here, and he arranged it.[2]

Well, we finally got out there. Of course it was pretty sad lot after seeing the tremendous things at home. But yet it had the same stuff at that. Mind you they make their pictures at an average cost of five thousand Dollars, where our cheapest will run $150,000. But they do a good job with what they have.

They didn't happen to be shooting that morning, said they had worked the night before. That sounded kinder natural. But we had tea, that was the minute we went in. They sure will load you up on tea if you do any visiting around. Just at the drop of the hat somebody will start bringing in tea. They started out to try and scare up some of the Stars. You know they have favorites over there just like ours, and some of 'em are big drawing cards.

Well we walked all around among the old buildings, you know theirs are all silent pictures, they have only made one or two Talkies, they don't like 'em so well, only the foreign ones.

Then they dug up a Screen Star and she was pretty. They had a Camera man that followed us around just like they do at home, where he is on publicity and snaps everything in the world that will never be used. I often wondered what they do with all the Pictures over home that Photographers take and that are never used.

None of them spoke any English and none of us any Japanese. But we bowed and giggled and pointed, and drank more tea, and had a fine time and I had quite a thrill of visiting a Japanese Studio. Course then I did a lot of Picture going in what little time I had there. They get our pictures out there right soon after they are released, and the Stars that are big here are over there too. Chevalier's latest was there.[3] These Japanese sure will try anything, and get away with it. Everything at home we make or do, or wear, they got here, and make it.

Course they got lots of Automobiles around Tokyo, and good paved streets. But what gives you a scare is to be in one of these Rickashas and have 'em be going right down the middle of the street among about a million others and then coming right at you, and a Driver that is not sure he knows where he is going coming at you in an Automobile. Here you are sitting up there in this frail little contraption. Nothing ahead of you but this Bird hauling it, and here comes this big car lumbering at you. Sometimes I have seen 'em missed by three and four inches. I quit riding in 'em. I says to myself if two things is going to meet, me for being the biggest one, so I got into the car.

Then the Bicycles, you never in all your born days saw as many Bicycles. Fords were never as thick as Bicycles are over here, and carry stuff on 'em? Say they will move your grand piano any day and do it on a Bicycle. A person riding along over here on one without anything is just practically dead heading in empty. They have always got a Billiard Table, or a stove or bed, or a couple of mattresses on the wheel with 'em.

There is lots of green over here even at this time of the year, and they do love flowers. They all got a little flower of some kind, they can make what they got go a long way, and they are awful neat and clean. There is a lot of fine qualities about 'em, and they are just about the most ambitious folks you ever saw. They are for progress, no matter what it is. All this has been done in fifty years, and they are proud to show you their Country, and if you ever want to make a real trip don't overlook 'em.

478   DING! DING! NANKING

Well, all I know is just what I read in the papers, and what I see here and there. Now just looking out of the window, what do I see? I am traveling from Peking, (Peiping) all same place, to Shanghai, by way of Nanking. (Nanking is the Capital of China, that is it was. You see there is a place called Canton.)

Canton is where all the Americanized Chinamen come from, and they have taken the Government of Nanking over. They are the real Trouble raisers, of Canton, that is I mean they are the progressive ones. They want always to be stirring something up.

Well, the Nanking Government has fallen and the Canton crowd is in the saddle. But that hasent anything to do with this trip by Train from Peking, the old capital, and by far the most interesting town in China.

Well, I was to have flown down. That flown is a pretty big world, maby I better make that flew. I was to have flowen down, but there is a bear of a Snow storm here and there won't be any Planes for days, so I had much against my will to take a Train. It's not a bad train. They have these Wagon Lits cars.

Know what is the Wagon Lits? Well it's a French contraption where you sleep cockeyed of the way the train is going. There is a little aisle along the side of the train and then some little Compartments, sometimes there is beds for two and sometimes there is beds for 4 in them.

I wanted one alone so I had to pay more, to keep somebody from sleeping with me, or over me or under me. I have heard of these same cars crossing the Transiberian Railway where they are for 10 days on this train, and you might be in the same room with a Woman. I say I have heard of such things. It wouldent be my luck.

But as I was saying I am in this one all alone. We are pulling out of Peking. It's snowing and it's cold. The poor Ricksha "Coolies" are out there in the snow trying to make 5 cents in their money for a fare, and one American Dollar is worth four of theirs so that means they are trying to make one-fourth of five, which is a cent and a quarter, to pull you where you want to go.

This is in a deep snow, and they will pull you by main strength, in a trot mind you, for just a fraction over one penny in our money. Then we talk about hard times. Say, we havent seen hard times. They wear a little cloth shoe that is exactly like a house slipper. It's no more than a sock, yet there they stand out there, hundreds of 'em, and there can't be any more than one-tenth of them get a passenger, so you will see what China is like without even going any further.

They say they don't last long. It's their heart that fails 'em. You go at a run or fast trot, in all kinds of weather, with practically no clothes on, rain, snow intense heat and all, and you are finished before you are 30, so they say.

Well, I hear some people in the next compartment speaking English or something like it, so that don't seem so bad. We are to be on this Rattler two days, and two nights, that's if it's on time. This is the line where the Students have been laying on the line and obstructing the traffic, you must have read about that.

Well it's a terrible night and if any of them are laying out there tonight, they deserve to have a train not see 'em. You can't beat education for foolishness. They have been going down to Nanking to see the Members of the Government. They beat up two or three. Ain't that a mess!

Imagine Notre Dame going to Washington to beat up Senator Borah, or Yale lying on the track to keep a train from getting to Harvard. There has always been a problem, "Does education pay?"

Yes, it does, if you got a sense of humor, you got to pay for your laughs at a Show, so why not at School.

Here we go, a friend from the City National Bank of New York brought me down a package. They are the real banking institution out here, they are in all these towns. Let me see, what is in it? Oh Boy, it's two bottles (small ones, darn skinflint) of Champaign. He could just as easy brought two big ones. Course I just met him casually, so you can't expect everything.

There is sure a lot of Chinese on here, most of them in the second and third class cars. But they are like Mexicans, they sure do love to travel, and eat as they go. Every Station we stop at, they are hollering and yelling till it sounds like a Football Game, and of all the queer junk they sell to eat, they have little Charcoal stoves they have it cooking right there before you. Everything is done with Chop sticks, and say these old boys can do more with a pair of them than Bobby Jones with a Putter.[1] Some of these Chinese girls are mighty pretty, they are prettier than the Japanese.

Here is a bunch of Students. My friend next door, a Mr. Furgeson, an American that has been here just fortyseven years, he is giving me all the dope.[2] He says the students are taking up a collection for General "Ma" to fight the Japs.[3] Ma is the old General that fought 'em pretty good away up at Titzihar.

He is a sort of a Pancho Villa.[4] When there is no war with Japan why he just makes up his own local wars to kill time till something better turns up. Well the Students wanted to go up and join him, but he sent word that for them to just send some money. "Smart people these Chinese." All these Students have on Kimmonas or long robes, and the Chinese are giving too, they are very liberal, especially the old ones.

Well, I just come from up there, where they are sending this dough, and it's no use. The war in Manchuria is over, Japan has already got all she wants and more in fact. I don't think they will try to hold what they have as it would be too big an expense to patrol it. It would break any nation to police such a large area. For these Chinese bands that would be on their tails all the time are big Armies, not just a little band of Bandits.

More students with Banners, "Down with Japan." Graves all over the place, round mounds just scattered around like shocks of wheat, they tend the ground all around them. Just think here we are jogging along here on a train, over ground that the history of it is known for 4 thousand years. That's older than some of the jokes we use in the Movies.

479   SEEING THE MANCHURIANS
AT HOME

Well, all I know is just what I read in the papers. And say brother it's so cold out here in this Manchuria that you can't read even if you had something to read which you haven't. Sitting here in Mukden, that's the town that all the Japanese and Chinese war news comes from, you know it's been on the front pages of every paper for months and months. It used to be the old capitol of Manchuria when Manchuria was really a kingdom.

They have had Emperors and rulers here for 2 or 3 thousand years. It's kinder in the range of that old repscallion Ganghis Khan. He ranged up and down these parts. He captured everything from Japan clear on right to the very gates of what is now Europe. He got clear to Vienna, and did it all horseback.

Well, this is right up his alley this place. It's got an old walled city here, where they close the gates at night. Went down there yesterday with some newspaper men to buy some curios, that is rare jade. They have been out here for years and savvy jade, so they seem to know that they were doing. But I don't know how anybody would hardly get the best of a Chinaman in a trade, so I figure my friends dident get away with any bargain.

It was sure cold, and in each little shop there would be a whole family. When you say a whole family in China I mean all the sons he has, all the grandsons, all the other kin folks. They are great family people and they all live together. When the son is married he brings his wife home and there they all stay.

They have some wonderful old curios in these old shops. Course they might have been like ours made the week before someplace but they looked pretty ancient to me. You know what these Chinese was nutty about was clocks. They say most of them were made in France and Switzerland, as they never did make any out here, but they sure was cuckoo about 'em.

They live in the back end of these places. The way they work the heat or the stove is they have a little bit of a thing like a fireplace. It's generally right under their bed, and their bed is built down solid to the ground. It's not a bed, it's just a high platform built against the back of the wall.

Well, they have little openings, not pipes, but just little long troughs, or alleyways running through the masonry that makes the foundation of the bed, and this little heat from this dinky little stove, it runs on through these little passages, and that is what heats the bed. It don't have a thing to do with the house but at night they have enough fire till they can get to sleep. They all bundle up there on the one big long bed. It's a regular Brigham Young affair.[1]

The Japanese they sleep on a mattress on the floor, but the Chinese get up on this shelf. We also went into a fur store as they wanted to get a kind of a lap robe to use in a Ricksha. That's one of the little carts they pull you around in. They can just hit a long trot and take you to the end of the road. These fellows however don't live long. They are so poorly paid you have to give what would be less than a couple of cents in our money, and then there is so many of 'em, the business is overdone. It's like everything at home, overproduction.

Well, you ought to have seen these furs, if they dident have some of the queerest looking old pelts in there, and what do you think they were, well, they were every kind of fur in the world, but they were all dog fur.

That's what they really were. Of course, there was fox and beaver and Kolinsky and mink, but all made from practically the same dog. You see those old dogs up there are kinder semi wild, and they roam the country and they are raised in the villages, then when the family get broke why old Fido is executed, and his hide brings in some rice, and his meat brings in all the neighbors, and they have a feed, "Come tonight we are eating the flea hound."

There is no two mutts colored alike. They look like everything that ever wore hair, and on these Chinese streets they don't sell hardly anything in the stores, they move it all out of the streets. Of all the junk they are cooking right there before you on a little charcoal fire. All kinds of fish, and queer do dads.

Then the barbers are out there. The tonsorial parlors are right in the middle of the road. They also wash out their ears too, all in the same sitting, that's one of the places they have to wash, as they get so stopped up they can't hear. When they cut hair, boy, they do it with a thing like a cycle or scythe. They get it off and you are cleaned as far as the hair is concerned. They don't wear the cues anymore, that is you do see a few but not many, it's kinder old fashioned, and is kinder like wearing a derby hat.

Did I tell you how they traded? Well, they wear great long kimonos, with sleeves about six inches longer than their hands, and in cold weather they run each hand up each sleeve, like a muff.

Well if two of them are trading, one each runs his hands up the other's sleeve, and by feeling each other's fingers they telegraph how much is offered and the other one how much he will take. Well, if they are a couple of good quick traders they can get the price of a pair of sox agreed on along about the middle of the afternoon.

Course the time means nothing to 'em, neither one is going anywhere. They are, everybody says the sharpest traders that there is in the world. There used to be a Jewish settlement many years ago, and these just finally wore them out and gobbled them up, they couldent start with the Chinese.

No pigeon English up north Cina where we are. That is down south at Canton, there is where all the American Chinaman come from is Canton. I sure am going down there. I want to see the home town of some of these. They are a great people they don't care who has got Manchuria, all they want to do is just to get you in a trade of some kind and they are fixed. They are not what we call "sharpers" they are just good legitimate traders. You got to be good to live among 400 million others.

480   WANTED—A NEWSPAPER

Well all I know is just what I read in the papers, and say, wasent I glad to get back home and read some papers! I mean some Papers! With some news in 'em and printed in language that was about 50 per cent intelligible to me.

Honest there was times on that trip when I would have given almost any amount of money to just have had that day's American newspaper. They don't print a bit of American news, even the big papers in England won't have two date lines from America.

Why our country newspapers have more European news in one edition than their big city ones will have of us in a month. No wonder the world don't know anything about us. They don't get a chance to read it, and if it is in there it is just about Al Capone, or some Gangster, or anything that is in any way detrimental to our Country.

They keep publishing that we are going to go off the Gold. Well so many of us over here haven't seen any Gold in so long that we don't know if we are off it or on it. But honest it was good to get a newspaper in my mits again. A breakfast without a newspaper is a Horse without a Saddle. You are just riding bareback if you got no news for breakfast.

I have just read since I been back till I am blue in the face. Everything that has happened in three months was news to me. Why do you know that I used to send Mrs. Rogers cables from Japan and China asking her about different National events.

Here I was all hopped up over my good friend John Garner. Now

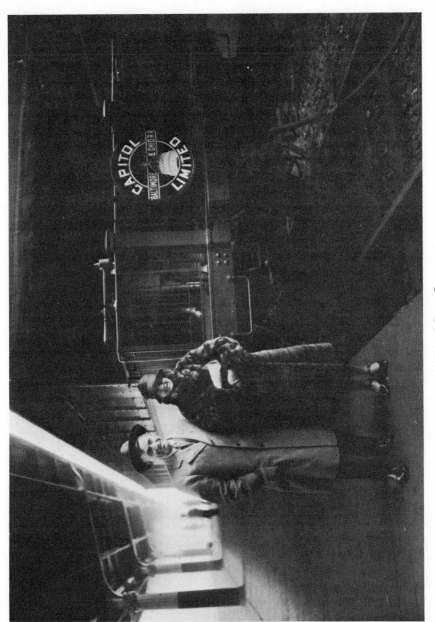

Will and Betty Rogers

I dident know if he had been made Speaker of the House or not. News like that meant nothing to a Chinaman, but it meant something to me. Notre Dame and Southern California, I couldent find out if it had been called off on account of rain, no attendance, or for the good of the order.[1]

Did Mayor Jimmy Walker get Mooney out?[2] Or did Jimmy just get out of New York? All these things I couldent get head and tail of. So I would cable Mrs. Rogers, now at $1.25 a word, naturally my news was scattering. So if I talk about things that don't mean a thing to you any more why they mean a lot to me for I just found 'em out. So what I am getting at, don't underestimate your paper, I don't care how small it is, and how little news you think it might have in it at that particular issue. Lord kiss it, for the news that it does bring you.

Why I have seen times when I would have given $100 for the "Claremore Progress" or the "Claremore Messenger," and that's just two of the smaller papers of Claremore. Take my ham away, take away my eggs, even my chili, but leave me my Newspaper.

Even if it just has such purely local news as "Jim Jones came home last night unexpectedly, and bloodshed ensued," or "Jesse Bushyhead, our local M.D., is having one of the best years of his career practically speaking. But they just won't pay him when they get well."[3]

"The County seat was packed yesterday with prominent visitors from out of town, attempting to renew their notes," "Election ain't far off and everybody is up for office that can sign an application blank."

Now all that don't seem much news to you. But it is news, especially when you know the people, and they are your own folks. So no matter how punk you might think your local paper is getting, why just take it away from you and see how you feel. The old newspaper I think is just about our biggest blessing. Course the car will strike some of you as better, but a Horse and Buggy was a mighty fine substitute for the Ford. But there has been no substitute for the old newspaper. Then look at the difference in the cost to us.

Then you see too we are living in such an age that we have to pick up the paper to see what Countries have gone to war, what one have Revolutions, how many Billions our Congress has appropriated. Never since the oldest inhabitant was born have we lived through such exciting times. The great war was just local. It was all in France. But today news, excitement, is everywhere. Nations are furnishing the news nowadays, and not just Peggy Joyce and Al Capone.[4] So let's all read and be merry, for tomorrow the paper may not have enough adds in to come out.

126

481   WILL SEES THE EARLY CANDIDATES

Well all I know is just what I read in the papers and what I see hither and thither. Did quite a bit of prowling around since I landed from Europe. Course went down to Washington a couple of times to see what the hired help was doing. They was just appropraiting right and left. The U.S. Treasury to them is just a rainbow. There is no end to it.

You see appropriations for the boys back home is what gets you the votes. Putting on taxes to get them money to appropiate is a sure way of losing votes. So this being election year, everybody is handing out, and nobody has the nerve to vote to replenish what they are taking out.

You see what makes it bad for our relief this year is that both sides are just bent on getting in in November. So they naturally got an eye for their own employment and not for the unemployed now.

They voted two billion bucks to help out the bankers but from the looks of the line when I was in Washington there was two billion bankers. So they will only get a dime apeace. Everything was politics there. All you could hear was "Who is going to run?"

The Democrats have got more candidates then they have voters. Every place wants to run a different man. The Republicans are just as bad. They want to run everybody too, but they can't run anybody but Mr. Hoover. If they run anybody else they would be repudiating their own administration, so they are up against it.

If things pick up Mr. Hoover has a good chance, but if they don't he is kinder snowed under. I bummed around from Washington, went over to Cleveland by air with secretary Dave Ingalls of the Navy.[1] Dave is running for the governorship of Ohio. He dident act like a real candiadte to me he was so complimentary about his Democratic opponent.

Dave said "Why Will he is a fine man, good friend of mine, he is a Democrat is about all you can have against him." Now that's no way for a young man running for his first office to talk. He has to cut that out and start telling what a schroundel he is. Voters never heard anybody complimented. They want to hear you knock 'em. He outside of that is a very capable young man. I think we ought to have some younger men in public life. Don't want to knock any of the older ones out of a job, but lots of 'em been in for years and years and they never have shown much, so if they havent in all this time why it looks like they won't. So it's no use monkeying with 'em. Went on over to Detroit and Chicago, then down through Oklahoma.

It looks like Garner is coming mighty strong. He has made

tremendous gains in the last two or three weeks. He is going to make some of those first mentioned candidates hard to catch. He is one they can't get much on. Everybody both Republican and Democrat have a lot of confidence in him. He has been right in the mouth of all the things that have happened, and should know more about it than anybody. If everybody knew him personally they would be for him.

Then I had a nice chat with Mr. Newton Baker.[2] There is a smart, pleasant, fine fellow. He did one great job for us and should be able to do another if he gets the chance. He is a very level headed fellow, perhaps the best orator of the lot, or any other lot.

Then I get on around into Oklahoma and go and see "Our Bill."[3] Now there is a guy that will fool you. When you look at him, you wouldent bet much on him, but if you go up and feel of him and examine him, and ask him some questions why he starts improving on you. His answeres will kinder make you forget his looks. Bill is mighty shrewd. He is especially cagy on state rights and laws. I bet there is not a govenor in the land that knows just what his state is entitled too as much as Murray. His not bragging on his chances, but he is out to do all he can, and if he can talk before enough voters why he will win a lot of votes, for he has some mighty convincing arguments. He is a sticker for the little fellow. Well there never was a time in our history when there was as many little fellows, so he ought to do mighty good if he can get too 'em.

Saw Al. He was feeling great. He is not out just to stop Roosevelt. He is out the same as the others, just to be nominated if he can. Lot of 'em blame him, but I don't see why. He has got a tremendous lot of friends in the country that will always vote for him. Look at Bryan.[4] There is people voting for him yet, and it will always be that way with Smith. He is the kind of man that he gets your supoort and friendship why you are for him for life.

There is lots of men that you are for just for the momenet, or just while some certain thing is on, and then there are others that you are just for, now, then and forever, no matter what it's for, when or why. Well that's Al Smith.

I dident get up to see Mr. Roosevelt. I know him and admire him very much. He is a very human fellow. Ask Warm Springs, Georgia if he is not quite a guy. Then this late affair with Tammany Hall, when he threw out a sherriff that had been "hoarding" the city's money for 'em personally. Why that will boost his stock in the provinces. Even if Tammany was to change and get respectable the world wouldent believe it.

Now that brings us to Mr. Ritchie.[5] There is the aristocrat, the gentleman, the good fellow, the politician, good state executive, champion state righter, one who saw that prohibition was a flop, even before it was. Younger than the others, great personality, and in case two or three of the others get into a deadlock at the convention is liable to make a great compromise candidate. He won't perhaps enter the convention with the amount of votes that some of the others will, but if the Democrats get in a fight there, and the only thing that will keep 'em from doing it, is if the convention is called off, why during the fight anything can happen. Then too you see the candidates I have enumerated to you, they are just the eary bird variety. There will be dozens and dozens come in from now on. The harder the times are the more will come in, mostly through starvation, and partly through thinking that the Democrats can win with practically nothing, and there will be some enter the race later that will qualify for nothing.

482   A NIGHT PHONE CALL

Well, all I know is just what I read in the papers, and what I hear one way and another.

One night out at my little ranch where I live I was awakened out of my sleep about 2:30 in the morning by a phone call. It was from New York and was from William Randolph Hearst, Jr.[1] I had been out to a dinner at the home of the neighbor, Oscar Lawlor, Los Angeles' best lawyer, who had just won the biggest case the Standard Oil had ever won.[2] It was over the Elk or Kettlemen Hills Oil Field. It wasn't a celebration, for he is too modest for that. It was just a lot of friends gathered together to "blather" and eat.

So naturally no one turned on the "radio," as everybody was pretty well fixed for toothpaste and mouth wash. My one tube had run me for years. So I went on home about eleven feeling that all was well with the world, outside of China, Japan, India, Manchuria, Russia, Germany, England, France, Italy, Spain, South America, Nicaragua, and the United States, including a two and a half billion deficit in one year and a worse year coming up.

So I felt that the world was really sitting pretty, outside of everybody not working, and nobody buying anything, and nobody knowing what the morrow might bring forth, but even if it brought it forth it wouldn't surprise us, for we were prepared for what we thought was the worst.

Well, the phone rings. You know how that scares you away in the night? You think of the ones that are not there with you. Mrs. Rogers was with my sister in Chelsea (twenty miles from Claremore).³ She didn't fly home from the East with me. She don't mind short flights of a couple or three hours but when they run into days, she believes that old man Pullman had a pretty good idea how to cross the continent, and she has made it so much that she knows every jack rabbit or coyote from California to Kansas.⁴ Her being away when the phone rang, and two boys scattered around in schools, of which we hadn't heard from since Christmas.

But when I am half asleep and nervously grabbed the phone and it was young Bill Hearst from New York, I couldn't think what in the world it was. I had just been up to his father's ranch about half way between Frisco and here, and I thought maybe I did something up there that I shouldn't. Maybe some of the silver is missing. Maybe there is an old William the Conquerer tapesty missplaced.

In fact, there is so much devilment up there that a country boy could do, that I couldn't think of what it was I had done. I remembered riding off horseback with the cattle boss, and spending the whole day, when I should have been maybe with the other guests at the castle. But there was lots of lawyers among the guests, and I knew cows better than I did lawyers. There is a way of studying a cow and learning all about her, but a lawyer? There has never been any course at college devised where you can take in "What Makes A Lawyer Like He Is?"

This young Bill Hearst, Jr. is a mighty promising young fellow, and looks like he is going to pick up W. R.'s trail and keep the ink smearing over half the pulp wood of Canada. Then when he says, "The Lindberg baby has been kidnapped," well, that put a different complexion on life.⁵ What did General Honjo taking Manchuria amount to?⁶ We could give the whole mess of candidates on both sides for the return of the baby.

It was just one of those things that hit you right between the eyes. It was then five-thirty in the morning in New York, and he said they had been up all night working on the case. He said that he had just had Arthur Brisbane on the wire for a couple of hours down at his home in New Jersey, and Mr. Brisbane wanted him to get me, that I was the last newspaper man to have seen the child.⁷

And would I tell 'em some more about it? So I told him what little I knew over the phone, which didn't take me long. It's as I have told you in my little daily blurb, we had spent the day out there, not at the Lindberg home, but at the Morrow home, where the Lindbergs live most of the time.⁸

In fact, my wife and I discussed going home that evening as to whether the Lindbergs would ever live at their new home. You see it was started before Mr. Morrow's death. But since then, of course that puts a whole new complexion on all their lives. Mrs. Morrow is naturally crazy about the baby, as are all the family, and they have this great big lively home at Englewood, that this baby and the family all being there would just help to make up for some of the loss of Mr. Morrow.[9] It is just a sad state of affairs, for here was this man Morrow who was as sure to be one of the pillars in our destiny as night was to follow day.

You didn't find a public man like that once in a lifetime. He had ability combined with common sense. Everything that come up he just took all the "hooey" out of it and brought it down to just an every day problem. The bigger the problem the easier it was to solve diplomatically with him, for he knew it only took square dealing on both sides, and the other fellow knowing how on the level Morrow was, why naturally he turned "straight" too. We all know a lot of these little old one horse papers in New York have taken digs at Lindberg. It made a lot of them sore because he didn't want their publicity. They can't understand anyone that don't want their name in the papers. He did his stunt and he wanted to be let alone, and live his life the way he saw fit. But no. These birds must start tormenting him, when he don't do like they want him to, then the little scandal sheets started "gunning" for him.

Why there is nothing that he has done since his flight that has not reflected credit on him and the whole people who are proud of him. Heroes are made every little while, but only one in a million conduct themselves afterwards so that it makes us proud that we honored them at the time. As I have always argued that fellow has a native intuition to do the right thing. In China, Japan, Mexico, France, or New Jersey, he hasn't made a wrong move yet. His wife has proven a lovely sweet American girl. She has at the risk of her own life taken up her husband's profession, and anything said against them in any way, must come through nothing but jealousy.

483   CHEER UP! THERE'S NO TAX
FOR BEING HAPPY

Well, all I know is just what I read in the papers. Poor old papers. While the Lindbergh case was at its heighth they even had to cut out some of the ads.[1] Let's see how is the world going anyhow.

Has depression scraped the bottom, or is it anchored there?

Things happen for a few days in a row that make you think, well maybe she is turning. Then the next week all that is washed up and it looks like we don't know a thing.

They are getting a lot of more people employed, due to some splendid work of some very able and public spirited men. I have a friend in the east, one of the big international polo players, Cheever Cowdin, and he has done a lot of fine work along that line.[2]

You know this darn thing has made the whole country better off in a lot of ways. It's done away with four flushing. If a man hasent got it, he don't mind telling you right out that he hasent. It's made poverty fashionable. It's brought out some mighty good qualities in lots of people. There is a spirit of better fellowship among everyone I think.

Things really are not as bad off as some paint 'em. That is I mean if the ones out of work could get jobs. Course there is lots of things that are making money, but they are not suffering so much. Everybody is living cheaper, still there is lots of things that haven't come down in comparison to other things.

Rents are still high in comparison to food, but everybody is trying to make the house or apartment pay a return on what it cost them at the time of the boom. They are not making any money out of the houses, according to the cost price, but the cost price is not liable to ever be what it was. Other businesses have charged it off and called it a day, and started in on a new scale.

The darndest crime of the whole thing is farm machinery we are now paying on. Never did a farmer have as little, yet never has his machinery cost as much. I think their earnings have kept up during all this hard times. They know an old boy has got to have a plow, so make him pay for it. Most men that I have talked to that ought to know, (but Lord that don't mean anything). Well, most of them are of the opinion that things will never be as they were, and I don't suppose anybody wants to see that "cuckoo" stage again, but these men seem to think that things will be more like they were away along before the war. This is in prices. Things you have to sell will be cheap but things you have to buy to eat, wear, and use will be in comparison.

I can remember when cattlemen made plenty of money and got ahold of all their big ranches on three and four cents a pound beef, but other things they had to buy and use were in comparison. Land taxes is the thing. They got so high that there is no chance to make anything. Not only land but all property tax.

You see in the old days, (I am speaking of when I was a boy back in the fortys') why the only thing they knew how to tax was land, or a house. Well, that condition went along for quite awhile, so even today the whole country tries to run its revenue on taxes on land. They never ask if the land makes anything. "It's land ain't it? Well tax it then."

Millions and millions of people don't pay an income tax, because they don't earn enough to pay on one, but you pay a land tax whether it ever did or ever will earn you a penny. And the taxes we pay now are on "After the war valuation" when things you raised were at their highest.

Now we got some kind of a big overhauling on this tax thing. Different conditions make different taxes. All taxes should be on income, and where there is no income either personally, or on your property, why you shouldent pay anything. You should pay on things that you buy outside of bare necessities.

I think this sales tax is the best tax we have had in years. It's what they call painless, that's when you don't know you are paying it. Course that's just a name, no tax is really painless. Then get the income tax high. You got to earn big money or you don't pay it, so there should never be any holler about that, but there should be a distinction between earned and un-earned income. For instance a man that earns every dollar by his work or efforts, then another earns the same by having enough money invested to bring him in that much. One has his principal to fall back on, and the other has nothing to fall back on when his earning capacity has diminished.

Oh, but the tough part of our whole system is the amount of money they are spending, hundreds, thousands, practically millions that are working for the state, the city, the federal government. There is hundreds of different branches, and bureaus, that everybody knows is not essential. But they were politically created to give jobs, and no politician has the nerve to do away with 'em. Lord, the money we do spend on government. And it's not a bit better government that we got for one-third the money twenty years ago. But we will do like the British, we will muddle through. We are kinder like China we are so big and powerful that we get along in spite of all the bad management we have.

Gosh wasent we crazy there for awhile! Why the thought never entered our head that we wasent the brightest, wisest, and most accomplished people that ever was on this earth. Hadent we figured out "mass production?" Couldent we make more things than any-body? Did the thought ever enter our bone-head that the time might come when nobody would want all these things we were making. No, we had it all figured out that the more we made the more they would want.

133

Honest as we look back on it now, somebody ought to have taken each one of us and soaked our fat heads. Bought everything under the sun that anybody had to sell, if he would sell it on enough payments. Where was our payments going to be if we lost our job? Why that had never entered our heads. Why should we lose our jobs? Wasent all our big men telling us things was even going to get better. Was our government or our prominent men warning us?

If we had had a "Prominent" man he would have but we just dident have any. But we can't lay the blame on to that, we all got to lay it on ourselves. Each one of us individually as we look back we can see what a mess we made, but the drunk is over, and this sobering up is terrible, but as bad as it is, it's better than any other country. So cheer up! That's the only thing they don't tax you on.

484   THE SMART SWEDES

Well, all I know is just what I read in the papers. Did you ever see a war so completely washed off the front page as that Japanese-Chinese one was by the Lindbergh case?[1] Gosh, people are human after all, ain't they? Sometimes we think we are not, but I don't know, when the real showdown comes why the toughest of us will bob up with some human trait. Did you ever read as many rumors to the square inch?

Had a couple of famous suicides the last few weeks. Mr. George Eastman was quite a surprise, as it was thought he had retired from active business and was taking things easy and not worrying.[2] But it seems that it was his health. You know after all I bet that old constant thought of feeling that you wouldent get well would just be too much for you. Well he had had a great career, and had done some wonderful charitable things.

He built a beautiful theater and concert hall of some kind there. Well, I was playing there four or five years ago on my concert tour. I was in an old hall. The manager said to me, "We would have done better tonight if it wasent in this place. People have got in the habit of going to Mr. Eastman's new theater. You know it's too bad he dedicated that to art or you could have gotten in. He had a jazz band there last week, and Earl Carroll's vanities the week before, but he just happened to dedicate it to art.[3] And so a Monologist can't get in."

Well I went on and did the best I could in the old place to the bunch that dident mind missing art for one night. We just had some laughs and wouldent have known art if we had met it face to face.

Then that Swedish match fellow, Kruger, that was quite a blow to the financial world.[4] You know those Swedes sure worked their loans the right way. When some nation wants to borrow from us why we just go ahead and loan it to 'em, in fact from what I heard in Europe they dident have to express a wish to borrow. Our folks were over there practically forcing it on 'em.

Well those Swedish match people made more loans around the world than anybody. But they didn't just dole it out like us. No sir! They made the loan with the distinct understanding that every time a fellow lit his stove, or his pipe, that it was to be done with their matches. Instead of taking a note that wasent any good, they just made a agreement that there was to be nothing "struck" there but their breed of matches. Just think what a collosal business was built up just by such a little thing as matches. It was one of the biggest businesses in the world. All founded on the theory that no cigar or cigarrette lighter will work.

But just look at the monopolies that we could have tied up. My goodness Henry Ford could have made a few million loan to each nation and they couldent have even put out a wheelbarrow without it was a Ford. Why some of these nations over there that had borrowed from this Kruger's firm, it was punishable by death if they caught a person using another match than this Swedish. Just think if Ford had made 'em a loan. You could have shot a man in England for using a Rolls Royce instead of a Ford.

Look at the countrys Listerine could have tied up? Why you couldent have gargled a thing in the world but it in Bulgaria, if their Board of Directors had been wise. Let the individual business concerns make the loans and make monopoly in return. A small loan would have made every Spaniard use our hair oil, a couple of millions loaned to the Russians and a safety razor would have been in every home. A half million out at 6 per cent would have put a blue jay corn plaster on every Checho-Slovakian with not a chance of any other plaster sneaking in under it.

Just think of the booze we made and sell. Why if Capone had dished out a few millions in long term loans to Europe why look at the pleasure they could have gotten out of our home brew and mountain dew, we could have been even with 'em at last.

We got loans scattered all over Europe, and they never even spent a cent back with us. They took the money to pay off the interest on what they owed to us. Look what the U.S. Steel, the oil companies could have tied up. You know there is just an awful lot of people all over the world smarter in lots of ways, and this Kruger was one of 'em. Talk about mass production. When you can make that many matches why you have done some mass producing. But it's no use telling 'em that now, the poor fellows are in such bad shape they got nothing to loan now.

But I think we just about been cured on foreign loans. The big boys have come in for such a rawhiding from all over the United States that it's made them realize they better "Give the lads here at home some Jack." I guess there is no race of people that it is so universally agreed that they pulled a boner as the International Bankers. We really ought to differentiate. (There is a pretty good word by the way for me.) As I just said, we really ought to differentiate (it's still a good word) between the International Bankers and the local product.

Our home bankers, both large and small, are in bad just through the bad times and an over expansion in good times, but the International one is in bad through malice aforethought. His devilment was premeditated. He knew he was loaning on no security in Europe, cause there is no security over there. He got his commissions for peddling it out so what does he care? But I guess they are about as good as the rest of us. We was all cuckoo and hog wild, but brother they are taming us. Did you ever see the cockiness taken out of a nation so quick? We will sure go in and bring sticks out of the water now for anybody. We are humble galore.

485   DIAMOND DUST

Well all I know is just what I read in the papers, or who I happen to run into here and there. A couple of weeks ago out here in old L.A. I went to a little dinner party. I generally do my little dinnering at home, the eats are better, and my wife can make a better speech daily than all the other after-dinner speakers can on special occasions. Then we always got the children to argue with over old timers vs. moderns, but I did go to this one and enjoyed every minute of it.

It was John J. McGraw, Manager of the famous New York Giants.[1] I have known him many years. He has some of the finest human qualities of any man in any line of sports. John McGraw has helped more oldtime baseball players than all the club owners who have made money out of them combined.

You know it's a kind of an odd thing. There has never been a rich club owner either living or in his will who has done one thing toward the aid of the men who gave from ten to fifteen years of the best parts of their lives to our great national sport and pastime.

There has been some rich men owned teams, lots of 'em because they loved the game, but lots of 'em for the prestige and publicity that it brought them. But their love for it never seemed to extend to the man who had passed the age where he could field a bunt or paste a two bagger. I don't think it's non appreciation, it's just that there has never been anything formed in such a way that it would be a working organization that would really take care of them. Lots of them would liked to have left something if there had been a way to do it where it would do good. There is bound to have been some very liberal and big hearted men connected with the ownership of clubs that would have helped if there had been a way. There ought to be so many days in each city given over where a part or all the receipts went to a big relief fund.

We have had some fine characters in baseball, got fine ones now, just figure it out yourself. There is not much a ball player can do after his career as a player is finished. They can't one twentieth of 'em be managers, coaches, scouts, and trainers. I had a long chat that night with an old ball player, Chief Meyers, catcher for the New York Giants for ten years, a good Indian and not dead either.[2] I would ask him about old ball players.

In the old vaudeville days I used to be around baseball and ball players, and knew a big part of them personally. Well, just name after name I would ask him about, names that us middle agers, and old timers were almost raised on. Names like Hans Wagner.[3] Just think of what that man for twenty years contributed of enjoyment and thrills of American life. Chief Bender, the greatest strategist pitcher of all time.[4] Mordeci Brown, Johnny Evers, and dear Tris Speaker, perhaps the greatest outfielders of all time.[5]

Oh, I could just sit here and mention 'em by the hour. I don't mean the ones that were great, and then since have managers jobs, like lovable Walter Johnson, but the ones who did their bit for the best years of their lives to make America a better place to live in from three to five o'clock in the afternoon, and all over our land, either minor league or majors.[6] They were highly specialized men, trained from boys in a highly specialized field, eat, slept, and dreamed their trade.

Of course you will say, "Well they were well paid, why dident they save?" Did you ever try working six months, then laying off six, and seeing how much you could save? If they were thrifty they naturally bought them a home. Well they commence passing over the

137

hill of oblivion at the decrepit old age of perhaps 35. Why what was in store for him?

My goodness you can be specialized in any line of work in America and you can't get a job, so what is a ball player going to do? You don't ever read a paper where any of 'em took up our popular mode of living, crime and racketeering. Every one of 'em are highly respected citizens in their communities. Dozens of 'em, hundred of 'em havent any of the world goods, but they got their neighbor's respect.

Football is great. It's a great thrill, it's a fine recreation, but it's for a pastime and physical conditioner while our fine young men are in college. But baseball is a profession, it's an art that you don't learn in any four years just from September to December. We will never get things really righted in our country till every line of sport, industry, profession or trade have some system of everyone contributing while working to the welfare of the old and unemployed in his own line. I don't mean to put all ball players in an old ball players home, I mean a system of help where it's done and they retain their respect and courage and self esteem. Outsiders don't have to know they are being aided at all.

All the sporting writers from the east that are covering the Giants and Detroit teams training were there, along with our local boys. All a fine bunch of fellows. Tillie Shaffer, the old Giant who the world has of course been good to, Fred Snodgrass, Bucky Harris, a very smart manager and high class, capable young fellow.[7] Bozeman Bulger, the fine old sports writer, was the Toastmaster.[8] Eddie Mayer, our local fine fellow.[9]

There was a host of 'em. Among the new was Bill Terry, king of first basemen today, Freddie Lindstrom, all around player.[10] A mixture of the old and new, all giving or had given their lives to entertainment of the public, paying respects to McGraw who after all these years is still at the top of the heap, and fairy godfather to more old time ball players than any man living. All these have contributed to what made our country proud of its sports.

Good luck to 'em. Long may they live, and the Umpire Good Fortune give 'em an even break.

486   CONFUSION IN CONGRESS

Well all I know is just what I read in the papers, and what I see, but sure haven't seen much lately. You would think anybody living out here this near to Hollywood would see quite a bit. Lots of folks come from far and wide to look us over, but I think they go back kinder disappointed. Hollywood for real up and doing is mighty delicatessen.

Depression has hit the devilment just like it has hit everything else. The persuit of life and liberty has been checked by this slow return to "Normalcy." So as I say I haven't seen much lately.

Keeping mighty close to home, riding the old Ponies out in the hills and seeing how it was making out during this long spell of Republicanism. It just looks like everything is doing fine but humans.

Animals are having a great year, grass was never higher, flowers were never more in bloom, trees are throwing out an abundance of shade for us to loaf under. Everything the Lord has a hand in is going great, but the minute you notice anything that is in any way under the supervision of man, why it's "cockeyed."

And the more men that have anything to do with trying to right a thing why the worse off it is. If every man was left absolutely to his own method of righting his own affairs why a big majority would get it done. But he can't do that.

The Government has not only hundreds but literally thousands in Washington to see that no man can personally tend to his own business. They go there to do it for him, and a mob always gets panicky quicker than an individual. They hear so much of how bad things are, and that something should be done, and they immediately feel that it's up to them to do it, so they just get up in the morning determined to pass some bills that day that will attempt to do something. They don't know if they will or not, but they were sent there to pass bills, so they get to passing them.

That was one of the great things about Coolidge. Coolidge never thought half the things that are wrong needed fixing. You knew that over half the things just needed leaving alone. It's like writing a letter to everybody you hear from. He knew that if you leave nine tenths of 'em alone it dident need answering. Now here a couple of weeks ago Congress broke out and they just gloried in their devilment.

If some one could point out anyone that looked like a rich man going down the street, why they just passed a search and seizure bill, and went out and not only plucked him, but added a little tar and feathers when they turned him loose. Well they got everbody sore at 'em and the big ones said, "Well if they are going to confiscate what I may earn, I just won't earn anything. Why should I take a chance investing in something when I will only be able to keep one fourth of it when I win?"

Well after Jack Garner got his strangle hold back on the boys again, and after they had sobered up, why he showed 'em that the Government was after all a sort of a co-operative affair, and that it wouldent be a bad idea to sort of distribute the Cost around in proportion. Course everybody knows that one of our great ills today is the unequal distribution of wealth. You are either at a banquet in this country, or you are at a hot dog stand. There was no doubt that the ones with money were about the only ones that could pay anything, but after all these durn rich ones are the ones the rest of us got to live off of. If the Government takes all their money in taxes it don't leave any for the folks that work for 'em.

Then to add to the confusion of everything Congress turned down the Sales Tax, then turned right around and had the same tax come up under a different name and passed it. That's just like we do more things. The League of Nations everybody agreed that we had no business in it, but the first thing you know we were "advising" with 'em. The World Court, we wouldent put on a cap and gown, but we would sit on the bench with 'em.

We are always doing something through the Kitchen door. We like the glory, but not the responsibilities. But we are kicking along in spite of our handicaps. The East and the North have got to get like the South has been for years, poor and used to it. Us folks down there have had to catch a cat fish, or kill a possum before we eat for years. So the other part of the country have got to learn to look to nature and not to Wall Street for what goes in the pot.

They got to find some other way making a living besides looking at a list of names in the paper every day. Stocks and bonds have got so now they don't go up and down only when there is a reason, not like they used to, go up and down when there was a wish on somebody's part. But the whole Country is taking it in good grace at that. If so many of 'em are not looking at our pictures as used to, we are mighty grateful to those that are. If they are not looking at us it's because they are wise to us, and that's about the way it is with everything else.

487   WILL LOOKS AT
MOVIES AND A HORSE

Well all I know is just what I read in the papers, and what I hear as I listen in on a radio that the kids put in my room here. I never was much of a radio hound. I get my Amos and Andy and then wash

the other programme up, but as this one is right here I got it going.[1]
Hollywood is having one of it's "Openings," that's one of those things
where there is a new movie opening at some Theatre.

Well for sameness I don't suppose two airdale pups are any more
alike than all "Openings." They have a microphone out in the lobby
of the Theatre and an announcer and he tells you who is coming in.
He says "Here comes Mr Who's or Mr Jasbo, we will have 'em step
over to the micraphone and says a few words to you over the micraphone." And that's the last you ever hear of it, they never come
over and say, "Hello everybody, wish you were here," but it's the
studio bootblack, or some one that worked for the company that is
putting on the picture. It's got so that every studio almost sandbags
it's own people to make 'em go and make up the crowd. If it's a
Warner Picture everyone there is working for Warner. If it's Fox's it's
a typical Fox audience. Most of 'em have seen it at the studio, or the
studio preview, but they don't attract the crowds like they used too.
And most of the companys have done away with 'em. It cost a lot of
dough to put one on, and after all a picture does nowadays just what
it deserves.

You can open one down a dark alley and not let anyone know it
and if it's any good in a few days you can't get near the thing. It's like
a good restaurant, you can't hide it. This old boy announcing tonight
is having trouble getting anyone to announce that anyone ever heard
of. He is laying it onto the traffic. He says traffic is holding all the big
ones back. He is tireless though. He keeps making you think someone
is coming pretty soon. He says he has to hurry that they have to go
back to the studio and put on a programme for the Chervolett, they
want to sell some cars, they don't want to know who is at the
openings.

This is a commercial age, we haven't got much time for frivolous
things. That is a thankless job that announcer has. Poor fellow can't
dig up a soul. He will be glad when that Chervolett times comes. Oh
yes here is Chick Sales, you all know Chick?[2] He is a bear on canvas
or boards, then he had a mighty popular novel one time. Chick ought
to fit right into an opening. Chick you was a lifesaver for this poor
announcer.

Yep here comes the Chervolett announcement, "We are back in
the studios, have you compared Chervolett quality and prices with
other cars, if you haven't get up in the morning and do it." They are
playing a kinder pretty tune now called In the Valley where the
Lillies grow. It's gota mighty catchy swing.

Now we are at a Culver City Nighty Club. I worked at the old
Goldwyn Studio for three years back in 19 and 20, 21, and I never

thought Culver City would ever have a night club, so you can never tell what a town will turn out to be.

Speaking of music my wife and Mrs. Flo Zeigfeld, (Billie Burke) have gone to hear Padawriski.[3] Say try to spell that guy's name. Everybody can say it but no one can spell it. I wanted to go hear the old gentleman tonight. I never in my life heard him. That's almost a crime, for he must be the greatest ever and a very fine old character. I wouldent have known any more what he was doing than a prairie dog, but I bet I would have enjoyed a lot of it at that. I have stayed at his hotel in Warsaw, in fact occupied his suit there, and by the way Floyd Gibbons was there at the hotel with me at the time. That's where I first met him. He has had a great time over in China. Sure wish I had not had to rush back.

But still I am not so hot for that actual war stuff. I don't want to see it, no matter what tribes of people are fighting. Ain't it funny how that was dropped right out of sight. The Lindberg Baby ruined that war for publicity sake.[4]

And next in comparison to that was a horse, that Australain horse.[5] Did you ever see as many people interested in an animal? I am sitting here now in my den looking at a wonderful picture of him, given to me by the sports writer that come over with him.[6] He told me that he cabled back to Australia from fifteen hundred to two thousand words about Pharlap every day. That was all during the time that he was being prepared for the race, and after he won it. Just think of the cost of that. And the interest that must have been in him. Now imagine how they must feel.

I was in Australia many many years ago, and I have always maintained that they had the best horses, I mean horse for horse all over the country, that they had the best horses in the world. Racing! That's not only a sport with them, it's a mania. When the big race, the Melbourne Cup, is run every man woman and child in the land has some kind of a bet on it. This horse holds the record for it. He won it I think a couple of times and would have kept on winning it, but the handicappers put the grandstand on him. He was a very big powerful horse, his real distance was two and a half miles. We haven't got a thing that could have finished in the stretch with him over that distance. Imagine that little group, trainer, vetenarinan, jockey, grooms, and my friend Wolfe, the sporting writer going back all that long trip alone, a horse after all I guess is just about next to a human. Him and the old Dog.

Well all I know is just what I read in the papers, and you see quite a few things as you nose around here and there.

Floyd Gibbons, the demon war correspondent, was out to my little ranch to visit me a week or so ago. I sure was glad to see him. We sure did ramble over old times. You know I was the luckiest fellow in the world to fall in with him at Vancouver on my way over to China, for he is a great traveling companion. He has been everywhere in the world, and he really knows how to get around.

I have prowled around a bit in my time, but I never seem to get any wiser, or onto things, but Floyd he gets you where you want to go and where something is doing. He has a wonder ful lecture on China and the Far East. I went down to the theater to hear it.

I was the local annoyer who was to introduce him. My wife was so afraid that I in my long winded way would monopolise the whole evening. She said, "Now remember tonight, you are just a pawl bearer, you are not the corpse, and it's the corpse they are interested in."

Well, I really dident have time to do him justice. I could have stood there all night and told jokes and nice things about him, and I really felt that I left in pretty good time, that is for me, for I am notoriously long winded. I think that's where people get the idea that I ought to be in politics. But when I get started I do like to blather away, especially if I got a good subject to work on.

Floyd's main talk is that we haven't got any more business in these Far East wars than we had in the last European one. He thinks seven thousand miles is a long way to go shoot somebody, especially if you are not right sure they need shooting, and you are not sure whether you are shooting the right side or not.

Those monkeys out there are going to be fighting from now on. China will be kinder cocky because she made her best showing of her whole war career at Shanghai, and Japan will want a chance to redeem her "face," for she lost "face" in that scrap.

He said it was a great war for the convenience of war correspondents, for they could go out and see one army fight, then come back through the international city and go out and then be with the opposite army. Or you could get on a high building and watch the whole thing. In fact it it was the only war ever fought where they had a grand stand.

He says that the Japanese had the old German method, but the German methods of 1914. But that the Chinese had the German methods of 1918. It was a division from down South at Canton that did the fighting. He bore out another thing that I had predicted in my articles, and that was that you wouldent hear of many prisoners being taken on either side in that war.

Well, he said there wasent, for the Chinese have the reputation, even among their friends, for being the most cruel nation in the world, even to their own people. If one is only going to get his head chopped off he is tickled to death, that is a beautiful death with him. That he is not unmercifully tortured before death is his fear, and the Japanese are not far behind 'em, so nobody on either side is going to be captured while he had a way to disposing of themselves. But, it was as he says, "Their war and they had a right to fight it as they saw fit, without any advice from us."

He says that it's only a matter of time till Japan will have to fight Russia over Manchuria, but that Russia is not ready yet, getting enough to eat for the next five years is going to keep them pretty busy, but that when they do so against Japan that they will sure be loaded for 'em.

It won't be like they were before, you see Russia has spread out since 1905. Then Siberia and Manchuria was thousands of miles away, but now they are populating and arming, and fortifying that country, and they are double tracking the long trans-Siberian R.R. And then too they have a great Air Force, and big part of its force is away out there, so it won't be just one of those Port Arthur things, and nothing in between. He says China has no more government that a billy goat. They are just running around arguing and fighting with each other as usual.

Another fellow was out to spend the day with me, a friend of Floyd's, that come over on the boat with him, and is about the biggest financial man in China, also in India, Sir Victor Sasoon, of the House of Sasoon, which is about the Rothschilds of England.[1] He has tremendous holdings in Shanghai.

I bet this war threw a scare into him for awhile. He owns the wonderful Cathay Hotel in Shanghai, where we all lived. He still has great faith in the Far East and thinks that it will come out O.K. He also knows more about India than anyone, as he was there for years. He thinks that it was clever scheme in England getting Gandhi to go to the Conference in London, for that really showed him up as just being human, and not some God or superman. He says that Gandhi has no solution for anything, and that when he got there he had nothing to offer why it simply showed that he was no great ruler, or miracle man. And he thinks that Gandhi lost "Face" by going. He says that the boycott in India is still working, and that the same is true in China against Japan.

144

I can sure understand how those fellows get fascinated with that Far East. I guess it gets you like the desert. They sure are both interesting men to talk to, they have both been everywhere and seen about all there is to see, but they were both mighty anxious to see Hollywood, and me being the old "Night Hawk" here, I was the one could show 'em.

I took 'em into some of the wildest cafeterias you ever saw. I just kept 'em a-jumping from one drug store fountain to another till I bet it was a quarter of ten. We sure heard a lot of different radios. They been in Shanghai, Bagdad, Constantinople, Paris, and Harbin, but they will never forget Hollywood. You folks want to get out here this summer at these Olympics.[2] You will see things at night that are fast enough to be in the Olympic program in the day time.

489   GARBO, GHANDHI, KREUGER AND CONGRESS

Well all I know is just what I read in the papers. Congress just keeps us all on the jump all the time, waiting to see what they are going to do with us. One minute they are not going to have a sales Tax, but they put a Tax on about a third of the things that are sold. Then they were asked to explain why it was that they taxed a boot but dident tax a shoe, or why put a tax on caps but none on hats. That is just about as nonsensikle as the things they did do.

They tried to hang most of it onto the Auto buyers, or Gasoline buyers. Well they just as well put it on bathing suits, or chairs, or anything else that folks use, anything outside of meat and bread and a Gandi Breechclouth can be called a luxury, or a necessity which ever way you want to look at it. Autos may be a luxury, a bed may be a luxury. You can ride on a street car, or you can also sleep on the ground, neither one is an absolute necessity. Well it just looks like Congress took a list of everything made and shut their eyes and took a pencil and marks off some names, and said, "Well will tax everything the pencil marks across." They were afraid to have the sales Tax for fear the voters back home while they dident want any tax, they did want one that was equal in most respects. People when you get right down to it are fairer than most individuals, so it looks now as I pen you these few lines that Mr Congress will get their tax bill handed back to 'em with everything changed but the title, and then Congress will have to knuckle under for just what they had refused to do in the first place.

They been investigating Wall Street, but there has been so much devilment going on there that one Committee can't dig it all out. They wanted to publish the names of the Firms that were implicated in the "Bear Raids," and the list was 24 thousand.

England come out with their Budget and it dident make any allowance for paying their debt to us. Well we come out with our Budget without paying our debt to ourselvs. We can't seem to find any dough to do anything with, but England hadent any more than broke out till Senator Borah was right on their tail. He reminded 'em that there had been an oversight on somebody's part. Then he was joined by Pat Harrison, another old crony of mine from away down in Mississippi.[1] Pat told England she would pay or else she wouldent build herself any more Navy. Well England who was so tickled at balancing their Budget, they had plum forgot about us, but when they heard from the above two lads, they went back into "Conference." You see that's the trouble you just can't do a nation a favor, or they will want it continued, although I will say this England will pay, and did, quicker than any the rest of 'em.

France just has guys laying awake at night to think up reasons for not paying. They give guys percentage on every new idea he gets for new reasons. France's main reason now is that if she paid us she would have to use her gold, and if she had to use her gold, she wouldent have as much gold. But England is a different breed of cats altogeather. The old Englishman is mighty high type business man. Well we will hear a lot about it anyhow, for it will be starting to come due in a few months, and the campaign this fall will be so full of debt arguments that you will think the future of the country hinged on the outcome.

Hollywood is all excited, they hear Greta Garbo is going home, she might be at home for all we know, nobody has ever seen her out here.[2] In fact she may make her pictures over there and just be sending 'em over. She is supposed to go home now and take up this match king job.[3] He was the biggest man over there. And she is the biggest woman. So they figure she could put it on it's feet. Say by the way some slick "Hombres," why Europe can make a sucker out of us for "Fenagling" guys.

This depression has brought out a lot of crooked stuff where if things had gone on and they had been able to keep covering up they would never have been known.

Talk about running a Ford car into a Billion dollars, why just think of running a little tiny stick of wood, with some phospherous on the end of it into an establishment that controlled the finances of a dozen nations.

146

We all just kinder sitting around here waiting for the new Fords to be delivered, that's about the only event in out lives. We trade in the old ones and go in debt for the differences.

We are all talking Olympic games out here. We don't know what they do or how they do it, but we want to see it. Fifty-five nations are coming. It will either be a success or a war, one, so in either case you don't want to miss it. There is hundreds of women competing, only in this case they have to compete against each other, and not just against the men. It's going to be well worth seeing. Come on out, you are not doing anything anyhow. If you run a store or are in business why put your customer in the car and bring him too then you won't lose him. Remember the date? Well I forgot when it was myself, but it's sometime during the hot weather.

490   WILL THINKS MAYBE HE'S MADE A MISTAKE

Well all I know is just what I read in the papers, and what I run into prowling about Hollywood. You remember one time when I was on the radio and did a little imitation of Mr. Coolidge. Well, some of 'em raised cain. Said I shouldent have done it. I even went so far as to ask Mr. Coolidge if it had offended him and he replied, "Why I dident even pay any attention to it."

Well a couple of weeks ago I was asked to be master of ceremonies at the opening of that great big picture "Grand Hotel."[1] Syd Grauman, the manager of the Chinese Theater in Hollywood, is the manager, and he is not only a great showman but a fine fellow.[2] Then Mr. Louie B. Mayer asked me, and I was tickled to do it.[3] I had never been around any of these "openings" in fact had always kidded about 'em, for there is plenty to kid at one. The whole thing is the biggest "hooey" out here. The studios would like to do away with 'em for they bring 'em nothing but cost.

But it's a great "Yokel" show. This was an especially big one for it was the biggest cast picture ever made. Think of Greta Garbo, the two Barrymores, Joan Crawford, Wally Berry, Jean Hersholt, Tully Marshall, and about half the other payroll of Hollywood.[4] Well it was a bear of a night, judging by people standing on soap boxes, and folks inside with old overhauled ermines.

They have an intermission and everybody goes out and looks at each other and you can't get 'em back in again. They would rather look at each other than the show. But it was what the society reporter would call "The Elite," what the film fan reporter call "Aristocracy of Filmdom," and what the poor folks on the street would call "The Nuts."

But all joking aside they was our best bunch. New York hasent got it on Hollywood for clothes. It was lovely looking out there. And some mighty fine substantial folks. There is some pretty down to earth people in our business, and lots of 'em have been into it long enough to realize that it's a kind of business after all. This fellow Grauman had a wonderful prologue. He put on a two dollar vaudeville show, had Will Mahoney, just about the cleverest one man actor in vaudeville and musical comedies.[5] He had been for years the "Ace" of Earl Carroll's Vanities.[6]

Well, Will knocked old Hollywood batty. He does a dance on the xylophones with his feet that is better than I ever heard with the hands. In fact that would be a good way to get rid of this overworked xylophone racket, make everybody play 'em with your feet. I have heard folks playing 'em that it sounded like they must have been using their feet but this was the only time I ever saw it done. There was a bunch of clever acts.

My job was to introduce the cast that was in the picture. Now of course you all know about Greta Garbo? She don't go anywhere, or she may go everywhere, for no one gets to her home to see if she has gone anywhere or not, but she really I guess don't get round people at all. The studio that she worked for have to go see her in the picture when they want to see her. She is just like a hermit, and these writers that write stories about her they never even get to see a photograph of her. Now everybody out here knows that. They know that she is not going to be anywhere.

But that night after I had introduced all the principals of the cast except John Barrymore, who was not there, I announced that on account of the importance of the occasion, and the prominence that this particular picture had received, that Miss Garbo would break her rule and be there, and that immediately after the picture was over that she had consented to come on the stage and take a bow, and that I would be highly honored by having her there when the picture was over.

Well Mr. Grauman starts his shows. He thinks the later they are started the better they are. Syd don't know or has perhaps forgot that all the big first nights in New York are started on time anyhow, no matter when they are finished. Well this one dident start until nine-thirty, and was over, the picture, at one-fifteen. Now that's pretty good for a country town, and in all we are a country town. It's a big one, but it's country.

Well I had framed up a gag with Wally Berry who I knew would be a big hit in the picture that they had just seen, and he got some "dame" clothes. And he was my Greta Garbo. Sounds kinder funny don't it? Well it wasent to them.

Wally did it fine. He even looked like her, but not enough to satisfy that crowd. Now they should have known that Garbo wasent going to be there any more than Coolidge, but they go and believe it and then get sore at themselves for believing it. I dident mean any harm. Gosh us comedians must get laughs. But these first nighters don't want us to get 'em at their expense. They want to be the ones that do all the laughing. I think they got their waitings worth by seeing Wally Berry in skirts. What did they want?

Now about the only way I got making good is to produce Garbo sometime. Course I can't do it, but it's a good idea. I got to do something to get back into the good graces of my Hollywood. Maybe I can show 'em Al Capone some time. They all want to see him, but I will never fool the old home town again.

491 MAYBE MELLON WILL CANCEL BRITISH DEBT

Well all I know is just what I read in the writing papers.

Can't we beat the world getting all worked up over something as though the world coming to an end depended on it and then find it's settled in some little easy way, and a week later we don't know we have ever been excited about it. That affair in Honolulu when we heard they were convicted, why we all of us like to tore up the place.[1] Then all there is to it is the Governor over there pardons them, and it's all over.

Course every country has got it's laws, and everyone of 'em have a right to act them out according to the dictates of their own views, but we dident think they got a square deal in the case, and we raised a howl. Now here is the catch in it. If this husband had come up on those men at the time and had killed not only one but all of them, why he would have come clear with medals on him, but because he waited awhile to shoot him, why that makes him a murderer. In other words I must shoot you quick if I am going to. Well it was terrible mess and it's good it's ended. There was several bad angles to it on both sides.

That old Darrow is a great old fellow.[2] I have known and been friends with him for many years. I go to see him in Chicago. He is one of the most pleasant and entertaining men in America. You know for a real down right humanatarian I doubt if he has his equal in our Country. Color, creed, man or beast, Darrow has a sympathetic interest in him.

Lord, in this time with every kind of Shyster Lawyer that we have, he is notable exception. Poor old Honolulu, I hope they get this lived down, for it really was not their fault. Course I am for 'em getting their independence and run the thing like they want too. Darn this thing of being somebody else's country and taking it over. No good ever comes of it. We claim it's for protection sake that we hold it. That's a lot of hooey. It's two thousand miles away. If any nation can come two thousand miles across an ocean and then lick us, well we are good enough sports to say "More power to you."

Those little Japs would be so seasick by the time they got here they couldent sight a gun anyhow. Turn 'em loose them and the Philippines and give Nicaragua back to the Nicks, then come home and take the country away from the Republicans and give it back to the Democrats where it belongs.

Say, this political thing is getting more cockeyed every day. Here in California, it looks like Roosevelt was a cinch, then Garner comes in and beats him, and Al Smith who had had no press agent, or advance work done, why he runs right up there almost with both of 'em, and he was like the girl at the tacky party when they voted on the ugliest person and she won, and said, "Why I wasent even running."

You are going to find this Guy Smith has a very loyal following. They will always be voting for him. I met young Roosevelt's son out here the other day.³ He and his charming wife. He made some speeches for his Dad, and I wasent fortunate enough to hear any, but they tell me they were great. He has a lot of sincerity, plain wholesomess, and good common sense. His little wife was very nice. They have a six weeks old baby. They talked more of the baby than they did of their mission out here. This Roosevelt is a very fine human man, sometimes I think he is too nice a fellow to be mixed up in all this politics.

We don't know yet as I pen these immovable words, what is the things we will pay taxes on. Congress guesses at one thing, and the Senate reaches in the hat and drags out some other objects to be taxes. Mr. Hoover throws the dice and they bring up some more different numbers. Ogden Mills the Treasury's Secretary weegee board calls out some more names.⁴ Everybody is trying to get it over on the other fellow. They all want to put it on objects but they don't want to call it a sales tax. They only want it on what is sold.

The English sure have taken to Mr. Mellon.[5] He is the lion of the hour in London. They figure that he will cancel the debt. The "Pilgrims" society give him a dinner. That's a society that found the social going not so "hot" in America and migrated from ham and eggs and coffee, to tea and marmalade. Well they dined him, and the Statue of Liberty that was made in ice melted during the festivities and run into everybody's lap. Well if he cancels the debt he better do it with his own money.

France is still dragging gold out of our country by the millions and asking us to cancell the debts. And then they tell you a Frenchman has no humor.

We are getting all excited out here over the Olympics, and hoping you will come out and see us. We got 55 nations coming, war or no war. Of course depression will still be on us, but we will be used to it by then. It will be your only chance during your lifetime seeing one on in this country. Course you could go to Europe but you couldent tell what language they was running in.

492   SAILOR WAS COOL HEADED

Well all I know is just what I read in the papers. Wasent that terrible out here in Cal, about the Akron landing?[1] They had had all this tough time crossing the country, storms and bad weather, then when the sailors at San Diego tried to help 'em land there was enacted about the greatest bit of drama that we have read of in our time.

That bit of the sailor being drawn up there for over an hour and a half, now if there is a man living that had had an hour and a half of any more suspense then that, that was actual suspense, he must have been a cool headed customer to have thought of tying himself on like that. They figured they would have to go out to sea and drop him the ocean. There was a nice little thing to look forward too.

"We will drop you in the ocean." Being a sailor it would just be his luck he couldent swim. But that's what I call real drama. You know it's hard to tell about those big old suckers, as to whether they are a success or not. Course they do go places. Look at that one that went around the world. And this one had come all the way across our continent without gas, food, water, hot dogs, or a morning paper. Course it had been two or three days doing it, but at that it beat a train. But I will trust all that to our army and navy men to figure out. They know whether it's practical or not. Remember there is 84 men on that thing. That's a lot of men to carry across the continent in one load.

I tell you any experiment that is being made in the air is not a waste of time or money. Our defense, offense and all have got to come from the air. So these big dachunds are going to find some place in our national defense. You know that is a terrible job being in charge of that floating bladder. This guy Rosendahl has done a fine job of it.[2] Course when you want to land you can't always find two hundred sailors in all parts of the country.

Some parts of the country you have to fly around for several hours before you can see two hundred sailors. Lots of people living in this country for all their lives never saw two hundred sailors. I don't much care to cruise the air if it's going to take two hundred men to pull me down.

In an aeroplane it don't take anybody to pull you down. If fact most of the time you wish you had two hundred men to hold up. I have seen times in a plane when I have wished there had been men underneath with a net. But let's get on to pleasanter subjects.

Marlene Dietrick our movie heroine, has come to terms and won't go back to Germany.[3] Never had any idea going but neither has Greta, but it's a good racket if it works and it has.[4] They are still on my neck for not producing Greta at that Grand Hotel opening. As they say in the Far East, "I lost face." If I can dig Greta up some of these days it may get me back my lost prestige, but she is a tough baby to get ahold of.

Doug Fairbanks got back a couple of weeks ago from the Fiji Islands, or some outlandish place that he had been.[5] He took pictures of it. He said that down there you could live on 90 cents a week. That is about ten cents more than here, or what some have to live on here. However you keep reading about things getting better, but most of the articles are written by folks that are doing well themselves. With the elections coming on you are going to be fed up with a lot of hooey about a lot of things. Naturally the Republicans are to put their best "side" forward. They are just trying now to figure out which side is their best.

Roosevelt is pretty well sweeping the country for the Democrats but perhaps won't have enough to nominate on the first ballot. Smith combined with a few of the native sons would be able to block him. Then it would be just a wild guess as to who would be nominated. Mr. Hoover just goes right on wanting to stay in there. I had kept thinking that he would finally give up and say, "Well boys here she is. Take it whoever wants it. I have had enough."

But once a man is President he is just as hard to pry out of there as a Senator, or a town constable, or any political office. He had done some pretty courageous things lately in a political way. If he will get up and cuss the Senate and Congress out a couple of more times, he is liable to wake up a hero for never was "Cussing Congress" as popular as it is now. And the rascals I guess are not to blame for it either. Of course they are not doing the best they can but they are doing the best they know how.

Conventions will be on us now. They are like the locusts. They come every few years. Will meet you all there, at one or the other of 'em. It will be good conventions this year for both sides will be in doubt. And the people don't care.

493   GRAB THY HORSE

Well all I know is just what I read in the Congressional Record. They have had some awful funny articles in there lately. As our government deteriorates, our humor increases. They been arguing over the taxes, and that give 'em a chance to get some original views on where they was going to get this two billion bucks that they were overdrawn. They have just appropriated and appropriated till they was so far in the red, that it don't look they will hardly get out by Xmas.

They got to get the whole thing all straightened out pretty quick, for the conventions are here right now. They have to be there and tell the deligates what they have done for the country. Well I will be seeing a lot of you all at the shows (both of 'em). I don't want to miss anything.

Well I had a fine time here about ten days ago. I went with our Governor, Jimmy Rolph, and we, "We" accepted in behalf of the State of California, one of the most magnificent ranches you ever saw.[1] It comprises about seven hundred acres.

Course that don't sound so big, but that's land that is all piped and watered, and irrigated, and improved. It is the largest Arabian Horse Ranch in America. It has 87 head of pure breed Arabian horses, the most wonderful up to date stables and equipment you ever saw. It's a marvelous place, about 40 miles out of Los Angeles, near Pomona. It was given to the State University Department Animal Husbandry, and will be maintained by them. It was the gift of W. K. Kellogg of Battle Creek.[2] He has been coming out here for the winters for several years and built up this beautiful place. We had a big ceremony.

Mr. and Mrs. Kellogg turned over the deeds to the Governor.

They are mighty fine, plain, wholesome folks, the Kelloggs. Now here is the catch in it that makes the gift so marvelous. He also give $600,000 as a fund, that the income from it would be used to keep this place up. That's where I got fooled, I went out there to the ceremony just thinking that it was an event where a man was giving away a ranch. Well I have one in California, and one in Oklahoma, both mighty little ones, but still big enough to be noticed by the tax men.

Well neither one of 'em have ever made their taxes, so if either state wants another Animal Husbandry joint, why I will be more than glad to turn each state over some of the best tax infested land in both states, and I will give 'em some horses with 'em too. They may not be Arabians, and again they may be, for you can't look at 'em and tell what kind they are.

They told us out there at this ceremony that the Arabian horses had one less vertabra in his back, and one less in his tail, and the bone from his knee down is shorter. Well if this Arabian is short of vertabra, and that is giving it a nice name, I don't know about our shin bone being shorter. If it is it's because we have worn it out kicking at everything so much.

We have worn out about an inch of it just kicking poor Hoover alone. Maby he did need a few, but perhaps not as many as we aimed at him. Now I think we ought to commence wearing out, not the shin bone but the heel bone, by kicking ourselves a few times each day. Our kicks have always been aimed at somebody else for our own troubles. And a few good ones directed at the proper source would find us getting 'em right where they are deserved.

So these horses are really American and not Arabian. They also have another American characteristic, they are long winded. There is a Senator among every colt born.

An Arabian's nostrils are always distended. He seems to smell everything pretty good. Well we don't. There is things about our affairs that you sometimes think we have no sense of smell at all, or we would certainly smell some of the things that are being put over on us every day.

If we had had even an ordinary "Nostril" we should have detected an oder when our International Bankers were giving everything in the world to Europe. We couldent even detect the limburger on the bonds they sold us. So we have all the characteristics of the Arab horse but the distended nostrils and it's beauty. The mare of the human race has retained it's beauty, but the male has been a throw back. He has retained none of the springy movement and the grace and beauty of form and skin. Our only salvation is to raise just females.

Well, all I know is just what I read in the papers, and what I run
onto out here in the hills of Santa Monica. Been having quite a few
interesting callers lately, starting couple of weeks back. One morning
some of the members of the Japanese Olympic Horsemen rode over to
our place, which is only one mile from the Riviera Club, where all the
horsemanship things will be held. Course a Japanese on a horse was
always a kind of funny sight, for they are not a horseman nation, and
they will all ways get the biggest horses they can find in Manchuria,
they won't ride the little manchurian ponies, they want big old tall
horses. They think it makes 'em look bigger, when as a matter of fact
they look littler, but this bunch is liable to fool all these other nations.

They got 11 head of mighty fine looking horses. And they are
mighty thorough learning anything, so they may have got all these
stunts worked out that these horses are to do and have 'em down pat.

Spain is coming with some horses, Poland, Holland, and a bunch
of other countries. I don't see why Mexico don't come. They got some
mighty fine horsemen and some good horses. Course sending horses
to one of these things runs into dough. It's not like sending a footracer
who can run over and then if he don't win anything, walk back.

Well, the little Japanese gentlemen were very nice and cordial,
and outside of having a hard time getting up on top of those big
horses they were O.K. You know I believe that the horse end of the
Olympics will outdraw anything else. Our American team was up
here to our polo field not long ago and they brought their horses, and
put on an exhibition. We got some great horses, and great riders.

Major Chamberlain is one of the best horsemen in this or any
other depressed country.[1] Well, the Japanese had no more than rode
away till here come Tom Mix, not on Tony, but in a nice new car,
with his new wife, Mabel Ward, that is a wonderful aerial circus
artist, and a very very charming and pretty little lady.[2] And they had
Tom's little daughter, Tomisina, about 8 or 9 years old.[3] Tom and I
milled over old days in the Wild West show business. He is looking
fine, fully recovered from his illness.[4]

And then comes my old friend W. G. McAdoo.[5] I hadent see W.
G. in some time, and of course we had a lot of politics to mull over.
W. G. is going to run for senator out here and looks like he ought to
get it if everybody are as Democratic as they say they are. He had just
come from Washington. He thinks the way those other fellows will kill
each other off that that Garner has a fine chance to be nominated. He
don't think the Al Smith, Roosevelt thing will be patched up, so that
will mean a tough fight for either of them. No one knows who Al will

switch his strength too if he can't get it himself. He says that the state of New York has only gone Democratic once in 40 years, (the year Cleveland run) and that there has been several New York men nominated in that time and they couldent carry it, so a man from any part of the country has as much chance as any one else.[6]

You know they always preach that a man must be able to carry New York in order to give the Democrats a chance. But Lord who knows what a voter will do, when Texas went Republican. W. G. is a mighty pleasant well informed man, a very charming fellow. He told me some interesting things about Mr. Wilson and prohibition. He said that Mr. Wilson always could see that just such a predicament as we are now in would be possible, and he wanted more laxity in the framing of any prohibition legislation. He had always been a local optionist. But you get him to write and tell you all that Mr. Wilson told him on it. It's very interesting and showed that this man Wilson had some vision.

W.G. thinks that the Republicans will put a referendum in their platform. Then there will be some fun with the Democrats. The Republicans always get the first shot at what to do but the Democrats get the last shot at it. If they, (the Republicans) put the plank in first that will steal the Democrats' thunder.

But it won't be long now for here the conventions are right on us. Mr. McAdoo has his own plane and flies back and forth across the continent with his pilot all the time. As he drove out, Irene Rich and her daughters drove in.[7] We had finished a picture lately, Irene and I. She is one that don't try to always stay 18 and claiming the daughters are "adopted." One finished Smith College a year ago, and Irene gets up and announces it to the world.

Then Miss Winona Winters, a vaudeville and musical comedy friend of Mrs. Rogers and I, from back in the good old days, B. I. (before inflation).[8] Remember how pretty she was and used to do a ventriliquoal act along with her songs. She is the daughter of Banks Winter (White Wings), a fine old Southern gentleman.[9] He is out here hale and hearty and lives with Winona, who is married and doing fine.

Then we had here our son Jimmy, and his New Mexico Polo team, from Roswell, N. M.[10] Kids from sixteen to nineteen, and brother they did clean up out here. They beat everything they run into, they played all men teams, and big men at that. But after seeing kids play polo against big guys it only shows that the horse is the greatest equalizer in the world. No matter what you weigh, the little fellow is your equal on a horse. Tex Austin, son of the big rodeo promoter; Dick Waring from San Angelo, and Tommy Thompson from New York, had a mighty fine kid team, coached by Col Keyes, who developed at that same school the famous Arizona team, which is the best college team in America (equally mounted).[11] Maby we will know by the time this reaches you if Congress is going to help anyone out. I mean anyone that really needs it, they have helped everybody else.

495   BABIES IN HOLLYWOOD;
                SENATORS IN CHICAGO

Well all I know is just what I read in the papers, and what I have been seeing as I been prowling around conventionward. Course I been writing you a lot about them so we better dig up something more pleasant.

Hollywood is what I am asked more about back here than all the politics. Everybody has their favorites and they want to know how they are getting on. "How's Clara Bow?"[1] "Did you see Barrymore's new baby?"[2] "Is it so that there is no such person as Greta Garbo?"[3] "Why don't you make another good picture once in awhile?" "Who do you have to look like to get in the movies?" "If we go to the Olympic Games can we get in and see 'em make pictures?" Well they just ask you so many questions I dident hardly have time to tell 'em who was going to be elected president.

Now about Clara Bow. Clara is up on her ranch in Nevada. She married Rex Bell, a boy that played with me in "They Had to See Paris."[4] He was the sweetheart of my daughter (Margaret Churchill) before she went to Paris.[5] Then he also was with us in "Lightnin."

Now you have heard of "Ranches." Everything out here that is not an apartment is a "Ranch." If you got twenty feet in your back yard it's a "Ranch." If you got an old avacado bush, (no matter if it bears or not) why it's an "Avacado Ranch." "Lemon Ranches" "Orange Ranches" "Peanut Ranches" "Rabbit Ranches" "Squab Ranches," we even call mine a "Ranch," and there is nothing on it but an old polo field, a few calves to rope at, and some old cow ponies.

But what I started to tell you was that Clara Bow's is "a" ranch. It's right out in about the remotest settled part of America there is, the desert country out west of Boulder Dam. I never have been there, but I have flown over it, and know the country. Neighbors? I expect their nearest neighbor is the dam, about 80 miles away. And they got cattle on it. It's a cattle ranch. "Big Boy" Williams has one up in that country.[6] Their stock ranges for over a hundred miles.

Well Clara is getting ready to do a story at Foxe's. Sam Roark a very fine high typed man and a good producer is making it, and if he gets her a good story why it's a cinch.[7]

Now about Barrymore's new baby. I never did see the old one. Or has he got another one? I believe he has, but he's got a pretty wife, and he's not bad looking himself so they are liable to have a mighty pretty little baby. This baby thing has got to be quite an epidemic out here in the movies, there is more babies being born out here than in any time since I can remember. I don't know if it's depression or unemployment or what, but a lot of 'em that never raised any children before are doing it now. I guess there is fads in child raising just like in anything else. Paul Whiteman and his wife Margaret Livingston (I think that was her name) by the way she worked with me in a picture in the silent days, called "Water Water Everywhere."[8] It was Irene Rich's first picture with us.[9] It was a western, and I had to swim out into a river and rescue her from drowning. I was on horsebach however, and I had to take her up on my horse and carry her to town. Now a drowned woman that is all wet is mighty hard to carry with you on a running horse, and it's hard on the lady too. And I never see Margaret that I don't think of that ride. We took it in the Kern River out of Bakersfield. It's as hard to find a running river in Southern California as it is a drowning woman.

Well but what's all that got to do with babies? Well just this, I see where Paul and his wife announced their intention of having a baby. It was about the earliest announcements of that caliber I ever saw. This was along early in May, and they expect the baby along in March. That reducing is a wonderful thing. You wouldent hardly know him. He is skinnier than Chick Sales.[10]

And speaking of babies, I guess you all know that the old timers like Chick was right there with the baby raising. Chick had twins. He has got an awful fine bunch of children. He's got one boy that is about to shed off to be an actor. And there don't seem to be a thing Chick can do about it, so he told me.

Now about getting into the studio's. They say they are going to have some kind of an arrangement that on certain days that visitors will be allowed into the studios, I think the studios are all cooperating with the Olympic people and will do what they can to help entertain any of you folks that come out.

The athletes are drifting in here. Most of the runners are walking in. It's kinder hard to predict just how the crowds will turn out for that. It's a funny year. Just when you think people have no money and something won't do any business why it's packed.

We are living in an age of selected entertainment. They will be here if they want to see 'em, and if they don't they won't. Folks used to not know what they wanted, but they sho do now. We are getting everything cleaned up out here for the games. The place don't look natural. If nobody don't come we will just have had all this trouble for nothing. I will sho be glad when I can dirty up my place again. Committee even told us to curry our horses. Why I would as soon try to skin some of my old ponies as I would try to curry 'em.

They are even trying to get the high school students now to either change or wash those corduroy breeches. But they don't hope to get that done.

Well it's getting late, and I havent seen much of Chicago yet. So I think I will go find a couple of senators and see the town. I won't let anybody know they are senators then we can get into the best places. Everybody that you ever read of that manhandles our country is here. Both sides are trying to get their clutches on it for the next four years, so no matter what happens there is little hope for us. Sometimes you wish politics were like Hollywood babies, just a passing fad.

496   HERE COMES THE DEMOCRATS!

Well all I know is just what I read in the papers, and what I run into hither and thither. Well here we all are gathering in for the round-up of the Democrats. They are coming into Chicago by plane, train, Fords, buckboards, and on burros. The Texas Deligation arrived on burros. Headed by that fearless old statesman, Amon G. Carter, the genial dirt farmer of Shady Oaks Post Office, Texas.[1]

Amon is National Committeeman, deligate, alternate, steering wheel, banker, receiver, and wet nurse for the Texas deligation. They have taken over the Sherman Hotel, the best hotel in Chicago, and have generously allowed the California deligation to spread their bed rolls out in the halls, so they could stand guard over the Texas deligation. Both deligations are here to offset the effect of the Texas and California deligation which was here a couple of weeks previous. These feel that their state was naturally given a black eye by having Republicans at large roaming around with Texas and California on their badges, so these are trying to show that those were imposters, that they were not really from those states at all.

Oh say this will be a convention. Of course the old Republicans did the best they could with what little they had to work on, and as I think back to those old days we did have some fun at that. Would have had more if they hadent "bulldogged" that fellow France who wanted to nominate Coolidge.[2] I was sure pulling for it, for I can't help but admit that I am personally a Coolidge fan. And Grace![3] I am crazy about Mrs. Coolidge. I tell you all these other public men's wives could learn a lot from her. But the qualities she has are God given, they can't be acquired.

I, like lots of others, would like to see Calvin in there again. Course I doubt if he would take it at this time. Calvin knows when to take over a business, but anyhow this old boy France would have sure stirred up a hornet's nest if he had been able to nominate him.

Chicago is going to do herself proud just like she did with the Republicans. The last day of the Republican show they killed 4 gangsters for the amusement of the deligates and I know that being a Democratic city at heart she will do as much for the Democrats. In fact, I bet they do better. One of those they bumped off was named "Red" somebody, he was an alternate for Capone.

Lots of the newspaper boys are still here from the last show. They were afraid that they would close up the places if they left 'em, so they just stuck in there. H. L. Mencken, the Boswell of the Potomac, has stayed steadily at his typewriter ever since Senator France was manhandled from the Republican rostrum.[4] It was just about the last blow against free speech. And I expect there will be a paragaraffe in the Green Magazine denouncing the Republican method. He was the first on the spot back in the jail room where Mr. France was quickly incarcerated. They are fellow Marylanders. And Mencken said "You take him, you can take me too!" But Senotor Fess says, "I will take care of you personally."[5] So Mencken and Fess squared off with their typewrieters. And what a sucker Mencken has made out of him.

The California deligation originally started out for this convention as members of the Bonus Army.[6] In that way they come across the continent this far. Jewett Shouse is here guiding the destinies of the Roosevelt forces.[7] All you can hear is "Will they stop Roosevelt." Well they dident stop him from getting six or seven hundred deligates. But maby they can get 'em to change their minds after the deligates have seen some of the other candidates. And maby some of the other deligates will switch to Roosevelt after they have seen face to face their own candidates. Anyhow it's a good spot for a deligate to be in. Never was a deligate so much in demand. I am sure sorry that I dident decide to "Del." I had a chance in California. They wanted to make me one, only I think they discovered I had none of the qualifications of one.

Tammany is gathering in. This is their first trip away, with the exceptions of the ones that survived the Houston massacre.[8]

Ritchie of Maryland and his troop are here and on their way.[9] They are going to profit by the happenings of the Republican fracas and bringing their own policemen to see that they can nominate who they want. Al Smith is coming and will be the most pupular figure here as he is everywhere. Thirty years from now if he never held another office Smith would still be of great interest to everyone. For he has just got in him that something.

Mr. Roosevelt will be here when it looks profitable for him to be. Or that's what they say. What who said? Oh nobody said it, I just made it up, but when a writer or anyone wants to say something they are not right sure of they always preface it by saying "So I've heard." Well that's just a alabi, or "out" for 'em. They havent heard anybody say it at all, but it's an easy way to lay the lie on someone else besides yourself.

Well the noise is starting so I better jarr loose and go hear it. I don't know if it's a Rube Band, or just Amon Carter whispering about Jack Garner to somebody. Well, see you at the third party convention.

497   WILL GOES BOOKISH

Well all I know is just what I read in the papers and what little I get from just the names and taking little glances in books. You know I am the "durndest" fellow. People send me more books. Now I am 52 years old, sound of body, but weak of mind, and I never did read hardly any books. Oh ever once in awhile I will hear 'em all blabbing about one so much till I try to take time off and read one.

Now, that "Good Earth" I read that, and quite a little on the boat going over to Japan.[1] Floyd Gibbons had a couple of trunks with nothing in but books, well, he would tell me some that I should read, and he would give 'em to me and I would read 'em a little. I like to read but I don't have any time. If I got any spare time I like to go on a horse and ride around, or sit and blather with somebody.

I am an awful windy old talker and my wife says I bore more people than I entertain. She says I can do more talking away from home, and less at home than anybody, for then I bog down and get my nose in a paper. I do lots of paper reading. If I had put all my paper reading into books I might have been pretty well read but this book thing I am so far behind there is no use trying to catch up now. My oldest boy, Bill, is the book hound of the family. He is always reading something and he can remember it, too. Even if I read a book, I forget even the name of it.

But this is not what I would recommend to anybody else, for there is some mighty fine stuff in books, and some of the ones coming out now, I bet there is some good ones. Hard times, poverty, then is when the fellows can write their soul. Even if some of us could write we couldent do it, our stomachs are too full while we are not doing any too good, at the same time we are eating too much, and taking things too easy. We are satisfied, I get some awful nice personally autographed books. Lots of 'em from writers I don't know. Just like I could mention some movie star or cowman that they wouldn't know. But lots of these are evidently well known, and have written lots of things. It gives names of 'em on the fly leaves, and then lots of 'em are my friends that autograph 'em to me.

Well what I mean is that I don't sit down and write 'em and thank 'em like I ought to. I appreciate the books and prize my collection very highly, but I know that sometimes they must think I am a fine mess that they don't hear from me about it. Well, they ought to just know what a poor hand I am at writing. About twice a year I will have batches of letters pile up that I keep saying I will answer, and maybe I do and I send 'em off and get lots of 'em back saying the people are dead.

People write too much, anyhow, write too many letters, too many books, too much in papers. Papers would be twice as good if they was half as big. Books twice as good if they was 50 percent less, and the ones left half as thick. And letters, 90 percent of them are written for no reason whatever. It just looks like anybody that can dig up a stamp just feels like it will spoil if they keep it. They must get it off on a letter right away.

But I started out telling about books. Why just tonight out here at the ranch, six or eight books are here on my desk, not in my "Den" but in my "Dump." My old friend McAdoo, W.G. sent me his with a very much treasured written words to me, "Crowded Years."[8] Well, I have heard it's one of the best of the autobiographies. I read snatches of it when I can, and like it immensely. Then Warden Lawes of Sing Sing, a friend of mine, I played up there for 'em one time, and went all through and they all seemed to know my old mug from the pictures, and the Warden said I was better known in prison than out.[3] Well that book of his is a fine one. His book on Sing Sing is a very best seller. Tonight's batch is one by Ernest Kinyoun Hutchinson, "Science with a Smile."[4] I been glancing over it here and it reads mighty interesting. Then here is one by a lady (evidently) auto-graphed to the Rogers family, "In the Land of Bah" by Elizabeth Berger Nicholson, it's poetry.[5] I can't even read writing much less poetry, but I'll bet it's good.

"The Inside Story of the Harding Tragedy," autographed with "Respects from the Undersigned, Henry L. Daugherty."[6] Well I was so durn sore at those other Harding books, and it's funny how some people fell for that junk. Now look at old Means the other day.[7] He was the author of one of 'em, and got twenty-five years for swindling Mrs. McLean out of that money on the Lindbergh baby case.[8] And they took a book that he would write seriously?

"Only Yesterday" by Frederick Lewis Allen is another I been reading in it.[9] It's everything that's happened since Armistice. I just read the chapters on the stock market of the days of October 24, 28 and 29, 1929, and statements by prominent men during it. Honest you wonder sometimes how they got prominent. Then that little book called "Yeah," that's a Darb, that's the cleverest thing yet. It makes no comment it just pegs these big birds. And they have maintained the steadiest average you ever saw. They have been just 100 per cent wrong ever since it started.

Then here tonight is a pile of literature about South Africa. They dident know I was all over every foot of it with a circus, but I am going back there some day, and see it in comfort. Then here is one called the "Caballeros" by Ruth Laughlin Baker.[10] It's California in the early days, a great field for interesting and romantic writing. This one reads mighty interesting. It's about horses. I may read it plum through. I'll write you all some book reviews some time and keep you all posted on what the ignorant man should read. That's enough writing for tonight. People write too much anyhow.

P.S. Then the best book of this or all time is "The Old Texas Trail Drives" by George Saunders, of San Antonio.[11] I think it's published there. Each one tells his own experience in his own way. Two hundred original authors in one book. Don't miss it. That's the "Will Rogers Book of the Month" selection.

498   CUCKOO BUT HAPPY

Well all I know is just what I read in the papers, or here lately it's not so much what I read in the papers as what I had to listen too. Not over the radio, but right out loud first-hand, as you perhaps have gathered from a round-about way there has been lately held in the

Will Rogers addresses delegates to the 1932 Democratic National Convention in Chicago.
(Photo taken from tinted motion picture film)

City of Chicago a couple of "Seances" by America leading second sight artists.

Well, I was drafted to go there. Of course no one would have gone of his own free will and accord, and now that they are all over and I sit and think of the amount of "applesauce" and "hooey" that was spilled there you wonder that we are even doing as well as we are as a nation.

When you think of thousands of people in a hot stuffy hall away up till the early morning hours listening to "The man I am about to nominate has the qualities of a Jackson, the statesmanship of a Jefferson, and the homely common sense of an Abraham Lincoln." Then the next one nominated would have all these and then a couple of more, maby the looks of McKinley, and the oratory of Bryan.[1] Hours on hours of that, then they would all get up and march around the hall, part would march and part would hiss or be against the ones that was marching. Then all sit down and then some local prodigy would have to make a "Seconding" speech. And go all through the same stuff the others had, anything in the world to get to talk.

But with it all they were a good bunch. I guess just so much of that has to be. An Englishman sitting in the Press Stand, from the world's most liberal paper the Manchester (England) Guardian. I just looked at him when thousands were acting like newly corralled monkeys, and wondered what he must think of this odd way of arriving at "Democracy." I talked to him. Of course he was like all well-bred Englishman, very "Discreet," and wouldn't say anything against our system, but it would have been worth a lot to have had his real thoughts.

I guess there is no profession as "Crazy as politics. It's a profession all its own. Of all the "Trades" and "Deals" and "Under Cover" happenings that go on during one of those conventions. A state Deligation is with "Their" man, but are they? Maby their leaders have already sold out to some opposition man, and are to deliver to him after the next ballot is taken. They "Trade" all kinds of ways. "Bring your Deligation over to me and I will give you the vice presidency." To another he will promise the Secretary of Stateship. Then the deligations begin to slip sometimes without anyone monkeying with 'em. It's just human nature to string with a winner. That's what they call getting on the Band Wagon. They know they can't get any Post Offices out of the loser, so sympathy cuts no Ice. They quit him so quick there is nothing left but the campaign buttons, especially at this last convention where there was a Presidential Candidate to every ten votes. So naturally there was a lot of disappointed candidates.

Now you might ask, "Do these fellows really think they will get somewhere?" Sure they do. There is nothing that can kill hope in a candidate. He just thinks the breaks were against him that time, and that he will get in the next time.

But at that there is a lot of humor among them, and it's not all unconscious. There is some pretty good kidders among our leading candidates and politicians. They kinder take it serious before the crowd but when they are kinder off to themselves in a little bunch, why they can kid themselves as much as any one.

You meet some great folks at those conventions, Governors, ex-Governors, Senators, ex-Senators, all the names that you have become accustomed to in the past, and maybe haven't heard of in a long time, why you find 'em at these conventions. Its the Fourth of July celebration of national politics. It's a clam bake of big politicians. If they can't get on the deligation they come as mere spectators.

Then it's becoming a great trip for the women. They slipped her the vote, and she slipped off the Mother Hubbard and into the old "Organdie" and she is meandering her way through a solid week of gabbing. And having a great time. It gives 'em something to do. Every once in a while they allow one up on the stand to make some kind of "Seconding" speech, or something of a minor order, but the old "He" leaders are pretty careful to not give 'em too much rope. They sorter keep 'em like a well-regulated family does the small child. It's supposed to mostly listen, and every once in awhile if a lull comes to maby ask some little inoffensive question, but never allowed full leeway. Course the women are more serious with it all. When they do get a chance they try to make their very best of it. They are generally more brief than the men. I can't tell whether that's from choice, or from the fact they are always limited to just so many minutes.

But it's a show that no American should miss. It's entertainment, and it's enlightening. It gives us a kind of an idea that most men that emerge from it with any spoils, were more lucky than competent. A good campaign manager can do more than an able candidate. "Trades" make Presidents, more than ability but as bad as we are, and as funny as we do things, we are better off than the other Countries, so bring on more conventions. The bigger, the noisier, the crazyer, the better. No nation likes and "Hooey" like we do. We are all cuckoo, but we are happy.

Well all I know is just what I read in the papers. and what I run into here and there. I made a little "Razee" around among some old friends down in Texas along after the Democrats had done their "Durndest" at Chicago. First down into Oklahoma and then Texas. Fourth of July sneaked up on me before I had even a firecracker or knew the day was anywhere near me.

I was around the old home place at Claremore and they said the next day was a big "Rodeo" up at Nowata. Well that's right near. I knew they would be having a lot of "Calf Missings" at various towns on the Fourth, so I was glad to get to this one, for there I met a lot of old boys that I had been raised with. Some of 'em still roping.

They sure did have a nice little show. You know Oklahoma and Texas is the home of the Contest Roper. The North is the place for the bucking horse riders, but go south if you want to see 'em throw some mean loops.

Fred Lowry who is just about the best steer roper in all these United States was there.[1] In fact, it's right near his ranch, and he had furnished 'em the stock. They still have the real old steer roping, where they rope and tie down big steers. Some states cut it out, not on account of the humane feature, but on account of the old cattlemen kicking on 'em roping their fat steers to practice on.

Lot of these places are having what they call old timers roping contest. Now that's getting right up my alley. I am going to start practicing and see if I can't get in some of them.

I was just thinking when I was looking at that show the Fourth, it was at a little Fourth of July celebration at Claremore just 35 miles from this one, on July Fourth, 1899, (Boy that's 33 years ago) they had a steer roping, and I went into it. It was the first one I ever was in; the very first thing I ever did in the way of appearing before an audience in my life. Just such a show as I was looking at now, (only ours was not so skilled, all these things have advanced).

Well, as I look back on it now I know that that had quite an influence in my little career, for I kinder got to running around to 'em, and the first thing I knew I was just plum "Honery" and fit for nothing but show business. Once you are a showman you are plum ruined for manual labor again.

I had an awful good little horse that really put me in the business. A little Dun (yellow pony, called "Comanche"). All the old timers will remember him. He put you up so close to a steer that you didn't rope him, you just reached over and put a "Hackimore" on him. Some of the old timers brought him up there the other day.

"Jimmie Kane" rider who could throw a loop out turn it over and make the catch we called the "Johnnie Block" right on his head.[2]

This calf roping has all come in the last few years after they had stopped steer roping. A man might be good at one and not necessarily good at the other. And here is something you might not know, or have noticed. A steer roping horse, and a calf roping horse is not the same animal.

You see when you rope steers you catch 'em, throw your slack rope over his rear axle and then run your horse on by him, having him roped by the head, but the rope going over behind him, therefore jerking his all four feet from under him. Then the horse is sopposed to keep pulling and dragging him as he attempts to get up, that is pulling away from him, with his tail to the steer.

Now in calf roping the minute you catch your calf, the horse is stopped. You jump off and go throw the calf yourself, and the horse is to keep the rope tight, but his head is towards the calf, and he does it by backing up, instead of pulling away like with a steer.

Course you can in rare instances have a horse that you can work both ways, but most of 'em have two different horses, and say they mean about 50 or 60 per cent of the game, the horses do.

You know these celebrations are great things. They mean a lot to these folks. They are a regular get-together every year, and they bring their picnic lunches, and all meet and have a great time. Gives all the "Hands" something to talk and argue over for the next twelve months. Funny thing, the best roper on the range is not always, in fact seldom is, the best roper at the contest.

Some of these old real ranch hands that never miss a calf on the prairie get the old buck fever when the crowd is there, and naturally they all go home feeling bad about it, and get a good joshing about it till the next time.

The contests where everybody knows everybody is always interesting. That is the smaller ones where there is not much what you might call professional talent. (That is, boys who make it a business, and just follow that game exclusively.) Still they are a mighty fine, nice bunch of boys. I tell you there is lots of different ways the people have got to be entertained.

In years gone by no one ever thought splendid living would be made by exhibition of things that was a part of one's every day work, but the folks got to have amusement, and the old calf, the steer, and bucking horse, they don't care much, they go back to the range and tell their stay at home cronies what they did at the "Big Fair." Think of the hero a calf is when he goes home and says, "Bob Crosby missed me."[3]

Well I am going to practice up, and from now on if you see an old fellow with long beard roping in the "Centennial Contest," that's old man Rogers, coming to life again.

500   ALL ABOARD FOR THE OLYMPICS

Well all I know is just what I read in the papers, or what I run into. I have prowled around the world quite a bit to try and see a lot of different kinds of people, but right here yesterday almost on my own doorstep I saw the biggest conglomeration of breeds and nationalities I ever saw. The League of Nations has moved right to Hollywood. How it all happened I went out to the Olympic Village, that's the place all these foreign and domestic athletes are stabled. There is just about 160 acres of solid cross breeds. It's built on a high hill overlooking Los Angeles, and it's all laid out in streets, and the flag of each Nation is out in front of their Igloos. The little houses corrall four persons, a kind of two room affair that has two in each room, with a little porch out in front. They are not permament, but they figure they will last till the medals are all distributed, and everybody that dident get one will be on his way home sore.

But I tell you the Committee that has handled this thing has done a fine job. They have made it just about as pleasant and convenient as it would be possible to do with a couple of thousand folks. They spoke about 19 hundred languages. There was a lot of 'em there already when I visited the place. Finland come in that day. Nurmi is kinder the Greta Garbo of the whole affair.[1] They don't know now if they are going to let him compete or not. It seems over in Finland one time when he went to an Athaletic meet, he accepted too much expense money. They only allow 'em what they can live on, and they live on dried fish over there, so Nurmi took two more fish than he could have actually subsided on, and they call him now a professional. I would call him a "Glutton" on fish, but the Athletic Association still call it professional. Well if they don't let him run it will be like having a Democratic Convention and not have Al Smith.

These Finns, there is no Fords in Finland. Well there is Hellingsford, but no Model T Fords. And what we do in a Ford why a Finn can do on his feet. Instead of five or six folks going out on Sunday in a Ford, why five or six Finns just hit out in a high lope, and only stop at these fish filling stations, refule and run on.

The trouble with America is they are not "Running" minded, we are kinder "Riding" minded. Well these Finns are the stars of the show here. Then the Japs have the biggest bunch outside of our gang, I just kinder figure those little rascals will carry off the main end of the loot. They are here on horseback, on foot, in canoes, and every way. They will just try anything that anybody else will do. There is about 150 of 'em, all those that the emigration laws kept out got in as runners and jumpers.

India has a gang here all dressed like Gandi. The man running the "Round Up" of medal hunters, says you learn a lot about what the League of Nations is up against when you try to please all these. That is in laying out the cottages or who will be next to who. For instance they found they couldent put France and Italy on the same hill. They then asked France who they wanted to be near, and France said Germany. Well that was fine. Then when Germany got here they asked them, and Germany said they dident want to be near France. Finland dident want to be near Sweden. They have tried to arrange 'em in groups where for instance the English speaking nations are togeather, England, U.S., Canada, Australia, South Africa. Then all the Spanish American bunch in one group.

Each country has its own dining room and its own cooks. They just give their order to the head of the village what it is they want in the way of groceries and meats and fruits, and it's handed out to their cooks, then they prepare it for their gang as they see fit. I was in the Swedish kitchen and dining room, he said all they eat was fruit, that they dident eat two ounces of meat a day. He had twenty seven in there and said there was forty more coming. I asked him what he would do when they come and he said, "I will just slice up more fruit."

One old big Argentine boy that looked like Firpo was out near the village practicing the shot put, and heaved it toward one of these little houses and carried it away on his cannon ball.[2] Now they have sent him out on the desert to practice. He will about knock down Mount McKinley.

They have one big assembly room or hotel lobby affair where they all gather, and meet friends. They don't allow any women visitors in the inside of the village, you can go to this reception room and that is as far as they can go. There is some women athletes but they are going to keep them over in some cages some place.

The events are held in about a dozen different places so no one knows where to go or what they really want to see. But it's all done on schedule, so it is possible to see it. There is 48 Nations here, some with only one or two athletes some with a hundred or more. It looks like it will be a great show, you don't want to miss it. It's an awful lot of running and a lot of jumping for nothing, but as long as they enjoy

170

it why I guess it's all right. They give these boys all this for $2.00 a day, so that's cheaper than staying at home. So they just as well be here arguing with the judges as not.

501   EDUCATIONAL FRILLS

Say, any of you that have kids in school, either grammar, high or college, it don't make any difference, but can any of you parents get head or tail of what they are doing, what they are taking, what they are learning?

This modern education gag has sure got me licked. I can't tell from talking to 'em what it's all about.

All the kids I know, either mine or anybody's, none of 'em can write so you can read it, none of 'em can spell so you can read it.

They can't figure and don't know geography, but they are always taking some of the darndest things, political science, international relations, drama, buck dancing, sociology, Latin, Greek art. Oh, Lord, the things they go in for runs on by the hour!

But it's as I say, not only our brood, but none of 'em that I have seen can write, spell, figure or tell what bounds Korea.

Everybody has swimming pools, but nobody has got a plain old geography. Gymnasiums to the right of you, and tennis courts to the left of you, but not a spelling book in a carload of schools.

Then they got another gag they call "credits." If you do anything thirty minutes twice a week, why you get some certain "credit." Maby it's lamp shade tinting, maby it's singing, maby it's a thing they call "music appreciation." That used to drive my cowboy son Jim pretty near "nuts."[1]

He never could see how that would aid you to rope a calf. They give out these things at schools for anything that any one can think of. Some of 'em you get more "credits" than for others. If a thing is particularly useless, why it give you more credits. There is none at all for things that we thought constituted "school."

You could write, read, spell, figure, and give the capital of Rhode Island, and they wouldent give you a "credit" in a year. But you can tell where a Latin word was originally located, and how it's been manhandled and orphanized down to the present day, and say, they will claim that you have the nucleus of a "thesis," and you are liable to get a horde of "credits." Now who cares about the word, or what it has contributed to the welfare of nations that never minds to them.

You have got yourself the family tree of a word. Course you can't go out and get a job on it, but these old professors value it mighty highly. Some of these days they are going to remove so much of the "punk and Hooey" and the thousands of things that the schools have become clogged up with, and we will find that we can educate our broods for about one-tenth the price and learn 'em something they might accidentally use after they escaped.

But us poor old dumb parents, we just string along and do the best we can, and send 'em as long as we are able, because we want them to have the same handicaps the others have. We don't know what it's all about. We just have to take the teachers word.

They all think education is our salvation, but you could turn ten college presidents loose in a forest with nothing to eat, or nothing to get it with, and then ten old so-called "ignorant" backwoodsmen, and your presidents wouldn't last a week.

The smarter a nation gets, the more wars it has. The dumb ones are too smart to fight. Our schools teach us what the other fellow knows, but it don't teach us anything new for ourselves. Everybody is learning just one thing, not because they will know more, but because they have been taught that they won't have to work if they are educated.

Well, we got so many educated now that there is not enough jobs for educated people. Most of our work is skilled and requires practice, and not education.

But none of these big professors will come out and tell you that that our education might be lacking, that it might be shortened, that it might be improved. They know as it is now that it's a "racket," and they are in on it.

You couldn't get me to admit that making movies was the bunk either. None of us will talk against our own graft. We all got us our "rackets" nowadays.

There is just about as much "hooey" in everything as there is merit. The heathen live with less effort, and less worry.

Trying to live "past" our parents, and not "up to 'em" is one of our drawbacks. The old Chinese got the right idea along that line, but every once in a while some fellow does pop up and declare himself. Look at that college professor in Chicago University.[2] He said our learning system was all haywire.

He is a smart young fellow, that guy. I heard him speak at a dinner in Chicago during the convention. He knew a whole lot more than just where a lot of words "come from." This education is just like everything else. You got to judge it by results. Here we are better educated (according to educational methods) than we ever were. And

172

we are worse off than we ever were, so it's not living up to its
"billing." It's over rated. It's not worth the price.

It's costing us more than it's worth. They got to devise some way
of giving more for the money. All he is getting out with now is
"credit" and nobody on the outside is cashing 'em.

502   SMILES AND TEARS IN THE
                  OLYMPIC SHOW

Well all I know is just what I read in the papers, and what I see
as I mess around. Well with us right in the middle of the Olympics,
we are just bogged down in swimmers, up to our ears in pole vaulters.
It's been great fun, and a wonderful sight to see. Nothing like it
during our lifetime, being a young guy, but you old birds won't ever
see it again, unless you hit the high seas.

About ten days ago before it started why one day out at our
studio they brought all the girl athletes out there for lunch and to see
the studio. We have a big cafe, and it was full. You musent miss
meeting this Texas wildcat "Tex" Dickinson, she just believes that
she can do anything, and the funny part about it is she can.[1] There is
none of the sports that she can't do and do well. She is an athletic
marvel. Played ten games of golf and makes it in 82. They say that's
pretty good. I don't play the game, but they say it is. She is within
three fifths of a second of Helen Madison's record.[2] This old Texas
girl said she would ride, rope, or play polo against me, and I bet she
could beat me in any one of 'em. I sure don't want to get mixed up
with 'em in any of these games, or out of 'em.

Then I met that day Helen Madison, our great swimmer, then
Georgie Coleman, oh and dozens of others.[3] A big pretty blonde girl
from Germany spoke good English, said she was a javelin thrower.
Javelin? Why that's little light thing like a spear. Why this girl could
have heaved a horse, much less a javelin.

Two girls from Mexico, one was a fencer, one was a javelin
thrower. The Canadian girls I believe as a whole were about the
prettiest of any of our foreign visitors, and they had on the most
attractive sweaters. The Japanese had a great bunch, and funny thing
there was only one girl from France, just one here. I guess France is
kinder slow having women taking up boxing, and wrestling, and
running and jumping. Still they don't mind 'em doing a lot of work in
the fields. I have see 'em pitching hay and hauling manure to the
fields.

Course I don't know how this women thing doing all these games is. I mean I can't just get my mind made up about it. But I guess it's all right. They just as well be doing that as in some other devilment. It sure does make 'em take care of their health. Course some say that it will be bad for 'em in the long run, but I doubt it. You know women always could endure more than men. (Not only physically, but mentally, did you ever get a peek at some of the husbands?) But they are superior to the so called male.

So I reckon that it's only a matter of time that they will not only be doing the same games as the men but will be in the same classes. There will be no male and female classes, for the men are getting pretty punk as a race. We will be wearing skirts in another generation. I want to pass out just before they catch me doing some "Battick" work. You know there was some awful sad things out here in these Olympics even before they started. Take for instance the trials. I saw the track and field trials for the American team at Palo Alto, and the dissapointment of the ones that were beat for places. It's not so bad to beat in the Olympics, that means that you were the best in your country anyhow, but when you have built up a great reputation around your own home, college, and state, and your records show that your time, or the heighth of your jump is above certain other performers, then to train for months, even years, to make this Olympic games that are held here at home, then you deny yourself, train conscientiously, and then get to the trials and be beaten, maby by inches, and in lots of cases by men who your previous record showed was better than the time they beat you in, in other words, you know that you just happened to have an off day that particular day. There is no doubt that there is men on the American team that beat men that day that they couldent do it again in a lifetime. Well you take a loser like that, and darn it it hurts. If you absolutley knew in your own heart that you could beat the man that beat you, why that would sit pretty tough with you wouldent it?

Course that's not taking any credit from the men that won, but it's just one of those tough breaks of fate. They can't just let it go and make up for it at the next meet. The next Olympics is four years now. Four years is a long time in an athletic career. But they all took it mighty gamely. They smiled but they smiled through many a tear. I begin to think this athletic racket is a pretty tough thing at that. There is about as many disapointments as successes. I think us fellows that can't do anything are just as well off. We are never dissapinted.

503   THE TALE OF A HORSE AND RIDER

Well all I know is just what I read in the papers, or what I see hither and yon.

Lot of funny things happened out here during the Olympic games. They had a wonderful event one morning.

It was part of what is called the pantathalon. It's for army or navy men. It's supposed to be the real test of a good soldier. He is supposed to start out on a horse. I don't know how a navy man is supposed to be on his horse but it's some foreign devised event, so I guess they have horses in the navy. Oh, yes, it sea horses. (Don't shoot I couldent help that one.)

Well you are supposed to be in war, and you start out on your horse. He is supposed to be shot from under you. Now there are 26 in the race, and why out of all the 26 not a man should be hit, but all the horses should be shot was another European mystery. Well after your horse is shot you take your sword and fight the man that shoots him a duel. Then you are supposed to fight him a second duel, this first one having not proven a success on either side. So the next one is with pistols. Then you are supposed to either join him or break away from him! (The rules don't say what becomes of him, but you are supposed to swim for three or four hundred yards, all this supposedly having taken place by a river. Then when you land on the other side you are supposed to run on foot for three thousand meters (that meter is a French word and you will have to look it up yourself). So you see this is quite a war you are supposed to be in. It's a wonder that they dident think of having a rattlesnake bite him after this, or maybe get married or some other hardship overtake him, but in this one they had why this was all that happened to you.

The way they had it, each one of these events was supposed to take place every day for five days, the horse part of it was the start. Well the nation that is holding the games is supposed to furnish the horses for all of 'em. It's really not a game, it's a horse killer that's what it is. Well we had shipped (I mean the U.S. Army) about 35 head of our best army horses from Ft. Riley, Kansas. That's where our cavalry school is, the big one. They were a fine bunch of horses and all about equally good. Each nation was allowed to have three men in it. Lots of nations in it that dident bring horses over for the regular horse events. In fact you dident even have to have a saddle to enter this, the government furnished you that.

Now some of these fellows wasent so hot as riders. Maby they figured to get by on their fencing, or swimming, or something else. You see the general average of all five events were the winners.

Well they drew for their horses, and even the Americans dident know what they would get. They were to race about three and a half miles over rolling hill country, with jumps averaging almost four feet, and built out of solid logs, or two by twelve boards nailed solid, and if you hit you turned over. A Mexican started No. 1. He made a good showing, had one fall about the fifth jump, but his horse got up and him too and they went on and finished in good shape. They each went it alone. They would have to judge their own speed that the horse would be able to carry them and still be able to jump the last jumps. Well things went along fine till a guy from Portugal "De Frietas Branco De Heredia." Now if you think that name is kidding you are crazy. I just copied it from an old program. Then that was only part of his name for he was a titled bird too, a "Don" or a "Donna" or something. Well he wasent dressed like the others, in army togs of their various nations. He had on a regular hunting outfit, that he had seen pictures of in England. Red coat, white pants, plush cap, black. Well while he was waiting for his time to start he figured this horse was standing too still, he dident have enough life for a man with such a name, so he took his whip and give the horse a couple of cuts with the whip. Now he had drawn the very best horse of the 26 that was in the race "Sir Anthony" a horse that the real riders would have won with. Well when he did this to the "Sir" (who was somewhat of a title himself) why he just up and throws Mr. Portugese right into the Bay of Biscay, then runs away without a single Portugese aboard.

Well after miles of chasing him they finally got him back and boosted him on top again. And they started. Well I have seen riders fall off at jumps, but this fellow wasent satisfied with that, he must fall between jumps. It was just too much name to stay on one horse. He whipped and beat the poor horse till at the finish it took all the negro grooms in the army to hold the horse up. And the Portugese claimed that he got a bad deal. Nobody will ever know what he started whipping him for in the first place, but you can bet he will never whip another one. It was a terrible lesson to a Portugese. The moral is don't loan a Portugese a good horse. In fact don't loan him any horse.

504   GOODBYE OLYMPICS

Well all I know is just what I read in the papers or what I see as I prowl about. Well the Olympics are all over, everybody has run as fast as they can, jumped as high as they can, swam as fast as they could, and now they have gone home to start practicing to start the whole thing over again. It was the most wonderful two weeks of thrills and excitement. It kept you looking nine ways to try and see half of it. It was a great job well done, by everybody connected with it.

There was many a laugh, many that dident get into the papers. There one day Ireland would like to have run off with the whole stadium. Some doctor from away down in the south of Ireland just had one more throw with the hammer, (I don't know why they call it a hammer, it's round) I would hate to have to drive a nail with it, well he just took his last heave and like to knocked down one end of the Stadium.[1]

Then on the same day an old Long boy named Tisdall won the I think it was 400 meters hurdles, he and a Lord Burghley and by the way he was the most popular man at the games was this very titled Englishman named Lord Burghley.[2] He owns a place in England that has ten towns located on it, that's quite a few towns, in fact that's the first time I ever heard of a man just going in for raising towns. That may be the salvation of the farmer is to raise towns, in one of his Castles, (you heard me, one of his Castles). He has more Rembrandts than any man alive, and his hobby is footracing. He runs the hurdles or the flat, any kind of a race that England needed anyone to run why the Lord would get in it. Everybody liked the Lord, he was a real Democrat. And I hope he stays and votes in November, we are going to need all we can get.

But I must get back to my "Gag." Well this Tisdall won the race, and I forget where the Lord finished, but it was either third or fourth. Well sir he and this Irishman went into the most wonderful and spontanious embrace you ever saw. Think of it an Irishman embracing an English Lord. If that got back to Ireland why they wouldent let him land with his medals. Ireland had a great representation, some good boxers, too.

Brazil was playing Germany water polo, and they had a Hungarian referee and he kept calling fouls on Brazil. In fact he called 35 during the course of the game. Well after it was over Brazil made for him and he started to hollering for a cop, but it was in his own language, and our cops couldent tell if he was hollering or cheering, and Brazil got to him, and how. They hit for every foul, then another Foreigner tried to rush over and the cops thought naturally he wanted to get in the fight, so they took care of him. Well he was the head of the whole Swimming Federation in Europe, and was trying to tell 'em who he was. Poor Brazil they had come up here on a Coffee Boat, and after they had been out a couple of weeks why their Government changed hands, and the new Government was trying to find out

177

where the boat was. The Athletes dident know what Government or country they were really representing.

Then of course there is lots of jealousy down in South America among the different countries. Well when the Argentine won the Marathon why the other Republics wanted to know why their men hadent won it?[3] They thought there was enough Marathons to go round. Why here we was having the whole thing right in our own alley, and we couldent get near the Marathon with our three men, so what was poor Boliviar, or Peru to do. I saw that Kid that won that in his quarters at the village the next day. He is only nineteen and he weighed only 123 when he went in and lost eight pounds in the race. He come out weighing 115. He is a skinny slender kid. That was a remarkable thing. Those long races are generally won by old fellows, the same as the hard long races with horses are won by old horses. It's nothing for a horse 14 or 15 years old to win the Grand National Steeplechase in England, but these other South American athletes are afraid to go home now.

Met and got acquainted with a lot of our boys. There was one old Kid competing and I mean really competing, from right about twenty miles from Oolagah, my old home town called called Skiatook. He was a distance runner. What a place for an Olympic runner to come from, I can't imagine what he was running around there for. His name was Dawson.[4] And say an "Injun" would like to have won the Decatholon, that's the thing where a man is supposed to do everything. This kid was named Buster Charles who used to go to Haskell Institute.[5] He was ahead almost up to the last two events. Those big guys in that event some of 'em weighing well over 200 pounds, pole vaulted over 13 feet. That's a long way for a big guy to drop.

And say if Mr. Hoover had come out here and opened those games like he should have done he would have not been in Washington during that mess they had, in fact they wouldent have had it.[6] I saw some movies of that away back couple of weeks ago, and what made it look so bad was the army going in with tanks and full war equipment. I was just thinking of the effect of that being shown all over the world. We can never go around preaching "Dissarmament" and "Brotherly Love" any more. It does look like there could have been some more sensible way out than that. I am a believer when you are at outs with a man or a Group, is not to send somebody (they always bungle it). Go out and talk it over with 'em, and lay your side right on the line and say, "Here there is no money in the Treasury to pay it, we don't owe it to you till it's due, don't you think you have made a mistake coming here." Or whatever it was he had to say. But it's all over and they are big men and are supposed to know the right thing to do in big cases. Sometimes it makes you think we don't need a different man as bad as we need different advisers for the same man.

505   WILL READS THE PAPER

Well, all I know is just what I read in the papers and what I see as I prowl from hither to thither. The old stock market is trying awful hard to land back on the front pages like it used to be years ago. As they say in China, it "Lost Face." You know, come to think of it, there is an expression that I don't see how we get along without. Everything in the Far East is about "Somebody Losing Face." It really don't mean that a man has lost out, or failed to make good, but it means a hundred things. Anything in the world that happens to you in the Far East, mumps, measels, hat blew off in public, insulted by someone, shoes run down, throw three "craps" in a row—anything in the world that is the least bit "Dissconcerting" or embarrasing, why that is what you call "Lost Face."

Well, the old stock market has lost so much face that it's practically been headless for three years. But they are just stirring around among each other now, and the market is like a Mexican jumping bean, and nobody knows why it's jumping. Course it's jumping to get Republican votes in November and it's got a lot of jumping yet to do.

Of course New York thinks that that is just what the whole world revolves on, they think that if the market was good today that every man, woman and child in the country should celebrate, and have a big meal on the strength of the rise. When as a matter of fact Amos and Andy have more influence on the whole American public than the market.[1]

Now let's see what else has been agitating the natives. Jack Garner went back east a couple of weeks ago to meet his commander and lay out schemes and deadfalls to trip the Republican, and fix it so the Democrat could walk over it. Garner they say made a fine impression. He had never been further east than Washington before, and he got so he got around New York about as good as all the foreigners that live there.

Canada has a big Congress of some kind at Ottawa, and for a family that is kin why they get along pretty well. They all agreed to buy from each other and they will till somebody comes along and sells cheaper. But they are mighty patriotic, that English empire and when the real show-down comes they will stick together. Been reading a lot of criticism by our papers of what they did. But when it comes to running their own business that Empire don't need any great advice from us. Mighty long headed old boys in their government. Canada is a mighty good neighbor and a mighty good customer. That's a combination that is hard to beat.

The Irish free state and England are still at it over "The Irish taking the oath to the King." They opened their parliament and they always did play "God save the King" when the Governor General who is appointed by England comes in. But the old boy had to walk in to his own whistling this time. The orchestra had a tip not to give him any entrance music. England is pretty stubborn themselves about these little details of giving the old country it's traditional due. At the games out here, Canada was the only one of the countries that had their own national anthem. South Africa had several first winners and always played the king song. But Canada had their own.

This Hitler stuff over in Germany, I can't get the straight of it.[2] They are kinder like the *"Facistists"* but still they are against the German "Facistists." There seems to be about a dozen or more different kinds of parties and they are hard to figure out. That old man Hindenburg must be a great old man.[3] He is about the sole surviving hero of the big men in the war over there. Hitler's main strength, if I get it right, is that the present generation of the Germans had nothing to do with the big war and they should not be made to pay. Now there is a lot of foundation to that. Every man ought to pay his own debts. The only way for him to outlaw 'em is to die. If they did that it sure would help to discourage war. If countries knew that they were not going to be paid but just a few years and then no more, they would be mighty slow about going out to start something.

Reading in the papers what Lord Cecil said about aerial disarmament, I have seen the old man at every one of these conferences and he is quite an authority on "Why they don't disarm."[4] He made rather a unique statement. He said, "I understand there should be no bombing of Civilians but that does not eliminate aerial warfare. If bombing is to continue, I do not think that Civilians have any right to claim a particular measure of immunity." Now I don't guess we ever had thought of it in that way. War is just to kill, so one bunch can't ask for any more protection than another. He said that, "It is a great pity flying ever was invented." What about the autos, they kill more than all the wars. Their warfare is going on all the time. A War is started by somebody agreeing to fight, but the old auto just keeps on reaping 'em down with no previous agreement.

But everything will be fixed this fall, if you just listen to what the candidates say. In fact that's about all we are doing now is just listening to what the candidates say. So you see even our minds are not working.

506   WHAT'S THE EXCITEMENT?

Well, all I know is just what I read in the papers, or what I see here and there. You know it's been weeks since the Olympics finished, but for a couple or three weeks after it was over it felt out here like a kind of an old ghost town. We had gotten so used to going to the stadium every day, and we had seen the athletes so often, and the thing kinder got next to you.

Well one of the last to leave was some of the Japanese, and among them was little Nichi Baron Nichi.[1] He is the one that won the high jumps with his horse. He was just about the most popular little rascal that was here. They say he is tremendously rich in his own country but no one knew that till after the games were over. He was just "another" Japanese cavalry officer to everybody.

They made a lot of friends the Japanese did over here. That Shanghai and Manchurian thing had just about put 'em in the dog house as far as we were concerned, but they acted so fine and were such good sports that they went away in the good graces of everyone. Course they haden't any more than got on the boat till we read in the papers that Japan was taking Jehol. Jehol is a province in China. It's a kind of a "Buffer" province. It lays between Manchuria, and China property, and the Japanese claim that they have to have it as it allows the Chinese to be too near to their operations in Manchuria. They was messing around about it when I was over there away last fall. They are always going to have a lot of trouble over there, but it's a long way from our home. I sure wish our State Department was a far away from things as our folks are.

Politics is just a boiling trying to jell. I sit around and try to keep my ear to the ground. Nothing between it but a pillow, but I can't get heads or tails out of what's going to happen. Everybody on both sides if you talk to 'em will be so confident, that it makes you ashamed of how little you know yourself. They just up and tell you to practically a thousand votes, by just how many each side will win by.

Now I get this news from a fellow the other day and he is a man that should have some idea for he is doing nothing but just traveling around taking "hearings" on public opinion. "Have been since I saw you at the Convention in Chicago, in every city east of there, so have a pretty good idea of what will happen in the fall. First of all I think we will get a Democratic governor in Maine. Moses I think will be defeated in New Hampshire.[2] Will get the Democratic governor in Indiana but will lose the Senate to Watson, Roosevelt will get Ohio and Michigan by slim majorities but will lose both of them to Republican Governors.[3] The Far South don't even know Hoover is running. If he gets a vote south of the Mason and Dixon line it will be some stray kin folks of his. Virginia, West Virginia, Maryland, and Kentucky will all go for Roosevelt. Democrats haven't got a chance in Pennsylvania, but will take an even bet that they get Maine and Vermont. I have done 15 east and Mid-west states, and start off into the Northwest, and West right away."

Now you have it. He tries every way he can to get the opinions. He just holds a clinic over every voter. But a vote is a funny thing.

Bet the whole thing gives everybody something to gab about. What we do, what we say, what we think don't mean much. Just glide along with 'em, give a lot of 'em a job. One man could do what 10 of 'em do. There could be a quarter or third as many Congressmen or Senators, and we would pick better ones then. But it's the system that we have always used, and there is no use getting all overcome with prespiration over it. We get along pretty good, and things kinder run themselves anyhow. Most of our improvements are so big they can't carry 'em off, and our laws we have eo many anyhow that a couple of hundred passed every session don't mean much to us.

Our congress is just like an old stray she cat. She will drag in with so many kittens just when you don't want 'em, but you tolerate her, and know that she can't help it. Well that's about the way we feel about our two governing bodies. They can just cause us so much annoyance each year, and the only time we really get sore at 'em is when they do come with an extra big "Litter."

It don't make much difference who is in or who is out. They both draw the same salary. I have always claimed that they should be elected for life. The Supreme Court is our most respected gang, so it might work in our other branches. Now take this year for instance, what can they do towards helping the country? Nothing. They have all got to be trying to get back in.

This is the year when they really work, but it's for themselves and you can't blame 'em. They have had a taste of it and they like it. There is something about holding office that must just get right next to 'em. And they are seldom ever any good any more for anything else. But they are all likable cusses. You can't help but like 'em, and they are always smarter than the people that elect 'em. So our

182

election every four years is just what we need. We don't know what we need it for but it's for something if it's only to get one-half of our folks sore at the other half every four years.

507   ROGERS ON LOCATION

Well all I know is just what I read in the papers. Been prowling around quite a bit lately away up in the mountains working on a movie. It's the first time we have been on location since we made "Lightnin."[1] That was when we was up at Lake Tahoe. That's the time Clara Bow visited us, remember?[2] But we better let that drop. Well this time we are making the old silent picture that I made twelve years ago called "Jubilo."[3] It is a tramp picture and everyone that sees me in my street clothes say that I excell in tramp parts. I like to play tramps. There is something about an old tramp that kinder hits me, especially a kind of a good natured one that don't take things too seriously.

Did you ever see a picture company on location? Well, now that we have to carry all that sound equipment and men with it, why it looks like Barnum's circus coming.[4] We have a very small cast, about five. Yet I bet there is about 50 of us. It takes lots of folks to make these things, even if when you see 'em sometimes you think they ain't so hot. And the funny part about it is that a bad one takes just as much work as a good one, for we have never found anyone that can tell when it's going to be bad. What I mean is that we don't make 'em bad purposely. They sometimes look like we did, but we don't. We do our best all the time, and all the crew, the cameramen, the carpenters, property men, sound technicians, and dozens of other expert men in their lines, they all do good work on all of 'em, but it's us actors, and writers and directors that just don't click in some of 'em.

It's kind of a cuckoo business, but trains have been full for twenty years of so-called smart people that were coming out here to fix the movies, and they have all gone back. There is things that look like they ought to be changed, but the wise ones can't seem able to think of any thing to improve 'em. It's sorter like our government, it's the cockeyedest run thing, we sometimes think, but darn it we keep living under it and nobody can scare up anything any different.

I don't know the older we get the more "standpat" we get. The only change we want as we grow older is a change back to the things of our early life. We don't want a lot of new ones. Just because a thing is new don't mean that it's better. Now take it right here where we are right in the edge of the High Sierras. Just a short ways from Mount Whitney, the highest point in the U.S. Now away back up in these high mountains, there is no automobile roads, so to get back there to fish and hunt, they have to "pack in." They hire horses and say they have the greatest time of their lives. So where is your old automobile? There will never be a time when the old horse is not superior to any auto ever made.

Like the other day at the studio they was talking about a story. Said it had to be changed a lot, that the old idea of the mortgage on the old farm was all out of date, that the villian robbing the train and hiding the money was all the hooey. They claimed that all stories had to be made modern and up to date. So I told 'em, say listen there never was a time in our lives when the fore-closing of a mortgage was as timely as it is today. It almost comes under the heading of standard equipment with most homes and farms, and as for villians being out of date, why villians are getting as thick as college degrees, and sometimes on the same fellow. No sir, there is no new situations. Wives are leaving husbands, husbands are leaving wives. Robberies where they used to take your horse and if they was caught they got hung for it, now they take your car and if they are caught it's a miracle, and they will perhaps have the inconvenience of having to go to court and explain. The old horse if the horse thief ever let him loose or give him half a chance he would come home. Our automobiles don't stay at home long enough to know where homes are, even if they could get back. So your movies won't be changed much more than your morals, or your taxes or any other of the things that you think should be remodelled.

There is one epidemic now that I think could be discontinued. I haven't got any kick with my friend Bill Hayes, but you sometimes do wonder if it's absolutely nessesary before a picture is released that it have the word "Hell" in the title.[5] Looks like if they had to have it, they could put more hell into the picture and leave less of it out of the title. There is a lot of these where most of the Hell is just in the title. They are taking perfectly innocent stories now and there is no more "Hell" in 'em than there is amusement, but the bars are down and the word "Hell" makes good reading to 'em, so it's just getting to be Hell to get a picture released unless it's name is hell, something or other.

But it's the old stuff. It comes from the preachers. Take any old preacher that is having a time drafting anybody to listen to him, and he announces that his sermon next Sunday night will be on, "Hell and Damnation," or "I am going to skin the Devil alive and showup Hell." Well that was just a lot of hooey like these titles are, but he knew that title would catch 'em. He knew that he couldent give the devil any more of a skinning if his title had been, "The outcome of a life without Christ." But he was looking for something sensational, and that's where the movies got the idea. Both of 'em ought to be made to cut it out. A picture that can't draw without hell in the title ain't much picture, and a preacher that can't preach without hell in his title is just as weak as the movies. Why don't they just for a change use the word "Dam" instead of Hell. It don't sound near as bad, and it's much more of a novelty. Instead of calling this picture "Tramping through Hell." I want to call it, "A Dam Tough Villian, Dam Fine Gal and a Pretty Dam Fair Kind of Tramp."

508   GOLD IN THOSE HILLS

Well, all I know is just what I read in the papers and what I see here and yonder. Do you like to just be in a car prowling around? I know you do, everybody does. I would much rather be in a plane, but if you haven't got one, and I haven't, more folks ask me about my plane. They think because I do a lot of traveling that way that I must have my own plane. Why I haven't got any more plane than Alabama has Republicans. I have always just used a regular organized line, walk up and pay your fare get in and go where you want to. It's just about the same price as R. R. fare, in most cases cheaper, and by the way, it is really being patronized now. There is big travel on plane lines, and if you want to go somewhere book your passage away ahead. I can remember when it looked to me like I was the only guy traveling that way. But I am lost in the mob now. But all this has nothing to do with planes. I am the greatest guy to start in on telling something and then switch over to something that has nothing to do with it at all. I get that from working in the movies. You notice it in our movie stories.

Well, I was up in a town called Bishop making a movie, and we got through with our outdoor shots (you see we went up there to get the beautiful scenery and get the mountains in the background). We could have taken 'em at the studio in "minature" like they do, but we just wanted to show some real mountains for a change. Well we finished one afternoon and the next day being a holiday we wasent to work. The Company would be traveling back to the studio, so I had never been over into the South Western part of Nevada. So I jumped in my car that very evening and went over a range of mountains about 130 miles to Tonopah, Nevada, that's the old silver town. It's not a ghost town by any means because it has a couple or three thousand people living there yet and is a very interesting town. Used to be along in 1907 and 8 a big rushing thriving town of perhaps 10 thousand or more.

Well I stayed there that night and met a lot of folks, real folks. There is some great people live in those old western towns. Hope is their staff of life. If silver ever comes back, and Lord knows they ought to put some kind of real comparative value on it, for it's used as money in 20 countries to gold's one. Tonopah is one of the big silver diggings of the West.

Well up early the next morning and down to Goldfield. Now don't that name and place bring back memories. One of the well advertised towns of the West. In 1906 on Labor Day, was the biggest and best advertised and best prize fight ever held. That was the famous Gans-Nelson fight of 42 rounds that was promoted by the famous Tex Rickard.[1] It was the first big purse at that time $30,000. They kept the prize money all in gold in the window of the Northern Saloon and Gambling House, where all could see it. It was just exactly 26 years to a day when I was there. I had known two of three principals, Nelson and Rickard.

There is an old depot down where the fight was held, and the railroad of it has been torn up. The whole line is out of commission now, but there stands the depot right out here connected with nothing. It has now about 500 people in all that still live there. The Goldfield Hotel is kept up and is quite a place yet. It was a little city of twenty thousand in its boom days, and some of the fortunes of Nevada were made there.

It's a gold town, and they are working some of the mines by small leases. The government is investigating it as they think there is big pay stuff there yet. Now here was an experience. The papers had been full of a new strike at a place called Clarkdale, for a fellow named Clark found it. So off I went to it, a newspaper man and mining man went with me, and sure enough away out there in the hills on those desert flats was dozen of camps all around a hole in the ground. Lots of 'em had leased from the original striker, and the others had staked near around there. Well they say there was some real gold there. Of course till they get away down in they can't tell just how much, but the lead looked mighty good, so they said. Course to me it just looked hot and dry, but these old boys that was out there was real miners, they ought to know. It's like us trying to sell a bum movie to a modern audience, it can't be done. So I am going (trying to sell) to watch this new strike at Clarkdale, Nevada, and see how it pans out. But it was only two weeks old when I was there.

Nevada is a great old state to prowl around in. I went on down to another famous old place Ryolite, and another nearby called "Bullfrog." But it had jumped its last. Then on that same trip and that same day I drove into Death Valley and visited Death Valley Scotty's famous castle.[2] But that's a whole story in itself, in fact it's a book, but just get in your car and drive around some time no matter where you live, you will be surprised the old interesting things there is to visit. But don't miss Nevada.

509 GETTING OUT A COLUMN
OF OUR OWN

Well all I know is just what I read in the papers and as there hasn't been much in the papers why I am kinder stuck on something to write. I got it. I will do like those New York columnists do. I wish I could write like that fellow McIntyre.[1] I never miss him. Old Odd can make spinach appetizing in print. Then he has got one of the biggest herds of words to ride in and out from. He is so far ahead of all other columnists there is no comparison. Then for real humor Bugs Bear is the King.[2] Lord, how that fellow can think of all that?

Here goes on my first lap of trying to be a columnist. I hate red neckties and I hate to see a fellow without sock supporters, even if he has got a diploma. I would like to be back on the old street corner at Oolagah, Oklahoma, and have one of the boys come by and say, "Come on, Will, let's go out on the prairie and tie a couple of steers." I will never stay in the city long enough to get away from the old steer roping. What's become of the old-fashioned window pane that was out and we stuffed it up with gunny sacks?

Up betimes and at my stint. My first stint is a lot of sliced fresh peaches, then some ham and then some eggs washed down with about a dozen saucers of coffee. I lay late, almost till 6:30. The papers came, but having nothing but politics, I cared not one whit for 'em. It does seem that our country could be run much better by someone if we could only think who. Mrs. Rogers came down and we had the usual argument as to how late the boys stayed out. They have to drive over a cattle guard coming in and it's as good as an alarm clock as it rattles under the car wheels.

There was a big opening in Hollywood last night, but as I had nothing new to wear or say, I didn't go. Our Scotty dog has more fleas on him, weight for age, than any other dog in California. Son Jimmy came down at last to breakfast and said he was late, as he had to drive half the night to find some movie house where they were showing a double feature. I argue with wife over what little pieces of real estate investments we should try to pay on and hold, and which to let go back. As we blowed up higher than a Wall Street margin speculator, we said, "Put it in land and you can always walk on it." We did, but no buyers would walk on it with us.

Came by Clara Bow's ranch away up in the desert in Nevada the other day.[3] She's got a Hollywood home right in the heart of the desert. Got cattle on it, not a California ranch with rabbits or avocados. I love my navy beans better than any other dish, or half dozen dishes. Just old plain white navies, cooked in plenty of ham or fat meat, with plenty of soup among 'em. Not catsup or any of that stuff. Just beans and corn bread, old corn pone (white, with no eggs), with the salt and water it's cooked with, and raw onions. Those three things are all I want.

Winnifred Sheehan, a Buffalo newspaper reporter who made good in a big studio.[4] I used to love to sing coon songs and was the first fellow in Cooweescoowee district, Cherokee Nation, Indian territory, that ever did the cake walk. Who does the Kingfish and who does Van Porter—Amos or Andy?[5] McAdoo's daughter is very tall and very beautiful and very charming.[6] Greta Garbo is high hattin' Sweden more than she did Hollyhockville?[7] I love to stroll down in the old part of Beverly Hills because I know of old places that have been built for four or five years. Marie Dressler is my pet actress.[8] Charlie Chaplin is my pet actor. I got two teeth out away back, but they did adjoin, and it shows when I laugh too much in the movies. Why do they make the legs of pajamas so long? The fellow that wrote "State Fair" is out at our studio.[9] They have already got the hog that I am to play with in there.

I have about quit trying to play polo; depression and old age hit me the same summer. Dick Powell, Master of Ceremonies in one theatre in Pittsburg for three years, made good in a big Hollywood studio.[10] He come from Little Rock. His father sold harvesters since wheat used to be worth cutting. I used to have two ingrowing toenails. I know lots of people that used to have bad breath before halitosis was invented. There is nothing that will keep you awake more than a leaking hot water bottle. Every time I shoot a pistol I shut my eyes.

William Hearst has got the the biggest house I ever saw.[11] I used to know Paul Bern eleven years ago, but I never issued any statement to the press.[12] I don't know who is "Blessed Eventing" this week, but as soon as they have a baby I will let you know. I was never in a night club; not morals, just never had a card. Mrs. Ziegfeld spent the evening with us yesterday, as lovely and bright a person as one could meet.[13] Jim Rogers burned his hand roping a calf. I didn't; I missed mine. Just read a book called "The Stump Farm," as fine literature as ever I tasted.[14] Got in my petrol wagon and drove over half of Nevada.

Why, my article is finished already. This kind of stuff is a cinch. Of course, I haven't made it as interesting as they do, but it's true. I must get a little more scandal in the next one, and I know a lot.

510   SOME SWELL IDEAS TO
               IMPROVE THE WORLD

Well all I know is just what I read in the papers. Now there's not much use writing about politics, for it's just in about the same shape it's been in. If things get better Mr Hoover will be elected, and if it don't, why he won't. So that's all there is to politics.

One side is in and wants to stay in, the other side is out and wants in, and there is no difference between 'em, they are both good if things are going good, and both terrible if things are bad, so just throw up a coin and go to the poles.

Well let's see what's has been messing around out here. Roosevelt was out to see us, and a pleasant time was had by all, he made a very fine impression. He is a very charming man, we are always lucky with our candidates. All have been splendid fellows. Any of 'em could have served us well.

I always kinder hate to see an election, for it's tough on the defeated ones. There is lots of luck in the whole thing, from the nominating right on down to the finish.

I have always maintained that the office of president should be for six years with no re-election. It's not right that a president should have to "lectineer" and work on his next campaighn. It's not fair to him. He is naturally human, and going to use every legitimate means of staying in office, so that takes up too much of his valuable time. He owes the nation that time. He don't owe it to his political henchmen that want to stay in with him.

This don't apply to Mr Hoover. It applies to all of 'em. Besides, in six years that gives him time to do something constructive. Suppose Mr Hoover had two more years now, we wouldent be doing all this worrying, right when everybody's mind ought to be on how to help out of this, and not "How to Get Some Votes." Then let two new ones fight over it, see which could outpromise the other.

Oh, yes then I got another scheme, a president retires at half pay for life, that relieves his worrys of a personal financial nature and makes him feel in his old days that his work and devotion to his country was always appreciated. Now these are just a couple of Rogers bills, course they will never get anywhere but the Sunday supplement, but I bet you that any ex-president will say the idea is not so cuckoo.

But ideas? Ideas? Schemes? Everybody has some scheme or plan to save somebody or the country. I am just a-gabbing like the usual soap box guy, always trying to remedy something, and not try to make out with what we got.

Everybody has got a scheme to set the world back right again. Come to think of it, I can't remember when it was right. There has been times when it has been right for you, and you and you, but never all at the same time. The whole thing is a teeter board even when it's supposed to be going good, you are going up and somebody is coming down. You can't make a dollar without taking it from somebody. So every time we wish for something for our own personal gain, we are wishing somebody else bad luck, so maby that's why so few of our wishes come to anything.

But all this kind of "nut" thinking is not my business. It's for some economist, or some fellow that teaches in school, and all that stuff is his "racket." You know we all got a "racket" and we should-ent tread over into the other fellows. So I am not going to try and muscle in on some thinker's racket.

Our picture business is picking up, that is the studios are making more than at any time in the last few years. We are all making 'em in hopes we strike a good one. It's just like fishing, we never know when the public is going to bite. With all their unfailing judgement, the public has bit at some bad ones, so we keep on having a supply of them on hand, figureing that ours might be the sucker picture they would go for.

Some of the biggest money makers have been some of the biggest fakes. As far as being *real* is concerned. But on the other hand the good ones that have done business deserved to do it. The old public is pretty smart after all. They don't bite at a bad one as often as do a good one.

But what I am getting at is that these fellows that judge the public, make and sell the pictures, they must feel pretty certain that there is quite a few more dimes and quarters "just around the corner" or they wouldent be putting all these millions into these sliding chromos. Talking to a fellow that was just over from France, he is a producer over there, he says the Germans are making the best pictures in Europe. The big hits of Paris are some German pictures. England is doing better, Italy not so much, (this is all what he said, not what I said). Russia goes in for sort of "art" mixed with propaganda. You see art is when you do something just cockeyed from what is the right way to do it, then it's art. When you get to monkeying with art, why you just about left commerce behind. You can make a picture that is saturated with "art" but it's liable to not be even "diluted" with gate receipts. The mob knows that the old cat has kittens and raises 'em in about the same way year after year. Occasionally you will hit an old tabby that wants to be unconventional, but she generally winds up on the same back fence.

But it's as I say, they are making more puctures, now who is going to look at 'em I don't know. But I was just telling you, I thought it might make you feel a little better to know that somewhere someplace there was a few more people at work. We are not as high salaried as we were, we are not as cocky as we were, we are not as foolish as we were, but we are happier, saner, (we hope) and willing to take care of your wants in the picture line, and not our preferences. We are just a lot of hired help in a business that strives to please, for we are like the president, we want to stay in office as long as possible.

511   'TWAS A BIG DAY IN CALIFORNIA

Well all I know is just what I read in the papers. Or what I see here and there. There is an awful lot to see this year, if you just sit on the side lines and look on. The politicians never were in a bigger huddle.

A few weeks ago when candidate Roosevelt was out here you never saw such a bunch of Democratic outriders. You see out here in California it used to be hard to scare up a Democrat, and where you did he was scared sure enough. But now they are showing their heads shamelessly. Why you would think the RASCALS were the salt of the earth the way they acting up.

But it was a big time for 'em. Folks did give Mr Roosevelt a fine reception and a mighty good time was indulged in by practically all. The movies turned out and gave a big night for him, not because they was going Democratic. They are a little of everything and most of us not much of anything. We are all too interested in our "art" to give much thought to material things. Don't that sould like a real artist? Most of us don't even know who is running.

In fact, who is running? Well Mr Roosevelt said he was, and the way they cheered I think he was. We (I don't really mean "we"; I had nothing to do with it) but they did put on a fine show for him. They had what they call an electric pageant. That seems to be the "go" now is a pageant. It used to be called just a parade, but now it's a pageant.

Now here is a kind of a joke on us that I don't know if it's ever leaked out or not. We had about 15 beautiful floats with girls just "strewn" all over 'em. You would naturally say "Why those floats cost a lot of dough." And they did. That is they did when they were first used. They were built by somebody. I don't know who, but they were built for the Shriners convention and parade in Frisco, which was held a short time before, and we just hired 'em. If there had been any Frisco folks in the audience it would have looked like old home week to 'em, but that's one thing there is never any Frisco folks down this way. Here and Death Valley is two places Frisco folks seldom ever go. To them one is just about as desolated as the other.

Course we took the old floats and changed the name of 'em. Where one up there might have been christened "The Progress of Beauty" or something why we had Laurel and Hardy on it and called it "Laughter Will Pay."[1] For instance, up there one was all decorated with angels, and called "Virtue and Beauty Intact." Why down here it was loaded up with Hollywood "extras" dressed as bullfighters advertising Sam Goldwyn's picture, "The Kid From Spain."[2] Where they had featured beauty solely, we had combined it with a slight tinge of advertisement and had blended beauty and commerce. But it was done mighty cleverly. But Frisco had made it possible, and we want to thank 'em for it. So they can consider this official.

Then they had some polo games. They wasent so hot, on account of the size of the field, and they should have used an indoor ball, which is bigger and the people could have seen, and also that the players could have too. Then a few stunts of a rodeo that was put on by Tom Mix, Hoot Gibson, and all our wild west boys.[3] It was very good, the speaking was short and not "so hot" either. But we all did the best we could. It was for a good charity cause, and the audience was liberal and lienient.

We had lots of screen stars there. None of Metro's for Louie B. Mayer is a staunch Republican.[4] And they of course was afraid to come on that account. Lot's of 'em would have liked to have seen Mr Roosevelt even if going to vote for Hoover, but they couldent take a chance. But Louie is a good fellow and loyal.

It was kind of a chilly night, and it seems that it's an unwritten law that you can't put a girl on a float with any clothes on. In fact here is the ingredients of a "pageant." You first pick a cold night, then have plenty of places all over the "float" for girls to stand, but don't let 'em have anything on. That's the first ingredient of a "float rider" is to be totally naked. Now she must be able to smile through the snow and sleet. What she is up there doing, or what she is to represent must never enter her head any more than it does the man that arranged it. She is just up there to act naked, and hope that she is not frostbitten by the end of the journey. They are not really "pageants." They are early stages of pheumonia. They are endurance contests, to see how much a girl can stand and shiver herself off the pedestal they have her on. You see a thing like that is just right up these old fat Shriners' alley. They sit there in their warm overcoats and delight on betting when the girl will turn to an icicle. A "pageant" is a collection of bare skin, surrounded by pleanty of electric light bulbs.

Oh yes there is a P.S. A guy tried to jump a horse through a hoop of fire, the horse wouldent jump, and the man was without the shadow of a doubt the worst jumping horse rider in the world. He finally walked the horse up to and forced him into it. The horse knocked the whole contraption and fell in the fire. The man got no burns, much to the disgust of 80 thousand people.

512   LOUD AIRBUSTERS

Well all I know is just what I read in the papers and what I hear over the Radio, and brother if that old Radio ain't getting a beating. The politicians are giving that poor little old microphone one of it's toughest seasons since it's birth. I was just sitting listening in like millions of you have been all Fall.

When the Country ought to be working it's just listening. Even us that are fortunate to have a kind of a job, why we knock off to listen. Well one I remember was Ogden Mills, Odgen took over the Treasury when Mr. Mellon took over the buisness of introducing "Debutantees" to George and Mary.[1]

Men in America live, hope and die trying to become Presidents. If they can't make it they accept the booby prize and go in the Senate. But women just live, hope and die happy, if they can be presented at the Court of St. James.

Well as I was saying before, one of the ones I tuned in on the other week was Ogden Mills. He was out our way sprinkling some tacks in the Democratic road. Ogden is the first man I ever made a political speech for, and the last one. When I got through it he was running for Congress in New York City and the audience couldent tell if I was talking for Ogden, or Aimee McPherson, so they pronounced my speech pretty much of a bust.[2] But they elected Ogden, the only Republican candidate elected to Congress from the great City of New York. (And there is dozens of 'em from there.) At the time I made the speech I dident know that he was running on the Republican side, but young Teddy Roosevelt asked me to go say a few words for Odgen, and I have always been glad I did, for he has made good.[3] I always feel that he is one man that I sponsored that lived up to it.

He is awful rich and got an awful nice wife, and she is a good fellow.[4] She comes into Jack Garner's office and we had a political kowtow. Mills is a wealthy man and always has been, but he really tries, and does render some fine service to his Country, and especially to his party. Even the Democrats say that he has made a fine Treasury, not that the Democrats know much about handling money but Mills has impressed 'em tremendously. He can count the Treasury money without looking at it longingly.

Well he come out to California a few weeks ago and I wanted to see him and Mrs. Mills, but the Republicans were around him so thick, that I knew I would be disinfecting myself for days afterwards, so I dident get to see him. And I dident have a Republican registration card so I couldent get in even to hear him, but I went home and got him on the Radio. I missed 15 minutes of him, for Amos and Andy was on, but the minute Amos stopped singing "Is I Blue?" why I went right over onto Ogden.[5] He is a mild-mannered man in private life but when he gets on that diving board in front of that microphone, why he goes hog wild. If you dident know who it was, and just heard him, you would think it was a Southern Democrat. He orates, then he super orates, then from then on he just gets louder.

They used to call 'em Spellbinders. They ought to call 'em "Airbusters" now. But he had a lot of facts mixed in with the noise, and a lot of facts between growls. But here was the strange thing, he had the same things in his speech that Mr. Hoover had in Des Moines three days later. Now who copped who's act? We used to have that a lot on vaudeville. Some bird would get in the week ahead of you and do your same jokes. Well that's what Ogden had done with Herbert. He did his act the week ahead of him, all that stuff about the Gold Standard.

But it may have been Mills, for that was up his alley, that finance stuff. But he is a very able man and can make a lot more speeches if he will just take it easy. The fellows that rant have to do it to cover up ignorance. Ogden don't have to do that.

By the way you know the best speaker of all of 'em I heard so far this fall? Well it was the wife of Bob Shuler, that preacher that is running for the senate out home.[6] Most women's voice is not so hot over the Radio, but I tell you hers is the most natural, and she's got a lot of plain good facts. McAdoo looks like he ought to win out there.[7] He has really done things. But old Bob getting in there messing it up for both the others, why that's liable to make a difference. Well it won't be long now! Just three more weeks to Alibis.

513   CAMPAIGN DIRECTORY

Well let's take this Campaighn right from the jump. You might wonder "Just when does a Campaighn really start?" Well they really start about 15 minutes after the official returns are in from the last election, on about the fifth drink after the counting is over or the Radio has announced that "So and So concedes the election to his honorable opponent." That is the first hooey of the following campaighn. What he would like to concede to him is a dose of giant powder or a couple of hou-deuvers of Paris Green. Well right then is when the boys start laying their traps for the open office holding season, which is four years away, but they start cutting their bait right that very night. "Well Jim, I'll tell you where we made our mistake this year and how we can beat that 'Ham' in '36." So they start soaping the tracks right away.

Course the President, he is always conceded the nomination of the next election unless he has been notoriously incompetent. But all things being as they usually are why he of course can have the election if he wants it. And history has never recorded the one that dident. Coolidge dident but he had already had practically two terms. And there is a kind of unwritten law against that (like the one where if a wife shoots her husband). But it wasent a third term bugaboo that kept Calvin out, it was horse sense. He knew just to an inch how much American wind the financial balloon would hold and he got out just two days before it busted. Poor Mr. Hoover dident see the thing any more than poor Rin Tin Tin.[1] Or for that matter, the rest of us.

But what we are talking about is this campaighn. It was set that Mr. Hoover could have it if he choose, and he did choose, and how! They do love to be President. It's the toughest job in the world, but there is always 120 million applicants.

Now that brings us down to the Democrats. (What do you mean brings us down?) The Democrats can always furnish more candidates than the Republicans. There is less Democrats, but more of 'em are candidates. Just after the previous election, let us say the one of 1928. Well the next morning after it, every Democrat who has been elected to anything at all the night before, his local paper said, and he like a yap believed it, "Jim Jasbo swept all opposition before him at the polls yesterday. He will be the best Justice of the Peace the Democrats ever had in this country and the U.S. Senate is in his grasp and the White House is before him."

We have 96 senators in there, all of whom think they are only there till the next election when they will move to the other end of the Pennsylvania Avenue. Then the Democrats go through what they call a "Delousing" process, that is they remove some of 'em's ambition. They ask 'em if they won't please wait four years, that they are young yet and that the office will be theirs four years later. Then we will say it's getting down near nomination time. It's been culled down to about one native son of each State. They get all they can out of him in the way of Campaighn trips, bands, and hotel bills. Then on a certain ballot they quit him cold and jump over to the fellow who was nominated the night before in the hotel room, and will be publicly announced the following morning.

Well the nominations are over now. The disgruntled ones start in: "Wrong man," "Will never make it," "Punk." But as the weeks drag along and their complaining is getting them no campaighn funds why they begin to "see the light." They have "heard the Candidate's speeches and he is sound and we are going to support him."

Now the Campaighn is going. The Democrats must attack. He is the "Out" as usual. He has to tell what he would have done. Finally the "In" must come "Out." He must tell "Why he dident do it." Now it's up to the voter to believe one man's promise or another man's alibis. One fellow is in and he don't want to get out the other fellow is out and he wants to get in. Nobody knows what the one that is in would do if he continues in, for no man knows what he would do till a condition arose, and he really faced it. But this thing has been going on for years, 150 I think it was, when George started it. But we always have good men on both sides so just let the voters guess their head off.

514   OVER YOUR SHOULDER

All I know is just what I read in the papers or what I run into as I prowl like a coyote trotting along looking back over my shoulders to see what's going on behind me. You know Ed Borein, the great cowboy etcher of Santa Barbara, Calif.[1] Ed makes the best western etchings of anybody. He is a real cowpuncher, and knows the California "Buckaroo" and the old Mexico "Vaquero" better than any artist living. He has been in Mexico a lot, and in California a lot more. Old Ed swings a pretty mean loop himself and goes to all the calf brandings around Santa Barbara.

I went with him one time down to the Hearst Ranch in old Mexico.[2] He had worked on it many years before. We were with Archie Parks, the manager of the big ranch in California, that the castle is on "Sam Simeon." Archie used to run the Mexico outfit, and it was his first visit back there in years. We sure had a big time. It would take me a week to tell you all about it.

But what started me on all this was telling about what Ed told me. He said an Indian told him that the reason a white man always got lost and an Indian dident was because an Indian always looked back after he passed anything so he got a view of it from both sides. You see the white man just figures that all sides of a thing are the same. That's like a dumb guy with an argument, he don't think there can be any other side only his. That's what you call politicians.

You can learn a lot from what that Indian told Ed besides just how not to get lost. You must never disagree with a man while you are facing him. Go around behind him and look the same way they do when you are facing him. Look over his shoulder and get his viewpoint, then go back and face him and you will have a different idea.

So lately I been trying to look back over my shoulder like a wolf and an Indian. I just been making a trip down through Mexico, Central and South America, and even in an aeroplane, I would look back. (Of course it was mostly looking back at the last place that looked like we could land if the engine stopped.) But I did do quite a bit of looking back.

Now for instance I looked back at Hollywood as I left. Now you would be surprised at Hollywood if you look at it from both sides. As you come up to it and its people, and you see the movie side, all the pain and glitter and makeup, and make believe houses, but as you look back at it, why a lot of those houses have backs to 'em, and people live in 'em, and they don't have any make up, and they eat and sleep and fret and worry about work, and about their children, and everything just like any other place. But you got to look back to see it. Yes sir, there is a lot of pleasure in looking back, and peeping around and trying to see the other fellow's angle. Every guy has an "Angle" on living, and on life, and on everything.

Take the election. Now one side couldent or wouldent want to

Will Rogers and Robert Woods Bliss, United States ambassador to Argentina (second from left), at a dinner given by members of the American community in Buenos Aires in October of 1932.

know really what the other side could do or really thought they could do. Both sides just spent the whole summer hunting up things to cuss the other side on. That the other side might be right in a lot of things never entered their head, in fact they wouldent let it enter it. A politician is not as narrow minded as he forces himself to be. Nobody is going to spoil the country but the people. No man can do it, and all the people are not going to do it, so it's going to run in spite of all the mistakes that can happen to it. Any people that can raise more than you can eat and wear is set for life anyhow.

Sure everybody hasent got as much, but everybody don't need as much. Flying along over Mexico, see all the little adobe huts, raising a little patch of "free hollie beans" a little patch of corn to mash up some meal into and make some "Tortillias" (bisquits to you). Now at first you will say "What in the world kind of an existance is that?"

Well now let's look back over the shoulder and see if we can't see a little more than just the hut, and the Mexican family sitting in the sun. In the first place you never hear of one jumping out of a window when General Motors drops ten points. What the Japs do in Manchuria is no more of his business than it is ours. Only he won't worry about it. A "Burro" in a lope is as fast as he ever went, and he thinks that's fast. A passenger aeroplane at (maybe) 140 is as fast as most of us ever went and we think that's fast. But not to Doolittle or Hawkes.[3] You see everything is by comparison. The old Mexican sleeps at night. Nothing bothers him except maybe a flea, but he can scratch him off. He knows how to reach him, but we don't know how to reach overproduction, unemployment, second mortgages, poor movies, and a thousand and one things that bite us and keep us awake at nights. And we don't know how to scratch 'em off for we don't know just where they are biting us.

No, sir, the world has got a million millionaires that would give a million apiece to the old Mexican to have nothing bothering them but just fleas, and other kindred spirits. So Viva-la-me-he-co.

515   IT WON'T BE LONG NOW

Well Boys it won't be long now. This is the last week of Democracy's campaign. If the boys haven't corraled the votes by now, why they just as well figure that the ones that are out yet are out for the money. The boys that haven't decided by now are waiting for the best offer. From now on till Tuesday is where dough counts. You don't win these late deciders by arguments. You got to lay it on the line for them. They have all, perhaps, collected from one side already and are laying for the other one.

I think the people as a rule have been mighty patient all this summer and fall. They have heard the country saved in every possible form and dialect. There has been men talking over the radio that their own families couldn't understand. Tammany Hall leaders spoke before the microphone without interpreters, which should never have been allowed. Poor old Tammany, as her figure grows less, her dialect becomes more pronounced. She has never been able to make a dent nationally.

Well, I guess after all it's been what they call a clean campaign. A clean campaign is one where each side cleans the other of every possible vestige of respectability. Mr. Hoover rarely if ever mentioned his opponent. He has kinder worked on the "Totally Ignored" system. That is, "I suppose I have an opponent, but as far as I am concerned he does not exist." Roosevelt took the other tack. He knew he had an opponent and he wanted people to know who the opponent was even if he did know some of them had forgotten.

They personally fought very clean (in all but the clinches). Then of course it was each man protect yourself. Mr. Hoover early in the campaign when he first went out to Iowa to speak, asked "For some degree of sportsmanship to be used." It seems they had been saying that he had no ear for the suffering that had gone on during the last three years. Well that was pretty bum propaganda and he had a right to speak out in church to stop it, but it is too bad that politics can't be conducted on a little higher plane. They just won't pay even one atom of credit to the opposition. They are just horse thieves and that's all there is to it. Well they are, but aren't we all?

Now this naturally brings me back to my "Platform." Every party and everybody must have some platform formed even if it's in their minds. Mine is that a president should hold office six years, with no re-election. Stop this thing of a president having to lower his dignity and go trooping around asking for votes to keep him there another term. He has to do it, naturally, but a six-year term with no re-election will be the remedy. Six years gives him time to do something. It takes him four years to find out who is his friends in the senate and house. There is a lot of senators in there for six years. Well, where do they get that way? Look at the saving of all the money, all the time, all the uncertainty of another election. It lessens it one-third. Then pay the man when he goes out one-half of his salary for life. The country should keep an ex-president from bankruptcy if it can keep a railroad or a badly managed bank. Course the cabinet wouldent have much to do on their last summer in office like they do now, but they could hang around their offices and kill time.

The boys have worked mighty hard during this campaign. Pat Hurley boasts that he used to work in a coal mine down home in Oklahoma.[1] Well he never shoveled as hard as he has this summer and fall. He did his all for his boss. Ogden Mills, all of 'em.[2] This cabinet thing might be a cinch for three years, but the last one you earn your oats.

I am anxious to see how the state elections come out. My good friend Dave Ingalls in Ohio, is as fine a young man as ever entered politics, got a tough opponent.[3] Governor White is a good man and there is a real race.[4] There's class to that. Whoever wins that can be proud and the loser need not be ashamed. Trubee Davidson in New York is another fine young man.[5] Course Lieut. Governor is kinder like a co-pilot. After him and the pilot he has to jump and pull their chutes, there is not much he can do. But it may lead him to a better landing some day.

An' we will know lots more in a week from now than we do now. There is going to be a terrible lot of people fooled. I have always said voting is a funny thing, a fellow will lie about it as easy as a golf score. Every candidate in the race on all sides have had enough promises to elect 'em unanimously, but you wait till the votes are counted and let them tell you how many liars there are of legal age.

516   A GRASS CROP AIN'T SO
EASY TO GROW

Well all I know is just what I read in the papers, and we will all be so dog gone glad to be able to read something in the papers from now on. I'll bet there was more useless ink wasted on this dog fight that just ended than there was on the same length of time in the war.

Now honest did you ever read, hear or see as much bunk and applesauce piled into one campaign? There wasent any more truth in over one half of what any campaign so called "Orator" said. If it wasent a "Deliberate Lie," why it was an "Exagerated Falsehood." Now can you tell us that ordinarily intelligent men can stand up there day after day and say, "If the Democrats win this it will bring hardship to every fireside in America, the grass will grow in five hundred streets. It will retard Progress for 100 years." Now a thing like that dident have to be said. Half the towns won't grow grass even if you quit using 'em, that's why they decided to use 'em as towns was

201

because they wouldent grow grass. And as a matter of fact if they would grow grass they would be worth more as a Range than they would as a Town. This thing of growing grass is a kind of a tough job. Did you ever try it? Well you wait till you try to start a lawn sometime and then see how much truth there is in Mr. Hoover's "Grass" speech.

I remember one time out in Higgins, Texas, there was quite an "Amiable Gentleman" worked out on the "Box T" Ranch for the Doyle's. This was in the Winter of 98. (I forget who run that year, but I guess it was Bryan, he was the only name the Democrats could pronounce along during that generation.)[1] I had been temporarily incarcerated in a military institution at Boonville, Missouri.[2] The warden was a mighty fine old gentleman named Thomas Johnston, in fact he is still living and occupies the same position, and has since enlarged his place till its one of the outstanding penal servitudes for Academic learning in the whole middle West, and receives inmates from almost every quarter of the Literary Digest Pole.[3] It was a splendidly organized and conducted place but it dident exactly agree with my high ideals at that time so we severed relations. It was mutual in my part and practically "Super" mutual on theirs.

Having never worked cattle in the Great Lone Star State of Texas, why Billy Johnson, of Canadian, Texas, a cell mate of mine at the time, advised me to go to Higgins, Texas.[4] (Just got word the other day that Billy had passed away. Too bad, fine fellow.) Well Billy told me to go to Frank Ewing's Ranch at Higgins, and he would give me some employment as maid of all work to a group of Texas Heifers.[5] All this is just to tell you how I got to Higgins, for Higgins is a town that you have to explain why and how you got there. All this is gradually leading up to this famous "Grass in the Street" speech of Herbert Hoover's.

Well the "Box T Lad" (that's this sturdy old citizen that worked for 'em out there and had for generations) well the Box T Lad come in for Ranch provisions, driving four awful good mules, and had brought a plow in to get it fixed up to plow a Garden patch at the Ranch on his return. You know in 98 Volstead was still plowing corn up in his home state.[6] In fact he is right back where he started and plowing the same corn, so there was good cheer in a Town in those days. The Box T Lad got full as a goat during the latter end of the evening, after all others were under the table for the night he went to the feed yard and by the assistance of the mules themselves got the harness on 'em, hitched 'em to the plow and in the dead of late night proceeded to plow up the streets of Higgins, the Main Street, the side streets, the cross streets, which in those days were all merged into one, if you plowed up the Main Street you practically had the town turned over. It wasent a long street but it had width. It was built for traffic, so four mule team pulling a trailer wagon could turn with ease. Next morning when the folks got up and found their "Main Stem" thoroughly turned over, suspicion gradually drifted to "The Lad." And between eye openers he remarked, "I thought I would plow her up and sow her in grass, she wasent much good to anybody like she was." So I think that's where Hoover's famous Campaign slogan come from. It was originated with the Box T Lad of Higgins in the Fall of 98.

Some of the other remarks and slogans of the various speakers God knows where they originated, but wherever they originated they will die at the same place, for none of 'em will live. The last campaign brought in religion. This one replaced it with fear. This time they tried to scare you into voting a certain way. Now take that fireside gag about "Affecting every fireside in America." Was it going to bring ruin and disaster to the Democratic Postmasters who would go in? How did he figure that it would affect Roosevelt's fireside? Not exactly dissaster I wouldent think. Well it's over and while everybody is not happy, everybody is at least glad, glad the thing is over.

It takes a great country to stand a thing like that hitting it every four years. When you figure that you have a system where you make business stand still and people go nutty for three months every four years, why somebody who concocted the idea of elections certainly figured out a devastating scheme. The locusts that I saw swarming the Argentine are house flys compared to the destruction to a business by a presidential election. The Candidates are "High Typed Gentlemen" till the contest gets close then the "Brute" comes out in 'em. What starts out to be a nice fight winds up in a street brawl. But it all comes under the heading of Democracy. And as bad as it is it's the best scheme we can think of. So let's all rest up for 36, mow the grass out of the streets, get that dissaster out of those firesides, and start another battle over those Post Offices.

517   REPORT OF THE POST MORTEM

Well all I know is just what I read in the papers and what I hear as I listen to Democrats like mocking birds in the tree tops. I kinder thought that when the votes were counted that we had closed the arguments, but we seem to have just started 'em, so as they are still going over 'em why we just as well join in. You can never be late with a Post Mortem, cause the corpse will always stay dead till you decide on what the cause of his death was. That's one accomodating thing about a corpse.

Now let's start from the beginning. What chance did Mr Hoover have at any time, even before the nominations? Everybody admitted "That if things don't pick up a whole lot why Mr Hoover hasent got a ghost of a chance." Well things dident pick up, everybody knew that. So why did they run him, or I mean rather why did he run himself, for naturally he would be called upon to by the party to run. They never care for the Individual. It's always the old hooey, "For the good of the party."

Now if Mr Hoover had just said, "Now boys I have done all I can for the good of the old Party. I have struggled with it, fought every type of hard luck that was ever invented, including some invented by my own party. Now I know the tide is against me, so why lead me to the slaughter? If people want a change as they evidently seem too, why maby we could lead them to accept a change in our own Party, so just let me drop out. In fact I don't care for another term."

Now you see where he would have been. Course you will say, "Yes Will, but this is a second guess you are making. It's easy to tell after it's all over what might have been done." But it's not a second guess. It was plain to him and all of 'em all the time. The whole thing hinged on "Things Picking Up." Well what was to make 'em pick up? If they hadent picked up in three years why were they going to pick up this Fall? A slight gain wouldent have meant a thing. It would have had to rained dollars to make everyone think that the real turn had come.

Away before the Convention in Chicago, I used to ask "Well why does Mr Hoover run? You all say that if the election was tomorrow that he would be overwhelmingly defeated, that the people just want a change. Why don't he step out and let me nominate somebody else in his place and save that beating?"

Well they would always tell me, "Well Will, don't you see that would be admitting that the Party had failed? And we couldent do that." You see it all gets back to the "Party." They couldent have the "Party" admit anything. No sir he must run, whether he wants to or not, "We must stand for our principals."

So another good man was sent out to bite the dust. I'll bet you that Mr Coolidge would have ducked 'em if he had been in there under these same conditions. He would have "Not Choosed" right in their face. He would have told 'em, "The running don't look good, and I am not going in just for the sake of running second." The

"Good of the Party" could have gone and jumped in the lake as far as he would have been concerned. They wouldent have made a Roman Holiday out of him. He would have said "Boys throw some other good Republican Christian to the lions. I see the handwriting on the wall in electric letters."

You see you could get over some such resignation as this, "Citizens I am afraid that my administration has not been entirely to your satisfaction, and there seems to be a decided element in favor of a change. I have no alabi's to offer, I have no excuses, I have done my very best. It seems that it should have been more. So for the good of all concerned I decline to be a candidate for re-election. Yours, Herbert Hoover."

But the "Party" wouldent have allowed such a sane and sensible course. It would have put them in the hole instead of Mr Hoover. He would have had the sympathy of everyone, but the "Party" kept hanging onto the idea that "Things" might pick up. They did. Democratic support picked up. But on the other hand there just seems to be something about running for President that you can never get out of a fellow's head. He never seems to figure his chances. It can be on an "Off Year" or an "On Year" or "Leap Year" and just nominate him, and he is perfectly tickled to death. That he will wind up by just being a defeated candidate never seems to enter his head. That "The time is not ripe for it" is as foreign to his thoughts as the moon.

But it's over and I guess everybody did the best they could according to what they had to do with. But I did hate to see a man that had been as conscientious as Mr Hoover had, take a beating like that. He dident deserve it, he deserved a straightforward declination to run again.

518   AND HERE'S HOW IT ALL HAPPENED

Well all I know is just what I read in the papers or what I see as I prowl hither and thither. With the election over everybody seems to have settled down to steady argument.

The old "Hide Bound" Republicans still think the world is just on the verge of coming to an end, and you can kinder see their angle at that for they have been running things for all these years.

I got a letter the other day from a very very prominent business man in Los Angeles, Mr. Frank Garbutt, the man that has made running of clubs a science, and not just a business.[1] He owns every club from the great Los Angeles Athletic Club to Beach Clubs, to Golf Clubs, to Polo Clubs. Now Frank is the longest headed man you ever saw. Yet he said there wouldent be a bank open in five months after Roosevelt took office. I don't know what these fellows figure the Democrats are going to do with the Country.

You would think a lot of folks would have their passage booked to some foreign land till the next election when they could get these Democrats back among the unemployed. Why they was in for eight years here not so long ago, from 1912 to 20. Course I was just a boy and can't remember back that far but I have heard my dear old Dad say there was some mighty good times including a war thrown in for good measure.

Personally I never could see much difference in the two "gangs." They used to be divided by the tarriff. The tarriff was originally supposed to aid the man that manufactured things. Well, the Democrats of those days dident manufacture anything but arguments, so they was against the tarriff, but the South woke up one day and saw some spinning looms advertised in a Montgomery-Ward menu card, so they sent and got some and started spinning their own cotton.

Well they had cheap water power, cheap coal, cheap labor, and the Yankees started moving their shops down from the North. Well the Democrats woke up on another morning with a tarriff problem on their hands. The South had gone industrial in a big way. Well they started talking about a tarriff in bigger words than the North, so now that the South has got 'em some smoke stacks where they used to have some mule sheds, why they are just tarriffing themselves to death. So, that left the principal dividing line between the two parties shot to pieces. You can't tell one from the other now. Course the last few years under Mr. Coolidge and Mr. Hoover there had grown the old original idea of the Republican Party that was the party of the rich. And I think that was the biggest contributing part in their defeat.

I think the general run of folks had kinder got wise to that. In the old days they could get away with it, but of late years the rich had diminished till their voting power wasent enough to keep a minority vote going. This last election was a revulsion of feeling that went back a long way ahead of the hard times. Mr. Hoover reaped the benefits of the arrogance of the party when it was going strong.

Why after that twenty-eight election there was no holding 'em. They really did think they had "hard times" cornered once and for all. Merger on top of merger. Get two nonpaying things merged and then issue more stock to the public. Consolidations and "Holding Companies." Those are the "Inventions" that every voter that had

206

bought during the "Cockoo" days were gunning for at this last election.

Saying that all the big vote was just against hard times is not all so. They was voting against not being advised that all these foreign loans was not too solid. They was voting because they had never been told or warned to the contrary that every big consolidation might not be just the best investment. You know the people kinder look on our Government to tell 'em and kinder advise 'em. And many an old bird got sore at Coolidge, but could only take it out on Hoover. Big business sure got big, but it got big by selling its stocks and not by selling its products. No scheme was halted by the Government as long as somebody would buy the stock. It could have been a plan to deepen the Atlantic ocean and it would have had the indorsement of the proper department in Washington, and the stocks would have gone on the market.

This election was lost four and five and six years ago not this year. They dident start thinking of the old common fellow till just as they started out on the election tour. The money was all appropriated for the top in the hopes that it would trickle down to the needy. Mr. Hoover was an engineer. He knew that water trickled down. Put it uphill and let it go and it will reach the dryest little spot. But he dident know that money trickled up. Give it to the people at the bottom and the people at the top will have it before night anyhow. But it will at least have passed through the poor fellow's hands. They saved the big banks but the little ones went up the flue.

No Sir, the little fellow felt that he never had a chance, and he dident till November the eighth, and did he grab it? The whole idea of Government relief for the last few years has been to loan somebody more money, so they could go further in debt. It ain't much relief to just transfer your debts from one party to another adding a little more in the bargain. No, I believe the "Boys" from all they had and hadent done had this coming to 'em.

519   SIGHTSEEING WITH ODD

Well all I know is just what I read in the papers, and what I see hither and thither. Was in New York here not long ago, and I rang up O. O. McIntyre.[1] Amon G. Carter (the man who unconsciously elected "Ma" Furgeson govenor of Texas) well, Amon was in New York at the time kinder dodging his own paper's editorials, so we visited O. O. McIntyre.[2] I hadent seen him in a long time, and I had heard he was kinder feeble and grouchy, and was doing well enough to have the gout along with it, so for old times sake I thought I would see if he was still living. My acquaintance with him went away back to the Zeigfeld midnight frolic days, when he was our press agent. All a press agent had to do for Mr. Zeigfeld was to see that the war got on the front page along with Mr. Zeigfeld's girls.[3]

Well Odd, (that's his name, Odd, Odd). Both O's stand for Odd. He was odd enough to stand for another O at birth. But his folks not knowing that he would get odder as he got older, thought double odd would be enough to start on. He comes from away out in Ohio. You see Ohio has two O's in it, too. When Odd was born out in Ohio their alphabet dident consist of much else but O's. So when they give a child an initial it had to have an O in it. He was born at a town called Golopolois, Ohio. So you see those Ohioans do the best they can on what O's they got. He left there with the first Ford and never gets back there much. You see when I first met him I was just a boy working in the chorus of Zeigfeld's show.

But let's get down to some modern data. I was in New York on my way from South America and I had heard so much about the Odd Odd McIntyre's apartment. It's one of the show places of New York, and it's located on Park Avenue, which is the fashionable street this year. Well he is away up in the top of one of those. It's where you can own your own apartment, even if it's in with a lot of others. His deed calls for apartment 96, located 345 feet straight up from where the ground would be on Park Avenue if there was any dirt on it.

There is more dirt on the people on Park Avenue than there is the houses are built on. Well let's get back to Odd's deed, it reads 345 straight up. Then the deed reads straight north till you hit apartment 97. Then you go west till you run into just space. Then the deed turns you south till you hit a bathroom, you come out of the bathroom keep straight ahead till you hit a Henry the Eighth crossed with a Roy Howard room, that puts you back at your original corner.[4] Then your deed in a thing like that has got to tell how high you run, after your floor originally started at 345 feet. It says you go straight up till you hear knocking on the next apartment floor above asking McIntire to keep those dogs still. Now that ought to give you a pretty good idea of the McIntires' apartment boundary. You don't need a road map to find it, you want a sextant and plumming line.

Well I looked up a sight-seeing tour place and got a ticket to go through this apartment. There is certain days of the week and certain hours that you can go through. Well Amon he was tagging along, he said he had been up there when you dident have to pay, but Amon kinder stretches things sometimes. Amon, never got in as a guest. Well there was a big crowd got off this bus we was on, and it took elevators to haul us all up.

Mind you, he don't get any money out of this. It's a kind a charity fund that goes to men who want pearl gray spats but can't buy 'em, but the whole thing is just a darn liberal and fine thing of Odds to let people see him at work and at play, and see his modest little home. There is a lecturer goes with you, and he points out everything and introduces you to Odd, and Odd is mighty gracious and nice to everybody the same as he is nice and considerate to everyone in his writings. Old Amon Carter was gaping all over the place, trying to find at which room Odd's property stopped and Vanderbilt's started.[5]

There was a series of glass topped tables, and desks, with nothing under 'em, just a kind of a skeleton frame of silver and glass all over it. No drawers or anything only just the glass top. It was built to look for things under, a collar button anywhere under it would show up like a spitoon. Everything looked awful clean, and in good taste.

Odd has on a kinda blue ensemble. (Jump on your dictionaries you Rogers readers.) An ensemble is a kind of a kimono, only it's got a belt around it and that makes it masculine gender. He had on kinder fur boots, very roomy and worth-while. His hair is just starting to turn black again after being white for years. I was awfully interested in his dog kennels. They are in the same place he lives in, and are kept just as clean and nice.

He has two dogs, one a bull dog that can't hear. Odd used to try his jokes on him and the dog went deaf purposely, I had never seen a deaf dog before. But he don't show his affliction at all. Just as many flees as if he could hear 'em on him. The other was a little white Sealingham. He can hear, I don't know why, but he can, so he hears everything then tells the other dog. One of 'em is named Billy and has been to Europe more times than Peggy Joyce.[6] The Sealyham has never been off Park Avenue. He is just a country dog. The maid had just had 'em over to Roxies to see the show, and she brought 'em in and cleaned all the Odd things off em.

Odd asked Amon and I to stay after the other tourists had gone, so we sit there for awhile and talked about old times, when people wasent ashamed to say they was Republicans. He is the most widely read writer on New York, or anywhere else in the U.S. He has got more clothes and more different words than any writer writing outside of a book. He has suits for every sentence.

I go all over the Country, and I hear him quoted more than any man. He has a lovely wife, but she was out that day.[7] Everybody knows him, and everybody likes him. He goes to all the first nights, and pays for his tickets.

He is not a critic, so he can see the last act. He's got a Rolls Royce car and he delivers all the high brow writers to their homes to give 'em a treat from the subway, I am sure glad I went. I think it's Tuesdays and Thursdays from three to five, and it's embraced in a tour that starts from the Waldorf Astoria Hotel. When we was coming down another party was going up. It was mostly friends, book and play writers who write about columnists and try to sell 'em. They was going up for a sandwitch. So don't miss this when you go to New York.

520   CHINA AND THE BUCKS

Well all I know is just what I read in the papers, or what I run onto here and there. I was just sitting here awhile ago reading a Literary Digest that was about a week old. I always read it and Time Magazine. Keep loaded up on them and you got a pretty good idea what's going on. The reason they are good is because in your local papers which you should all read, there might be things that they dident happen to cover. And these weekly magazines do.

Well I was just reading a long article in the Digest about Pearl Buck the author of not only the "Book of the Month" or book of the year, but the book of our Time.[1] Well just a few days before leaving New York just before the election I had the pleasure of Mrs. Rogers and I to spend an hour or more with this very remarkable woman. How it come about was that last year when I was over China, I had read her book on the boat, when I wasent argueing with Floyd Gibbons. Well I thought it was the greatest thing I had ever read, so I talked to lots of people over there about her. A Dr. Donaldson on the train from Peking to Shanghai, he had known the family of this girl for years.[2] He and they both were early missionaries out there.

Well I wanted to meet her while out there. She lived up at Nanking. That's the capital of China, or was that week. It used to be Peking, and if the southern crowd keep getting stronger I guess it will be Canton.

Well I wanted to go up to Nanking anyhow. I had come through there on the train from Peking, but dident get to see much. So I called up the school where they live. Her husband is a professor in a big University there, he has made a study of Agriculture, graduated at Cornell.[3]

By the way that always struck me as being the oddest place for an Agriculture course. You just kinder look for them out in the Middle West where they raise something. Well I got in communication with them up at Nanking and was to go up and see her on a certain day. Well I was going to fly. There was a line of sea planes that went right up the Yangste River. Well I got to the place to take off that day and it was raining and cloudy all day and I dident get to go.

I was leaving on the boat the next day for Singapore, then for the flight across India, and all points west. I talked to Mr. Buck, her husband, over the phone, but not seeing her out there was a great disappointment for she is one person that wrote a book about a country, and even that country liked it. I never heard a derogatory (that's a pretty hot word for me ain't it) word about the book. The Chinese say it was true to life and characters.

Well her publishers knew what a great admirer I was of hers, so when I landed from South America and Mrs. Rogers met me in New York, why they phoned us and said Mrs. Buck would be in New York at a certain time and would see us.

Well we were tickled to death. Well we went over to her hotel. Her husband is taking a special course again at Cornell. He is quite an Agricultural authority in China, and has held some very important government missions in regard to trying to get them straightened out on what to raise. Well she too I think was taking some course up there. So she stayed up there most all the time. She just come down to New York occasionally, she dident like it so much. She is not so hot for this hero worship business. She is very modest, wonderfully interesting to talk to. She almost speaks with an accent, she has spoken Chinese so long.

After "Sons," which was another powerful book, she is working on the third and last of the series that brings it up to now. You know if you know your Chinese there is quite a big communistic hold in certain parts of China. The influence is growing rapidly. Well they said they would like her in finishing up, or bringing this same family up-to-date. They want her to show that it was through communism that China would eventually be saved. (I don't know what they are supposed to be saved from. They got the best mode of life and living in the world now.)

But somebody is always "Saving China" from something or other. She said in "Good Earth" that while she dident write it in Chinese, that her thoughts were all in Chinese, that is her characters were all talking to each other in Chinese, then as she translated the very words into English before writing them down, that there is where some of the reviewers got the idea that it was Old Testament writing, or a throw-back from these words being the very ones the Chinese utter, with a literal translation.

This next one will bring in the modern things that have pestered China during our times, including the American missionaries I imagine, for she is like everyone out there. They doubt in their own hearts if they should have ever gone. She claims they send the wrong ones, the ones who couldent make a living here. She claims a dumb missionary hasent any more business in China than he has here, in fact not as much.

She is for specialists in that particular work out there. Well she was a-talking right up my alley. For from all I could ever hear abroad, and here at home, this thing of making Baptists or Holy Rollers out of some nationalities that has had his certain brand of religion when folks over here was living up in the side of a cliff like a mountain goat is not so good. Most of 'em are Christians over there just as long as the missionaries hand out the rice. The Sioux Indians could go out there and siouxise a bunch of 'em as long as they could demonstrate their religion with some grub. You can take all the Methodists who's eyes slant out there, and let 'em get a better offer for the old stomach and you will have a bunch of back-sliders on your hands. I think she feels that the same efforts, money, and time devoted on us local heathen here at home, and it would have been better all around. Course these folks here that work so hard to send them and do all this, they mean well, they are fine conscientious folks, they got a heart as big as anybody, but it's in the wrong country.

521   NOW, ABOUT THESE CRITICS

You know in the radio it's hard to tell just how anyone's stuff is going. That is they have no real way of checking up as to whether anyone is listening in or not. But us fellows that write on things of a political nature, we have an absolute way of knowing just who is reading our stuff. We can check up on it to the individual, because each one writes you a letter telling you how "Wrong" you are.

Everybody sure was "jumpy" during this late uprising. They had a vote in their pocket and chip on their shoulder, and any insinuation you made against their "hero" was just too bad for you. For instance, they would write to the paper, "I read Will Rogers, but why does he have to dabble in politics. Let him stay on funny stuff where he belongs." Well if they would just stop to think I have written on nothing but politics for years, you never heard me on a mother in law joke. It was always about national or international affairs.

Well I have been in almost every country in the last few years. I have talked with prominent men of those countrys, our Ambassadors, or Ministers, and I would have to be pretty dumb to not soak up some information. For instance I was in Japan, China and Manchuria. I wrote one paragraph that was copied all over the Far East, and editorials written on it. Well I couldent have done it by staying in Hollywood or in an editorial room. I had to be over there to learn it. It was, "China owns the lot, Japan owns the house that's on it, now who is going to furnish the policeman?"

Still you will read some letter where it says, "Why does Will Rogers butt into these international problems he knows nothing about?"

Where do these other fellows get all of their vast stores of knowledge. I never hear of 'em going any place. If I write about Mexico, I have been down there half a dozen times. Nicaragua, I been there twice and found out things that I couldent ever have by reading about it. Crossed India at the heighth of their troubles, been in Europe and talked debts till I had everybody's angle over there. There is not a state in this country that I am not in ever once in awhile. Talk to everyone, get the ranchers' and farmers' angle.

Those New York writers should be compelled to get out once in their lifetime and get the "folks" angle. I know and have known all the time that the real backbone people of America wasent going to cancell any debts. They would never have given the moratorium if it had come to a vote of them. All your Lippmans and all your cancellationists in New York can write their economic theories that want too, but they dident know a thing about our people.[1] They said "How you going to collect it?, Europe won't pay."

Any old farmer knew that if you owed a debt and had money and dident pay it, you couldent do but one thing and that was default, so the minute the word "default" was brought in why you heard a different tune. I learned on my trips to Europe and to South America too, that our international bankers had hotels full of their agents begging countrys to take a loan, then back home and sold them to the people, so they got their commissions both ways. Go to Europe and it's the first thing you will find out, but not here, you don't learn that.

I said that nothing would come out of the meeting of Mr Hoover and Roosevelt on the debts. A true guess, but at election time you make people sore if you tell 'em the truth. Republicans got sore at me because Roosevelt was elected, and the cancellationists got sore at me because they had to pay. I guess that was all my fault? Now as far as showing any dissrespect for our presidents or high officials, that is only an excuse, it's something I am saying that they don't like, it's not something I am saying that the President or some official don't like.

I have told more jokes than would go in this room if they were written on tissue paper, about Mr Coolidge, yet he knows that I have the greatest regard for him personally, and for his ability. Mr Hoover I wish every critic had to read every nice thing I have said about him during his administration. I know him, admire him, and I think he will tell you that I have been fair. I have spoken hundreds of times about the bad breaks he got. We have been a fortunate nation, we have always had good presidents.

You are going to find from now on that this party thing is a lot of hooey. People are voting policies now, not partys. We are living in a time when if one or the other of these partys don't start delivering an economic government to the people, they are both going out on their ears. The Democrats are only in for a trial. If they don't make good out they go. It's perhaps too bad that sentiment plays no part in our elections, but it don't, it's results, or out.

Now I read politics, talk politics, know personally almost every prominent politician, like 'em and they are my friends, but I can't help it if I have seen enough of it to know that there is "some" Baloney in it. Now I am going to be like an umpire, or referee. I am going to keep on doing the same as I have in the past. I am going to call 'em like I see 'em. If I don't see things your way, well why should I?

I hope I never get so old that I can't peep behind the scenes and see the amount of politics that's mixed in this medicine before it's dished out to the people as "pure statesmanship." Politics is the best show in America and I am going to keep on enjoying it. If there is some people that can't enjoy it why they are missing something.

So on with the show. We will have many a laugh in the next four years, for there is one thing about the Democrats, they never put on a dull show. But always remember this, that as bad as we sometimes think our government is run, it's the best run one I ever saw.

So this winds the whole thing up. There has only been two that has dissagreed with me, the "rabid" Republican, that was just sore at the world anyhow, no matter what you said, and the other is the cancellationist. My lack of humor, lack of English, lack of good taste, and all the other things they accuse me of, is a lot of bunk. Let the same things be said in favor of their opinion, and I would be a great guy. So now we got the whole thing straightened out. He is a "die hard" Republican, or a cancellationist, but you are still going to get the truth.

214

Well all I know is just what I read in the papers, or what I run into high and low. We had a big time out at our studio the other day. The Fox studios where I labor is the only studio that has been built entirely since the talkies come in. It's all new and all talkie. Well in most studios they just have little cubby holes or places for writers. That is the writer has never really had a place in commemoration with his surroundings. Well Mr. Winnifred Sheehan conceived the idea of building them a real building all to themselves, nothing in it but writers, and we had a big dedication of it the other day.[1] Mr. Rupert Hughes the eminent author come over and spoke in behalf of the authors.[2] That is he took it, he said he would be glad to receive it in behalf of the authors for they had no "club house" as it is, and that this free one was very acceptable to them. I know you have all read Rupert Hughes, but you missed much if you have not heard him in one of his delightful speeches. He was at his best on this day.

I can remember when he come out here first it was with Mr. Sam Goldwyn's "Troop of Eminent Authors."[3] Among them was even Materlink, "The Old Bee Man."[4] I was working at Goldwyn's Studio at the time. Of course none of them were brought out for any of my pictures, but I could at least talk to them. A fine bunch of fellows you never met. I never did get to read that beestory of Materlink's, but I met a "Bee Man" on the boat going to China last year with a contingent of bees and he told me that just reading the book had put him in the bee business. He claimed a bee was more interesting than a person, and he looked me right in the face when he said it. I am going to read it sometime, it's got love, and sex and gangsters bee's and everything in it.

Well, Rupert Hughes stuck out here, and it's part and parcel of our industry. We hate to call it that, it sounds so sordid. He is really a co-artist with us, in this constructive photography we carry on.

Rex Beach was another that was tremendously successful, and is yet with his stories for the movies.[5] Rex was responsible for my little toe hold on this eighth science. I played by request of Mrs. Rex Beach in one of his storys called, "Laughing Bill Hyde." The part was rather that of a crook, who received money under false pretenses. Mrs. Beach had seen my little act in the follies, so she decided that I was the one to do naturally this crook who obtained money under false pretense.

Rex Beaches "Spoilers" are made or remade every time a company had to absolutely have a new batch of dough. Beach was and is today a "Natural" screen writer. His stuff is pictorial and it moves.

Well then that day another great favorite appeared and helped us out on the dedication. It was Fred Niblo, the monologist, lecturer, traveler.[6] And great screen director. He made some of the biggest screen hits of our times. Fred is one of our top hole masters of ceremonies, and that's taking in a lot of territory, for Rupert Hughes and Conrad Nagel are just as good.[7] In fact they are three ties.

Fred spoke in behalf of the directors who have to "do" the authors pieces, no matter what kind of rooms they have been written in. Fred said he could remember the days when they were all under foot, that folks were tramping on 'em, loads of 'em would come from New York, and no one knew who or what they were. Then some detective would discover they were authors. Then the laugh would be on the studio. He never thought he would live to see the day they would have a house of their own to write in. In fact he doubted if they could write under happy and beautiful surroundings. Mr. Hughes thought the place resembled an institution where you confine people for various maladys. Niblo thought it a fine place to hide from the producers.

It is a beautiful building, and when you tourists come to the coast you must see it. It's more French than Shakesperean, as the French plays rather lend themselves to "Box Office" than the Bard's stuff. Lots of people like to read Shakespeare, but that's the trouble, he appeals to the people who can read, and not to the ones who want it read to 'em by an actor, either on or off the screen. The successful author is the one who can write for the ones who can't read.

We have some splendid men out here from the East and everywhere and I am sure that they will under such pleasant surroundings turn you folks out some fine screen entertainment, so if they don't why you write 'em and tell 'em that I told you that they had lovely quarters, and that you looked for something great. As to the acting, that is of course as always "The Same." Little Miss Janet Gaynor did the unveiling and while she dident lay the cornerstone she did unveil it.[8] In fact two, we had two cornerstones. That was in case you was standing where you couldent see 'em unveil one you could see the other. She did a gracious and dignified act with it. The whole thing has kinder led me to decide to take up reading. I mean reading in English, not newspaper reading.

A book dropped into my hands the other day called "The West Is Still Wild" written by our ace writer of the coast, Harry Carr.[9] No one knows our Southwest like this man. He came with the Mission Padres and will leave with the last movie camera. What Materlink can do with humanizing the bee this fellow can do with a rattlesnake, broncho, or a Mexican hoot owl. He knows the scandal of the cliff dwellers, he is the Walter Winchell of Prehistoric cavortings.[10]

Oh I tell you I am going to read more. I am at least going to read the titles of some of these books anyhow. We have all got to read more and remember less. The trouble people used to read something then remember it, but things are changing. So many books are being published that you couldent possibly remember 'em, so you just got to read 'em. Then books are not written to be remembered anyhow, they are written just to be sold, not even to be read.

523   ## WE GOT SOME FINE STATES
IN OUR COUNTRY

Well all I know is just what I read in the papers, or what I see
here and there. Well we finally all of us about got X-mas out of our
hair. Our little troop of children come ganging in here from the four
corners. Got one boy, Bill Jr., the oldest, at the University of Arizona,
a very fine school, well liked and spoken of by everybody that knows
about it. You know that Arizona is going to really be understood and
get somewhere some day. It and New Mexico, they are similar in lots
of respects, but they are different from all the other states. They have
great climates; almost any kind you like. They have a romance in
history that out dates anything we have in our whole country, and
there is just enough Indians to keep the whole thing respectable.

They are both states that kinder wear well on you. Don't just
look out of the train and condemn 'em. It just looks like nothing
couldent live by looking out of a sleeper window. They built those
railroads through the mangiest parts, so it wouldent spoil the good
land. You know you can just look out of taxicab windows in parts of
New York City and wonder what people live on, the same as you can
in Arizona. There is many a canyon in N.Y. where the grass is short,
and it looks like people packed their grub a long ways. Ah, but, darn
it, there is some great country everywhere.

There is a fine comedy picture out that shows what would happen if a bunch of people received a million dollars apiece. Well now
just suppose that by some good chance you did fall heir to a nice little
nest egg, and you wanted to go somewhere and build you a home, a
farm, or a ranch, and you dident previously have any particular place
or ties that bound you to one locality. I tell you if you was to have a
good car and the money to travel on, and also to build the place when
you found it, you would be absolutely "nuts" before you settled
down. We havent got a state in our whole Union but what has some
great advantages that no other state possesses.

New England, the most beautiful place in the summer time, and
for those that like their snow it's fine all the year round. Up state New
York is great. All the Middle West, with its rolling prairies and big

grain farms. The Northwest, just anything in the way of scenery you want, any crops, any views. The whole Pacific Coast and its adjoining mountainous states. California, the Chamber of Commerce will take that up with you. But Nevada, there is a state that should be given a whole paragraph on its own. Mining and stock raising! There is two bunches of folks that just "anybody" don't fit in with. They are kinder the aristocracy of labor. Nevada has a freedom and an independent spirit that is slowly reaching out all over our land. Utah is a great state and those Mormons are fine substantial citizens. Colorado is our grand stand seat to see our world from.

Texas? It's too big to be even under Jim Ferguson.[1] Texas has got everything that any other state has and then "Ma" and "Jim" besides. Oklahoma? A lack of vocabulary is all that stops me. I should have stayed in Oxford another year to really have done justice to Oklahoma. Alfalfa Bill Murray has taken what was once just a prairie dog town and he has populated it with emigrants from every political faith known to mankind.[2] Why there is Republicans who live so high up in them skyscrapers of Tulsa and Oklahoma City that they ain't been down to the ground since November eighth. Wilder than the Zulus in Africa. Bill has put a bounty on 'em now, and we are either going to house break 'em or yoke 'em up to a gentle Republican and bring 'em in. Kansas lays to our north, and there she lays, and you can never tell what she is laying for. It's got more good newspapers and less people that can read 'em than almost any place. They can read the politics, but they never was taught to read anything else cause there wasent nothing else in Kansas.

Old Missouri? Some mighty poor farms but mighty good schools. You can learn something, but you can't raise much. Boonville, (Kemper Military Academy) one of the finest Military schools anywhere. I was two years there, one year in the guard house, and the other in the fourth reader. One was about as bad as the other. Great old educator there, T. A. Johnston.[3] Famous and deservedly so. Neosho, Mo? The school I went to there has blown up, and I did all I could while there to assist it in doing so. Lots of politics in Missouri. Wherever you find poor soil you will always find politics. When you see you ain't going to raise anything, you just sit down at the end of the row and cuss the party in power. There is a lot of fertile ground in that historical old state too, but it's from the limestone ridges where the long winded old congressmen come from.

Arkansaw' scenery, vacation land, fertility, beautiful women. I traded a wagon bed full of hickory nuts for one of the prettiest ones in the state at Rogers, Ark., twenty four years ago. I expect with the depression on like it is, a gunnysack full would get you one now. But

219

not as good one as I got. Arkansaw has got a lot of gallantry mixed in with their good sense too. They got the only bonifide lady senatoress in captivity. She is a conscientious sensible little woman; Hattie Caraway, and Wall Street don't know her address.[4]

Was you ever down in Long Valley?[5] There is a wonderful, beautiful, poetical valley along the length of our great Mississippi River. Cities, beautiful prosperous ones, hanging moss from century old trees. Charming and delightful people in this valley. It's not called Long Valley on any of your maps, it's labelled Lousiana. But "Long Valley" is a much more beautiful name and every time election rolls around, the people signify the fact by writing "Long" from the top to the bottom of their ticket. You would love "Long Valley." It's a paradise. Some famous old poem was laid there among its people.[6] I don't just remember whether it was Ivanhoe or Gunga Din but it was a good one. Oh I wish I had time to go over all those old states. I been in all of 'em. I love 'em. Each as I said has got something. Something different. Look at Mississippi, with Pat Harrison and the state sales tax.[7] Not a senator. He is an institution. But I'll get into the others later.

524   SERMON TO A PREACHER BY
JUST A "COMEDIAN"

A preacher named Rev. Grant, of Simpson Methodist Church, of Minneapolis, Minn., wrote me, "I am speaking on you and your life's pholosophy at a Sunday evening vesper service, in our great Church of two thousand members.[1] Is there any word of greeting? I would appreciate it.

Yours, A. Raymond Grant, Pastor."

Well the same night I answered his letter I had to write my weekly Sunday article. So I couldent see why one "greeting" or "alabi" wouldent do for both. He had been mighty nice and I appreciated it. So I got strung out and in my long winded way, I sounded like a preacher without a stop signal. I wrote:

"Dear Rev. Grant: I got your letter saying you was 'speaking on me,' but you dident say why? There is an awful lot of different ways to speak on me, and all of 'em be pretty near true at that.

My life has got more angles than a cat. You may be one of these Republicans, (as most of the Ministers have gone into politics). You may be one that blamed me for electing Mr. Roosevelt, or you might be one of those Democrats who blamed me for electing Mr. Hoover four years ago.

This is kinder the public season to jump on me if anything has gone wrong, everything from a scarcity of skunk hides in the Northwest to a predominating amount of girl babies in Pennsylvania. You see, Rev. Grant, I think I am as independent as any one writing. I have as many Republican as Democratic papers, as many readers that can't read as can. The editorial policies of these great dailies mean nothing to me, I am going to call 'em like I see 'em.

I think I have complimented many a worthy thing in my time, and I have taken a shot at a lot of "hooey," I am not against it mind you, as it just seems that it takes so much of it in every business. And they are all my friends, I am proud of the fact there is not a human being that I have got it in for. I never met a man I dident like.

I got no "Philosophy." I don't even know what the word means. The Fourth Reader, (McGuffy's) is as far as I ever got in schools.[2] I am not bragging on it, I am thoroughly ashamed of it for I had every opportunity. Everything I have done has been by luck, no move was premeditated. I just stumbled from one thing to another. I might have been down. I dident know at the time, and I don't know yet, for I don't know what "Up" is. I may be lower than I ever was, I don't know. I may be making the wrong use of any little talent (if any) that I accidentally have. I don't know.

I was raised predominately a Methodist, but I have traveled so much, mixed with so many people in all parts of the world, I don't know now just what I am. I know I have never been a non-be-liever. But I can honestly tell you that I don't think that any one religion is the religion.

If I am broadminded in any way (and I hope I am in many) but I do know that I am broadminded in a religious way. Which way you serve your God will never get one word of argument or condemnation out of me. There has been times when I wished there had been as much real religion among some of our creeds as there has been vanity, but that's not in any way a criticism.

I feel mighty proud that you will discuss me in your tebernacle. The joke is more on you than on me. I thought the only time I would ever make the pulpit as a conversational subject was when I finished, and then only by one minister who's charges for kind words would be deducted from the estate.

I feel like I did the other day when they told me I was in the British "Who's Who." There was no way I could sue 'em or make 'em retract, and there is no way to keep you from gabbing around about anything you like. I heard a fellow preach one time on Jesse

James, the outlaw, and I left the Church wanting to hold up everything and everybody I run into.

So if you are such a persuasive preacher, you are liable to turn out a flock of Swedish comedians up around Minneapolis. Don't make the life too rosy, for with the politicians horning in, our comedian business is overcrowded as it is. I preached one time in a church in Cleveland, Ohio. But the collection dident warrant me carrying it on as a steady profession. Preaching should not only be done by a preacher, but by a man like Gandi, who can do fasting when necessary.

Minneapolis has always been one of my pet cities, they have been good to me on every occasion I was ever there. They have not only laughed at me, but paid to laugh at me.

Love to all your congregation, including the ones that are not paid up, it's just hard times, they mean well, Parson. They got just as much religion as the paid up ones, so you will just have to trust 'em, and give 'em a little preaching "on time."

You see preaching is one of the few things that folks have never been able to dole out exactly what it's worth anyhow. Some preachers ought to pay admission to get into the church themselves, but as rule preachers do a mighty good job and are underpaid.

But there is a lot of dignity about the clerical (newspaper) profession that you would have to work for years for in any other line. But you are sympathetic, useful, instructive, and the most worthwhile profession ever invented.

I wish your church a happy and charitable '33, or any other years. No use being stingy in our wishes. Pick out as many years as you want and I will wish you good luck with all of 'em.

Yours, Will.

525   FOOTBALL, BRALE, AND POLITICS

Well all I know is just what I read in the papers and what I see here and there. Well sir, last week I went out to our "Rose Bowl" to see a great football game. Our Rose Bowl is down in a rocky hollow; there is not a rose in a mile of it, but they do replace their roses with some mighty finely developed football players.

Pittsburgh come out here twice before and run second and it naturally was a hard blow to the boys to get such a beating again but say they dident get near that bad beating; they made a great showing. They were as game a bunch of boys as you ever saw. They had two ends that were in the Southern California territory so much that Coach Howard Jones wanted to put California Sweaters on 'em.[1]

Then they had a halfback named Heller, that was really that.[2] But they just happened to come on a bad year. This guy named Howard Jones out here can coach. He could take me for three weeks and have me throwing Red Grange for a loss.[3] And then California had a great team. A lot of the things we brag on out here is the hooey, but I want to tell you that this football team of U.S.C. is a pip. Pasadena put on their marvelous parade in the morning. They always do a great job of it.

Now, that's enough about California, what about the rest of the Country? That fellow Hiram Johnson, our senator from out here, made a great speech in the Senate on the war debts a few days ago.[4] Now there is a fellow that has always had the dope on a lot of our international affairs.

Hoover has always had an international learning, his life, his work, have always been of a European angle. Well Johnson seems to have always known that, and he has always had a bunch of facts to bring out at various times that just showed how the ball was rolling. And right in the middle of the argument up pops Borah, and brings out something that a lot had heard all the time, that was that there was some kind of an understanding between Lavalle and us.[5] But what does most of us know about those debts? You could argue 'em till they are paid and you wouldent get it straightened out. There never was a debt that wasent at some time or another missunderstood. Every debt, be it personal, or any other kind always winds up in one side feeling they got the worst of it. So debts are sorter like "Why are you a Democrat?", or "What ever induced you to be a Republican?" So we will leave the debts to those that can really settle 'em.

Say, by the way, I got the finest letter tonight. It was from a blind girl, and she sent me one of my Sunday articles and it was all written out in Braille. She said the article had impressed her and she wanted it handed around in her own language. Well, by golly, I sure did appreciate that.

She sent me also the alphabet. It has all the dots, (peruf-u-u) I can't speel the thing. I mean it had the dots punched pretty near through with something, and it leaves a raised part that they can feel of with their sensitive fingers. And just read it right off.

I must write to my friend Helen Keller about this article being all pushed through like that.[6] You know I don't know how long that system of writing has been out. It may have been before the Nobel Prize was given for outstanding achievement, but Braille or whoever she was sure should have had that prize.[7] It undoubtedly stands out as the greatest benefit to a handicapped people. Gosh, think of helping the world like that.

I prize it very highly. It was translated by Nellie Conger of Coshocton, Ohio, and says: "Presented to Will Rogers, the man who always writes the truth as he sees it." I wish I had time to try to learn to read that. I can imagine nothing more fascinating. But I never have had time to learn to read our other kind for the ones with sight.

Still getting straggling X-mas cards, mostly sent out I think by folks that found they had a few left over. But they were mighty welcome I tell you. Just on first thought a X-mas card don't mean much, but the older you get the more you like to open 'em and know that someone has remembered you.

Just got a beautiful pamphlet of the "Big Bend" Country down in Texas on the border, between El Paso and San Antonio. I doubt if America holds a more interesting place, and for you guys that like to hunt, my goodness, there is your star spot.

You talk about some wild old country. Well, that is about the wildest of the wild we got left, outside of the cities. Old Fort Davis must be one of the greatest of our old time forts. And smuggling back and forth across that line, why there is more danger, excitement and romance there than anywhere.

Anywhere around where there is some Mexicans mixed up in it always interested me. I think I like a Mexican because he can rope, or lasso as you would call it. They are the best in the world. We beat 'em in a contest at one thing. But in the brush or out in the open on all kinds of roping, they are the daddy's.

Well, I guess Mr Hoover is not going to take my advice and resign. He has had worse advice than that during his term. I talked the other day here at the ranch about that very thing with Mr McAdoo, and Mr George Creel.[8] Mr Creel is one of our foremost writers, he was ahead of all the writers of ours during the war. He had complete charge. He has a lot of humor in his stuff along with his vast sums of knowledge.

He and Mr McAdoo both admitted that it would have been a great thing to have done and would have put the Democrats in the hole, but there is just something about that being President, or even trying to be President, that once it's in your system it never gets out till you are carried out. But I still claim it would have made him a bigger man. He hasent got a chance with this bunch in there now. He is too conscientious, hard-working a man to have to put up with two more months of this. He is just like being in the pest house, those Senate and House hyenas won't even bring him food and water.

224

Well all I know is just what I read in the papers. Well we just can't hardly get over the shock of the death of Mr. Coolidge.[1] I had a great admiration for Mr. Coolidge, and as for Mrs. Coolidge I just thought she was about the finest woman in public life.[2] They were mighty nice to me. Right after I had written all those alleged jokes from Europe, "Letters of a self made diplomat to his President," why when I got to New York he invited me down to spend the week end at the White House. Well that was the biggest thing for me, for I had never been there, and I don't mind telling you that with all my jokes, I have a great reverence for our Presidents, and our White House.

Well the jokes I told about that trip were my biggest laugh producers anytime I wanted to tell them, but they were not disrespectful, they were touching on the little homely things that made people like Mr. Coolidge.

I have had many Republican politicians tell me, "Will, you are one of Mr. Coolidge's best boosters." Well I did like him. I could get a laugh out of almost all the little things he said, but at the same time they were so wise. He could put more in a line than any public man could in a whole speech.

I have visited them at the "Beeches," the home he died in. He had gone to New York that day, but I had a fine visit with Mrs. Coolidge. She showed me over the place. It was very homey and lovely. She just sat and chatted like your next door neighbor.

I was down to his law office, met his law partner, Mr. Hemingway.[3] He told me many stories of Mr. Coolidge. They all in the office had great affection for him. He dident take any active part in the law practice, but he always came to the office and transacted his private business. I know his son, John, who is an awfully fine young man, and his wife is a lovely girl.[4]

Here is a thing do you reckon Mr. Coolidge worried over in late years? Now he could see further than any of these politicians. Things were going so fast and everybody was so cuckoo during his term in office, that lots of them just couldent possibly see how it could ever do otherwise than go up. Now Mr. Coolidge dident think that. He knew that it couldent. He knew that we couldent just keep running stocks and everything else up and up and them paying no dividends in comparison to the price. His whole fundamental training was against all that inflation. Now there was times when he casually in a speech did give some warning, but he really never did come right out and say, "Hold on there, this thing can't go on! You people are crazy. This thing has got to bust."

But how could he have said or done that? What would have been the effect? Everybody would have said, "Ha, what's the idea of butting into our prosperity? Here we are going good, and you our President, try to crab it. Let us alone, we know our business."

There is a thousand things we would have said to him or about him. He would have come in for a raft of criticism. The Republican party, the party of big business, would have done their best to have stopped him, for they couldn't see it like he did, and they never could have understood until a year after.

Later in his own heart did Calvin Coolidge ever wish that he had preached it from the housetops regardless of what big business, his party, or what anybody would have said?

Now here is another thing, too, in Mr. Coolidge's favor in not doing it. He no doubt ever dreamed of the magnitude of this depression. That is, he knew the thing had to bust, but he didn't think it would bust so big, or be such a permanent bust. Had he known of the tremendous extent of it, I'll bet he would have defied hell and damnation and told and warned the people about it. Now in these after years as he saw the thing overwhelm everybody, he naturally thought back to those hectic days when as President the country was paying a dollar down on everything on earth.

But all this is what they call in baseball a "second guess." It's easy to see now what might have helped lighten or prolong the shock, but put yourself in his place and I guess 99 out of 100 would have done as he did.

Now on the other hand in saying he saw the thing coming, might be doing him an injustice. He might not. He may not have known any more about it than all our other prominent men. But we always felt he was two jumps ahead of any of them on think ahead. Now if he did know that the fire was going to break out and had he warned and warned, and shouted and shouted, he would perhaps have been impeached, but he would have gone down as "The world's smartest man."

But predicting, or no predicting, the thing was coming anyhow. But no one knows what passed through that wise head of his as he sat for three years on that porch up there and just thought.

527 WASHINGTON IS GETTING
INTERESTING AGAIN

Well all I know is just what I read in the papers. That Huey Long episode in our history like to took up as much of our political historical space as anything George Washington did. Huey made the boys a few preliminary remarks that lasted well into the latter part of January. Huey had it in for Carter Glass.[1]

Now if you know Carter Glass, and I have had that privalege for several years, he is a very high class, rather of the old school southern gentleman, but in addition to being a gentleman he has a tremendous amount of ability. Along banking and financial lines he is just about the most able man in either party in Washington. When they get all through argueing over "Who is the father of the Federal Reserve Act" why they will really find the sire to be none other than Carter Glass. Now eveidentally he had a very sound banking bill. Certainly knows what one should be. Then right in the midst of it to hear somebody crashing right through the Louisiana cane breaks with an arm load of adjectives that it would take a good strong voiced man a month to dispose of. Why naturally that was dumbfounding to the sensibilities of a man of the Carter Glass type.

But you can't blame Huey near as much as you can blame the system that allows a prolonged thing like that. It's not allowed in the House of Representatives, so I was a hoping that Huey might be the means of getting a rule like that changed.

I'll bet you another one or two of those "Filibusters" break out before this session is over. This Huey Long spree of consanants and vowels that he excelled in, why it's not the first one in the Senate by any means. Somebody is always trying to talk a bill to death in there. But Huey killed the bill and wounded the Senate.

Well poor Mr Hoover, they passed the Phillipine Freedom over his head. He sends suggestions up to the law makers, (no doubt some of them splendid) but they don't pay any more attention to it than they do an add over the radio.

It's a very humiliating position for a fine man like a president of our U. S. to be in. Here he is President but he "ain't." Roosevelt is President but he "can't" yet. Which brings me right back to my pet belief, and that is that I'll bet you if Mr Hoover had it to do over again he would have resigned after election and dumped the thing right into the hands the people voted to handle it. It would have been a grand exit. He would have gone out with more sympathy, and incidentally put the Democrats in a hole. All they could have done was say, "Well we was going to save the country but you brought it

227

on us so quick that we havent quite got our minds made up how to do it yet."

You see if the President had done that, why naturally his example would have had to be followed by enough other lame ducks that this session would have been Democratic overwhelmingly. Then you wouldent have to wait till after March fourth for a new session to be called, and then see what they will do. We would have known by now.

But that's all old time stuff. I guess he knew what he was doing better than some comedian. But these last four weeks is going to be the hardest.

I got a nice letter from Pat Hurley the other day.[2] Hadent heard from Pat since the election, and was mighty glad to get the letter. And some of the "local " news. Chances are Pat will stay in Washington. He has lots of financial interests there, and then he will want to be where he can make faces at the Democrats. It may be more profitable and more satisfying to belong to the party that's in, but it's certainly more amusing to belong to the party that's out. Pat's likable, and humorous, and can laugh now, where he couldent before.

I hear that Amon G. Carter, of Ft Worth Texas, owner of the biggest newspaper in the Southwest, will take Hurley's place in the cabinet.[3] Carter, from all I can gather from the "inside" will be the man that will draw that splended cabinet plum. Amon will make 'em a mighty fine man. He is mighty well liked by all the Democrats, and fifty percent of the Republicans. (Well I will say a dozen anyway.) He would handle our army mighty well in peace, and put us on a mighty pretty war if the occasion arose. So while all the other cabinet positions are more or less up in the air from what we can hear, why it's practically cinched that Carter will succeed Hurley, who by the way is a very good friend of his.

Carter has practically retired from active management of his paper, but sometimes has it sent to New York or Washington to read. He is by far Texas' most public spirited man. So with Garner daily inquiring as to the health of our President, and Carter at the head of our military hordes, why Texas will have received more than her share of the spoils of the late political war. All his old friends in Texas, (of which I almost consider myself a native of), we all hope this new honor will not make him break an old custom of years, and that was to always be in the Capitol, Austin, on all Furgeson innaugarations.[4] This Carter cabinet news hasent been generally broadcasted, but those who know, say it's "in the bag."

Well it's about time to write something about the debts again and get everybody all stirred up. I like to throw 'em a little piece of meat ever once in awhile and just sit back and hear 'em growl. We got

Americans that take the debts as serious as a postmaster did the last election. I will write a little "Gag" in a day or two and stir 'em up again. Yours. Will.

528   WHERE'S THAT NEW DEAL?

Well all I know is just what I read in the papers. The lame duck congress has been putting us on a mighty inspiring example of just how honery a congress can be, if they really make up their minds to be honery. We just got about four more weeks of show and then these boys go into what some writer has termed oblivion. Oblivion is a oneway ticket town.

But the minute these guys get out of there here will come another bunch, and take their places. Now whether the new bunch is better than the old bunch is just kinder like cutting off a bunch of sheep as they run through the gate, stopping 'em because they don't look so good, then opening up the gate and try out the other half of 'em to see this shearing anyhow. We had some old big horned babies that had been in that Senate corrall so long that their horns were getting kinder twisted, but some likable old animals at that.

Well we are all getting ready for the new deal. We don't know what kind of hand we will get, but we want it even if it's just duces. It will at least get us out of our expectant mood. Democrats been doing a lot of stirring around since they got promised work. Couple of weeks ago bunch of 'em went down to Muscle Shoals dam to figure out what they could irrigate, or imitate, or nitrate, or fertilate with it. That dam was built when it looked like the war, like depression, was going to run forever. We had an awful lot of things figured out to do with a big dam if we had a war, but we can't think of a thing to do with it only have another war.

Well Congress is working on that, too. I been down to that dam, I was one of the first to inspect it. I could have told 'em about it without 'em going down. Dams are pretty much alike. They all work on about the same principal. You stop up the creek or river at some point, then the water generally backs up away from it, and how far it backs up denotes approximately how much the taxpayers paid to keep it backed up.

This Mussell Shoals is an awful pretty dam. It's not like the Boulder dam. Mussell Shoals is a long dam, very long, over a very wide river. Boulder is over a very steep river. It's in the deepest narrow canyon you ever saw. Mussell Shoals dam is laying down, and Boulder dam is standing up on end, but Mussell Shoals has got the most machinery, and a mighty fine little city by there named Florence.

Both dams were really made for fertilizer purposes, Mussell Shoals to make nitrates fertilizer and Boulder to make conversational fertilizer for the Los Angeles real estaters if we can ever get our heads up from behind these mortgages. Every time the Government starts to run it to make something at Mussell Shoals, why the politicians from the water power States raise up and howl, "Don't put the government in the power business!"

They are always wanting the Government to spend the taxpayers' money to build something, then don't want 'em to run it. Why can't the government run it, or anything else they have built? They run the Post Offices and deliver a letter from the North to the South Pole for 3 cents.

Well anyhow, the Democrats and Senator Norris as a chaperone went down to see if the water was really there, and just see what we could make out of it, if we turned it loose.[1] Too bad it's not closer to Washington. We could use it for our Presidents to fish in.

This dam business is getting to be quite a racket anyhow, every congressman if he's got a little stream running through his client's pasture wants to get an appropriation to dam it up with a federal appropriation, generally under a racket called flood control.

If the politicians have their way there won't be a foot of water in this country that's not standing above a dam. We are sure getting sucked into a lot of things for the sole benefit of a local community, to be paid for by everybody. Just think of an old bird owning a farm away out in the country in most any out of the way place, no paved road, no dam, no rural delivery, yet through his taxes he is paying for every dam, every road, and every other dam thing that he is not using. But the Democrats are going to do something about it. Maby build some more dams and roads.

Huey has been mighty quiet here lately. Kinder resting up for the big show that will open some time after March. That will be held in the nature of a Democratic reunion. There will be scattering Republicans in there, but they will remain scattered. February is going to be a kind of standstill month from a geographical, mineral and political aspect. There will be slight rains but no heavy damage done till March. Everybody is thinking up things to do and say for the new Congress. Some of the members are going so far as to get a new shirt for it. Well the people can't attend. They havent got a shirt.

529   A GREAT PILOT GOES HOME

I made a fast trip in an aeroplane the other day. That is 205 miles an hour in a commercial plane, regular passenger run. Just pay your fare and get in. This was the Varney line on the coast. But it made me think of trips I had made in almost the same type of plane. Lockhead with the legs pulled up, that I used to make trips in. That was the famous plane owned by Hal Roach the movie producer that makes you laugh in the theatre after some of our long pictures have either made you cry or cuss.[1]

But making this last trip my thoughts naturally went to Captain Jimmy Dickinson, and it's of him I want to talk about.[2] One of the finest pilots, one of the finest men that it has ever been my fortune to meet and know. Here he was flying all around back and forth across the U. S. in a single day. Carrying Mr Roach or his business associates on the quickest business trips ever made in the world. He made the greatest flight to and across South America that has been made in that country. Every pilot on the commercial lines down there told me so. And today he is buried in the heart of Africa, at Victoria Falls, Africa's Niagra.

He was in that same plane of Mr Roache's, piloting Mr Edmund Loew, son of Marcus Loew of the great Loew circuit of movie theatres.[3] He and a friend were making a tour of the world to see their various theatres. They had shipped the plane to Australia, then flew all over Australia, then flew it all the way from there to China, then from China across India, Messopotamia, Persia, to Cario, then the whole length of Africa, and were on their way back into Europe, then home. So you see they were on the very home stretch. Bad field, and the engine stalled on the take off. Up only a little ways, no chance, crash, other two safe, he went. Why, none of us know.

Judged by every moral and manly standard that anyone who knew him could judge him, fate dident give him a square deal. But maybe fate don't run those things. Maby somebody sees somebody they need and they just reach out and get 'em. Well if our Supreme Being needed a real man, He used splendid judgement in His selection. He will be a worthy addition to that company, no matter how select it may be. They will be proud of Jimmy. He was an army flier, he was a graduate of Northwestern, Captain of their great swimming team, schoolmaster there with a wonderful little girl that become his wife. Two children, one he was rushing home to be there at its birth.

Used to always fly over his house coming in from a trip, dip down and let her know he was home again. He lived near the field, and she would hike for the car, and hike for the field. The love and devotion between them was beautiful. He flew Mr Roach, Mr Eric Pedley the international polo player and myself to Mexico one time.[4] Every day no matter where I was I would file my telegram to the newspaper syndicate, he would say well I got to file mine too. His was to his wife. A great companion on a trip. And what confidence he inspired in his passengers!

He was the only pilot that Mrs Rogers ever made a long trip with. He flew us out to see our son at Roswell, New Mexico. Flew over there by lunch time.

Mrs Roach and her friends who are not aviation enthusiasts at all, but would go to Siberia with Captain Dickinson. He is the only pilot that I know of that ever fooled a nation. Roach and Lowe flew to Santiago, Chili with him in four or five days, some maricilous time, to fly the Andes the next morning to Buenos Aires. They left earlier than they had expected. Well it's a military field, and they dident properly check out, or some tecnicality, (maby it was the starting of technocracy) but anyhow they just took off. The Andes to Jimmy was just a high hedge fence, and he took it in stride. He made Buenos Aires for breakfast. But Chili commenced getting hot, all kinds of stories, two movie magnates had taken a lot of gold out of the country, and all kinds of yarns.

Well they then went on up the coast of Brazil to Rio Janerio. Now I made that trip around and on up the East coast of South America from Rio Janerio, clear up to Cuba and Miami, but it must be done in a sea plane or amphibian. Theirs being a land plane solely, they had to come back by the West coast like they had gone down, so Chili figured they had 'em, because they had to come back through there, but they figured without Captain Dickinson. He looked on the map and saw that right straight west of them was Peru, but about three thousand miles away. Well he finds one landing field away out in there just north of Paraguay, at a place called Carambauy, which had only been approached from the south and not from where he was. So Roach said, "Let her go Jimmy! Anything you say! If you want to blaze a trail across Brazil in a single motored ship, O.K. Brazil we are crossing you."

And he did, Roach says it was the greatest flight he ever saw, and those American pilots on the regular runs down there say it was a masterpiece of navigating, and judgement. So he hit the Pacific Ocean north of Chili, and saved some outlandish fine.

If you dropped down in those jungles there was no hitch hiking to town. They after wards got it straightened up with Chili. It was all a missunderstanding. But that trip of Jimmy's was no missunderstanding, that was a real fact. Just before he started on this last trip he come up to my house to talk about a long hop of about nine thousand miles that I had just made a few months before, from Singapore, India to Cairo, Egypt. There is just one line across there like a western trail for the early 49'ers.

You see aeroplanes have kinder got to keep on a route to get the fields and the gas. Well I told him all I could remember about it, which wasent much for I slept most of the time. We was about nine days making it in a big three-motored Fokker on the Holland Dutch line. I guess he made it in about three. I told him to look out for sacred cows on the field at Calcutta. We like to hit one. If I had ever been able to own my own plane I wanted to steal him from Hal for my pilot.

Owing to various difficulties there was no way of getting the body home for burial, so one of America's finest men, member of that new and adventerous calling, lies buried with the great Victoria Falls as his headstone. The next long trip I make is going to be that trip from Europe to Capetown, the whole length of Africa, and I am going to those falls, but not to see the falls.

530   A CLAIM FOR CHARITY

All I know is just what I read in the papers. Get all kinds of literature about everything under the sun. If there is a man in this country that hasent had a pamphlet printed giving his views on how to solve the depression, it's because there is no more paper to print 'em on. Every stock selling scheme at cut rates. Then ads for all the things under Heaven and earth, but among 'em sometimes is worth while literature.

Here is one before me now that just come in the mail. It's a beautiful illustrated booklet of a cruise in the West Indies Islands, and it's on one of the most wonderful boats a float, the Belengenland, built especially for tropical comfort. Now that got my attention, for I never was on a pleasure cruise. I crossed and uncrossed about all the oceans we got, but it's always been because I wanted to get somewhere. It never was just really for relaxation and pleasure.

But wait a minute as my good friend Al Jolson says, "You ain't heard nothing yet."[1] This is a special cruise not only for people who can afford it, but its profit is for a great cause. Well that got my interest still more. I had never heard of anyone thinking up the marvelous idea of hiring a boat and putting on a cruise and giving the profits to some worthy charity, had you? Well anyhow I hadent. The whole scheme of the thing struck me as being unique and extraorinary.

Well what was the charity that would risk such a collosal undertaking, for it takes money to charter a real boat, and when you charter a floating castle, athletic field, swimming pool, church and night club, why brother you have done yourself some chartering. Well, it's the Frontier Nursing Service. Never heard of it? Well I am practically world famous for my ignorance. But I certainly do know something about the Frontier Nursing Service, I was Nursed on the Frontier, but it was before they had any service. We was just born and raised Ad. Lib, our poor mothers pulled through away out there, just through good fortune. But somebody realizing the hardships of what pioneer women had to undergo in child birth without benefit of anything that even looked like a white apron why this party conceived the idea of organizing a nursing service that would touch the pioneer woman. You will rise right up in meeting and say, yes, but it's fifty years too late for this, there is no pioneer women to nurse.

Yeah. Well you follow these nurses on a dark night with them sitting not on the seat of a Ford or at the wheel of a Chevrolet. But all that nurse has got under her is a mule, and there ain't a stretch of pavement between her and Lexington, Kentucky, for this is in the mountains of Kentucky that I am alluding too. All our lives we have read of the feuds and the moonshiners back in those mountains. It's the last stand of primitative and hundred per cent Americanism, (leaving out us Injuns, which of course they always do. Left 'em out so long till they are perpetually out.) But these are the real stock of the early emigration to America. A foreigner to them is a man that come into their country after 1750. He is what they refer to as a Johnny Newcomer.

Well we have all read of those old boys that could take an old long barrell brindle rifle and shoot the hat off a revenue man almost as far away as he should be shot at. But no thought has ever been given to young of the specie. Where was any doctors? A Nurse was as foreign to 'em as a French payment.

Well then this party conceived the idea of these nurses to go away into the mountains and relieve the suffering and death rate of these pioneer women. Their home is as primitive from birth to death as any covered wagon ever invented. There is not hundreds of companions accompaying them. They are born alone, live alone, die alone.

I had just read a book, which you all should read called "Nurses on Horseback," by Earnest Poole, it's of Mary Breckenridge, a member of one of the old families of not only a state but our country.[2]

Mary, the name alone means something don't it? Always helping someone. My mother was named Mary, my only daughter is named Mary, and I hope she does some good for someone.[3]

Well they have these Nurses that go in all hours of the day or night to lonely Mountain cabins and assist that greatest of all operation, our coming into the world. Now they are having this cruise it lasts 15 days, with a minimum rate of 177 apiece.

My goodness, you can't stay home in a good Hotel for that price, or even stay home. And a trip through the West Indies! I have flown over them by plane, and they looked so pretty that if I had had a parachute I would have jumped out and spent a few hours or days. Cruises are one thing that depression has helped, for they are so reasonable they are a money saver. I would like to be on this particular cruise for they will be a great bunch, congenial people with the added satisfaction that they are going to perhaps assist in the saving of a young life, maby another Lincoln. He was born amidst just such surroundings. They said February 25, for 15 days. You will see Spanish colonies, Dutch, French, British, and may see some of our Marines prowling around somewhere.

531   WHO CAN BEAT LINCOLN IN SPEECH-MAKINGS

Well all I know is just what I read in the papers, now just what has been agitating the natives here lately in the way of printed matter? Mr Hoover's speech couple of weeks ago is still fresh in the minds and editorials of our press, but no man should ever make a speech after someone at the same dinner has read or recited, (this woman did a kind of a cross between the two) Lincoln's Gettysburg Address. You see it was Lincoln's birthday and the Republicans in New York were celebrating.

If it hadent been for Lincoln the Republicans in N. Y. would sure be short of a cause for celebrating. Well preceeding Mr Hoover's speech some woman read Lincoln's speech. It's only about three hundred words long, and the plainest words. There's not a child or even a comedian that can't understand it. Well Mr Hoover got flowery, all long words. Honest Lincoln just as well not made his speech as far as it has had any effect on other speakers. He left it as an example, but no one ever followed it. You know this radio gives you a pretty good line on just how things go over. Now the President got a tremendous reception at all references to him by the preceeding speakers, and a great hand when he arose to speak, but when he got into his speech, which was on affairs as they pertain to us, why not a ripple did he get.

I just don't believe one tenth of those people knew what he was talking about. You take an audience like he would draw, all of rich New York Republicans, and I bet you outside a few of the men present they dident get him at all. When he got into Gold Standard and finances, why those women dident care a thing about it as long as they already had on the sable coat, and dident have to worry about where it was to come from. The President said things in his speech that I know they would have applauded if they had known what they were.

I have played to audiances all over this country, cities, towns, and right on the bald prairie, and lots of swell charity affairs in New York, and if you talk about international or political affairs, a fashionable New York audience is the dumbest one you can assemble anywhere in this country. Small town people will make a sucker out of 'em for reading and keeping up with the news. I will never forget one time I went over to Sherry's, a fashionable restaurant, after the Follies show one night to play a charity affair for one of the Vanderbilt ladies, and I thought I had some good material at the time. The League of Nations was in the heighth of its argument, Ireland and England was fussing, dissarmament was a headline topic. William Randolph Hearst was sitting with a party of friends at one of the tables.[1] Well he had heard these same little jokes of mine over at the Follies Show, and I breezed out there rather cocky thinking I had some sure fire material. Well you never saw jokes hit a ball room floor and slide off like those did. Those old dowagers, and those young debutantes had no more read a paper than I had Shakespeare. Mr. Hearst was dying laughing, but not at the jokes. He was laughing at me out there dying. He had heard these get big laughs with an out of town audience at the Follies, and he got a kick out of 'em laying an egg there with that bunch.

So I can appreciate what Mr. Hoover was up against. They dident know who was on or off the gold. They knew they were on velvet was all. Then two nights later after that fiasco one time I went to sing and did a show for them and I never had as well read audience in my life. They dident muff a gag. Ever since then I have always felt we had the wrong bunch in there. They have papers and magazines in there and read all the time.

Talking about Mr Lincoln and his speech that day at Gettysburg, he was not what is always humorously referred to as the "Principal Speaker." And this little speech of Lincoln's dident go over so big, but this other old man that got up there and raved for an hour, they thought he was great. Now nobody knows his name or a word he said. He just talked himself right into oblivion. They say Lincoln wrote his going up on the train in a day coach, on the back of an envelope. Every speaker that goes to commerate something or other should be locked up in a day coach and if he comes out with over three hundred words then he should be put in a cattle car and make it to the stock. It's funny how they use these famous men of ours birthdays to not pay tribute to his memory, but put over some party hooey. That the man in the grave if, he could hear it, would get up and denounce the whole affair. It's "Lincoln and the great Republican party, and Jefferson and the great Democratic Party." Neither man would know his party if he come back today, and neither one would admit it if he did know 'em, so Mr Lincoln you and Mr Jefferson have got a lot to answer for.

532   OVER THE MODERN
                 CRACKER BARREL

Well all I know is just what I read in the papers, or what I hear see or imagine. Here a week or so ago I attended my first thing called symposium. I dident know if it was going to be a circus, burlesque show, or a preaching. Well it was all three.

It seems that this symposium is a racket. It's carried on by colleges mostly. It's where some given number of men talk on some subject. They get it discussed from different angles. I guess that's about what they are that's what this one was anyhow.

I went because my friend Will Durant was going to be one of the symposers.[1] He was to talk on the hopes and fears of Russia. Chester Rowell is the editor of the San Francisco Choronicle.[2] Well he was to speak on the hopes and fears of China. Then there was a Japanes, I don't know his name but it don't make any difference they all have the same names anyhow, he spoke on the hopes and fears of Japan.

Then there was a fellow from Australia that was supposed to give a summary. Well he did but it was of Australia. Instead of explaining what the others had been talking to us about for the last two or three hours, why he sold tickets to Australia, and durned if he dident do it pretty good too. He said Australia was purely a white man's country, and that they were trying to make a high class country out of it. They wanted immigration, but immigrants with some kind of "Who's Who" record behind 'em. He said that Australia was the only country that was going to feature class in population. He showed that it is a very fine country.

Well he dident need to tell me about it, I have been over more of it than he had I expect. I was with Worth Bros. circus and we played everything from Wyapuckerou, in New Zealand to Killgooly, or something like that away out in the west of Australia.

Australia is a fine place. It's beautiful, the people are congenial and hospitable, and no one making a tour of any length should miss it. There is only six and half million people there, but that's enough people. Who wants more people than that? I wish I had lived in this country when there was only six and half million. I may yet. You can't tell. A lot of 'em that have the fare are walking out on us mighty fast.

But I must get back to the hopes and fears of all these nations. I wanted to get up and enumerate some of the hopes and fears of the Democratic party. We are more interested in them than in all the hopes and fears of Russia, Japan, and China combined.

Well it wouldent have taken me long to give that. The Democrats hope they will do something, but they fear they won't. They hope 50 percent and fear 50. Now you can't be any more fair with your hoping and fearing than that, can you?

Well first was Will Durant. He is just about our best writer on Russia. He is the most fearless writer that has been there. He tells you just what it's like. He makes a mighty fine talk. One of the most interesting lecturers we have, and a fine fellow.

He said Russia hopes to make Russia industrial like us. They want to manafacture everything. Well that will be the end of 'em if they get like us. Their fears seemed to be by the ones in charge afraid the other 139 million would get wise to 'em, because there is less than a million running the country, but Lord they claim there is less than a dozen running this country.

Chester Rowell who spoke for China made a fine talk. Course he had the best subject. There is something about a Chinaman that everybody feels sorry for 'em, and there is no nation in the world that needs sympathy less. China will be getting along when people of the 25 Century will be digging and wondering what kind of apes inhabited this country along about the ninteenth century. Rowell showed that China had no fears of the ultimate future, but was just a little uneasy about local conditions for the moment.

Well then come the Japanese who spoke. He was a very pleasant man, they all are. They are the nicest people over there you ever saw. Hospitality toward you is just plum suffocating. Well this fellow said that it was Russia that they were afraid of, and that was why they were taking over Jehol, and Manchuria, it was to keep Russia from gobbling 'em up, as they have already done with Outer Mongolia. He of course couldent offer much reason for his country taking all this, but he was nice and pleasant about it, said he knew his country was in bad as far as public opinion was concerned, and they give him a big hand at the finish.

All in all it was fine symposium. Dr. Von Kleinschmidt the president and producer of the best football team in America, the Trojans, was the toastmaster, and did a lovely and gracious job.[3] He gave 'em all a nice boost and asked 'em if they had a son that was a good athlete to send 'em to U.S.C.

All this exchange of talk is a lot of hooey. It changes nobody or effects no opinions, but it's kinder like weather talk it does no harm. But a symposium is pretty good. If one ever travels through your town and plays there go hear it. It's the old cracker barrell arguments over again.

NOTES

428   McNaught Syndicate (McN) copy; published: *Tulsa Daily World* (TDW), March 8, 1931. The texts of the Weekly Articles (WA) published herein come from Rogers' original manuscripts when such documents are available. In all other cases, the texts of the articles are taken from the *Tulsa Daily World (TDW)*, from some other reliable newspaper, or from the copy issued by the McNaught Syndicate. The dates given indicate earliest publication. The headings accompanying each article are from the original manuscript or from the newspaper cited.

[1]Alfonso XIII, king of Spain from 1886 to 1931. Although Alfonso enjoyed some personal popularity, the monarchy was threatened by considerable social and political unrest. Alfonso was forced to abdicate in the face of a significant electoral victory by republicans on April 12, 1931. He died in exile in 1941.

[2]Edward Albert, prince of Wales and heir apparent to the British throne. Immensely popular, he succeeded to the throne in January of 1936, but was forced to relinquish the crown later that year because of opposition to his impending marriage to an American divorcee.

429   McN; published: *TDW*, March 15, 1931

[1]George William Norris, Republican United States senator from Nebraska from 1913 to 1943. A liberal Republican, Norris was the author in 1932 of the Twentieth Amendment, which abolished the "lame duck" session of Congress and changed the date of the presidential inauguration.

[2]Although veterans of World War I were due to receive bonus payments in 1945, many ex-soldiers sought depression relief through early payment. A congressional act of February 27, 1931, did not provide payment of the bonus, but did make available low interest loans for veterans holding the adjusted service certificates.

[3]Smedley Darlington Butler, major general in the United States Marine Corps and winner of two Congressional Medals of Honor. Butler provoked a minor international incident in January of 1931 when he publicly slurred Benito Mussolini, the Italian dictator. Although threatened with court martial, Butler escaped punishment with only a reprimand.

[4]Aimee Semple McPherson, popular and controversial American evangelist of the 1920s and 1930s; founder of the International Church of the Foursquare Gospel.

Roberta Star McPherson, twenty-year-old daughter of Aimee Semple McPherson, married William Bradley Smyth, the purser of the S. S. *President Wilson*, on March 4, 1931, in the midst of a tour of Asia.

[5]Sawtelle, which was adjacent to Los Angeles, was the site of a large veterans' hospital and convalescent center.

Jamaica ginger, popularly known as "jake," was a beverage of ginger and sixty to eighty percent alcohol that had a crippling, paralyzing effect on the extremities of its victims.

[6]Albert Einstein, noted German physicist who received a Nobel Prize in 1921 for his work in theoretical physics, notably on the photoelectric effect. He served as a visiting professor at the California Institute of Technology at Pasadena during the winter of 1930-1931.

430   *TDW*, March 22, 1931

[1]Herbert Clark Hoover, president of the United States from 1929 to 1933. A Republican, he previously had served as secretary of commerce and in other public offices.

[2]John Jakob Raskob, wealthy American industrialist who resigned his executive position with General Motors Corporation in 1928 to serve as Democratic national

chairman and as presidential campaign manager for Alfred Emanual "Al" Smith. He received much blame for Smith's electoral defeat.

[3]Alfred Emanual "Al" Smith, Democratic governor of New York from 1919 to 1920 and 1923 to 1928; unsuccessful Democratic nominee for the presidency in 1928.

[4]Joseph Taylor "Joe" Robinson, Democratic United States senator from Arkansas from 1913 until his death in 1937.

431   McN; published: *TDW*, March 29, 1931

[1]William Rogers, Jr., eldest son of Will and Betty Blake Rogers; known as Will, Jr. He attended the University of Arizona in 1931.

[2]Andrew John Volstead, Republican United States representative from Minnesota from 1903 to 1923; author of the Volstead Act of 1919, the enforcement legislation for the Eighteenth (Prohibition) Amendment.

[3]Willis Chatman Hawley, Republican United States representative from Oregon from 1907 to 1933; ardent protectionist.

Reed Smoot, Republican United States senator from Utah from 1903 to 1933. Smoot sponsored the Hawley-Smoot Tariff Act of 1930, which raised the tariff to the then highest protective level in the history of the United States.

[4]Henry Cabot Lodge, Republican United States senator from Massachusetts from 1893 until his death in 1924. Lodge led senatorial opposition in 1919 to the Versailles Treaty and American membership in the League of Nations.

[5]Dwight Whitney Morrow, Republican United States senator from New Jersey from 1930 until his death in October of 1931; ambassador to Mexico from 1927 to 1930; attorney, banker, and international financial expert.

432   McN; published: *TDW*, April 5, 1931

[1]For this and all further references to Herbert C. Hoover see WA 430: Note (N) 1.

[2]John Calvin Coolidge, Republican president of the United States from 1923 to 1929. Coolidge attended the Sixth Pan-American Conference, which was held in Havana, Cuba, in 1928.

[3]Theodore Roosevelt, Republican president of the United States from 1901 to 1909.

[4]Charles Spencer "Charlie" Chaplin, famous English comedian of silent films, known widely for his "Little Tramp" character.

[5]For this and all further references to the Prince of Wales see WA 428:N 2.

William Edgar Borah, Republican United States senator from Idaho from 1907 until his death in 1940. Staunchly independent, Borah exerted great influence as chairman of the Senate Committee on Foreign Affairs from 1924 to 1933.

[6]The Federal Farm Board, an agricultural marketing agency, was created in 1929.

433   McN; published: *TDW*, April 12, 1931

[1]Knute Kenneth Rockne, football coach at the University of Notre Dame from 1918 to 1931. Personable and popular, Rockne compiled a record of 105 wins, 12 losses, and 5 ties with the Fighting Irish. He and seven other persons perished in an airplane crash in southeastern Kansas on March 31, 1931.

[2]Harry Stuhldreher, quarterback at the University of Notre Dame from 1922 to 1924 and member of the immortal "Four Horsemen." Stuhldreher subsequently played professional football for one season and then coached collegiate football for several years.

[3]Joseph A. "Jumpin' Joe" Savoldi, running back for Notre Dame from 1928 to 1930. Savoldi, who played on two national championship teams, was expelled from school in 1930 for breaking university athletic rules against marriage.

[4]Frank F. Carideo, quarterback for Notre Dame from 1928 to 1930. A two-time unanimous All-America player, Carideo quarterbacked the 1929 and 1930 Irish teams, which Rockne considered his best.

[5]Howard Harding Jones, head football coach at the University of Southern California from 1925 until his death in 1940. His USC teams won two national titles and five Rose Bowl games.

[1]George Ade, Indiana humorist, newspaper columnist, author, and playwright; author of the plays *The County Chairman, The College Widow,* and *Father and The Boys.*

[2]The earthquake that struck Managua, Nicaragua, on March 31, 1931, took 1,450 lives. United States Army engineers and Marines stationed in Nicaragua rendered valuable service during the subsequent relief and clean-up operations. Rogers spent three days in Managua and personally contributed at least $5,000 to the relief cause.

[3]Francis Monroe "Frank" Hawks, American aviator who established numerous transcontinental and point-to-point speed records in the 1920s and 1930s. Hawks piloted Rogers through the Southwest on a benefit tour to raise money for drought victims.

[4]For Aimee Semple McPherson see WA 429:N 4.

[5]Clara Bow, American film actress whose sexuality and vivaciousness made her one of the most popular stars of the 1920s.

[6]Douglas Fairbanks, Sr., American stage and screen actor famous for his agile acrobatics and flashy smile. He starred in numerous screen spectaculars during a successful, twenty-year film career.

[7]Mary Pickford, American motion picture actress who in the heyday of silent films won renown as "America's Sweetheart"; wife of Douglas Fairbanks, Sr.

[8]Charles Partlow "Chic" Sale, American comedian, vaudevillian, motion picture actor, and writer; author of the bestselling book *The Specialist.*

435   *TDW,* April 26, 1931

[1]Betty Blake Rogers, wife of Will Rogers. The couple was married at Rogers, Arkansas, in 1908.

[2]Luís Terrazas, wealthy Mexican cattle baron and patriarch of the Terrazas family, which figured prominently in the country's politics and finances from 1861 to 1913. His 70,000,000-acre estate in Chihuahua state was a frequent target of insurgents during the Mexican Revolution. He died in exile in 1923 at the age of ninety-four.

[3]Francisco "Pancho" Villa, Mexican bandit and revolutionary leader. He almost succeeded in drawing the United States into war with Mexico in 1916 when he raided Columbus, New Mexico, killing sixteen persons and burning much of the town. He was assassinated in 1923.

[4]Joshua Reuben Clark, Jr., American career diplomat who served as ambassador to Mexico from 1930 to 1933.

For Dwight W. Morrow see WA 431:N 5.

436   *TDW,* May 3, 1931

[1]On his return from the Virgin Islands in March of 1931, Hoover remarked that the United States had obtained "an effective poorhouse" by its "unfortunate" acquisition of the islands in 1917.

[2]Alphonse "Scarface Al" Capone, Italian-born American gangster and racketeer whose crime syndicate terrorized Chicago during much of the 1920s. Capone was convicted and imprisoned for federal income tax evasion in 1931.

437   *TDW,* May 10, 1931

[1]William Wallace Atterbury, president of the Pennsylvania Railroad Company from 1925 to 1935; director of construction and operation of American railways in France during World War I.

[2]Amon Giles Carter, publisher of the *Fort Worth Star-Telegram* from 1923 until his death in 1955; prominent philanthropist and civic leader.

[3]"The Peanut Vendor" ("El Manisero"), popular Cuban song which was introduced by Moises Simons and his orchestra in *Cubanola* in 1929. It made its American debut in 1931 and quickly became a "hit."

[4]Charles Michael Schwab, founder and chairman of the board of Bethlehem Steel Corporation; major spokesman for the American steel industry and big business.

[5]Andrew Carnegie, American industrialist and philanthropist whose Carnegie Steel Company dominated the steel industry by 1900. He died in 1919.

[6]Roy Wilson Howard, chairman of the board of the Scripps-MacRae newspaper chain from 1921 to 1936 and president from 1936 to 1952. The company changed its name to Scripps-Howard after Howard became a partner in 1925.

[7]Robert Paine Scripps, associate editorial director of the Scripps-Howard newspapers from 1925 until his death in 1938; son of the founder of the chain, Edward Wyllis Scripps.

438   *TDW*, May 17, 1931

[1]*A Connecticut Yankee* was released in February of 1931. It was adapted from the popular story by Mark Twain.

[2]William Harrison "Will" Hays, president of Motion Picture Producers and Distributors from 1922 to 1945; Republican political figure; known as the "czar" of the motion picture industry.

439   *TDW*, May 24, 1931

[1]For this and all further references to Betty Blake Rogers see WA 435:N 1.

[2]Smith (see WA 430:N 3) served as president of the corporate enterprise that built the Empire State Building in New York City. The 102-story structure, which was opened in 1931, was for many years the tallest building in the world.

[3]James Larkin White, young New Mexico cowboy who "discovered" Carlsbad Caverns about 1900. The site was made a national park in 1930.

[4]Thomas "Tom" Boles Jr., superintendant of Carlsbad Caverns National Park from 1927 to 1946. Known as "Mr. Carlsbad Caverns," Boles mastered the art of publicity and, in so doing, made the little known opening in the earth internationally famous.

[5]Walter Guy Attwell, associate engineer with the National Park Service; was chiefly responsible for the installation of the elevator shaft at Carlsbad Caverns between 1929 and 1932.

[6]Thomas Carroll "Cal" Miller, assistant chief ranger at Carlsbad Caverns. Miller served in several capacities at the park and in other National Park Service areas between 1926 and his retirement in 1961.

440   *TDW*, May 31, 1931

[1]George V, king of Great Britain and Ireland from 1910 to 1936. King George was an outgoing and active monarch, well-liked by the British people.

Mary, queen consort of Great Britain and Ireland; daughter of the duke of Teck.

[2]Charles Gates Dawes, United States ambassador to Great Britain from 1929 to 1932. A Republican, Dawes served as vice president of the United States from 1925 to 1929 and in other major governmental positions.

[3]Louise Behn, daughter of Hernand Behn, president of International Telephone and Telegraph Corporation. She was presented at the Court of Saint James on May 19, 1931.

[4]For King Alfonso XIII see WA 428:N 1.

[5]For this and all further references to Calvin Coolidge see WA 432:N 2.

[6]Marie, queen consort of Rumania from 1914 until 1927. Queen Marie made a highly-publicized good will tour of the United States in the fall of 1926.

George Higgins Moses, Republican United States senator from New Hampshire from 1918 to 1933; loyal supporter of the Coolidge and Hoover administrations.

[7]Emily Price Post, American writer and columnist, famous for her advice on manners and social etiquette; author of the bestseller *Etiquette* (1922).

[8]For this and all further references to Charlie Chaplin see WA 432:N 4.

[9]Patrick Jay "Pat" Hurley, United States secretary of war from 1929 to 1933; Oklahoma attorney and oilman.

Andrew William Mellon, United States secretary of the treasury from 1921 to 1932; ambassador to Great Britain from 1932 to 1933; prominent Pittsburgh industrialist, financier, and philanthropist.

[10]Alexander Hamilton, American statesman who served as the first United States secretary of the treasury and who planned and initiated policies establishing a national fiscal system.

[11]David Sinton Ingalls, United States assistant secretary of the Navy for aeronautics from 1929 to 1932. Member of a prominent Cleveland family, Ingalls is noted as a superb pilot.

[12]Augusto Cesar Sandino, Nicaraguan revolutionary leader who waged guerrilla warfare against United States marines in Nicaragua from 1927 to 1932, declaring that the attacks were motivated by a patriotic desire to end American intervention. Sandino was assassinated in 1934.

441   *TDW*, June 7, 1931

[1]William H. Bonney, known as "Billy the Kid," notorious nineteenth century outlaw of the American Southwest. A legendary glamour surrounded his career.

[2]John Clinton Porter, Republican mayor of Los Angeles from 1929 to 1933. Porter and seventeen other American mayors visited France in May of 1931 as guests of the French government and the city of Paris. At the first official reception for the visitors, Porter, a prohibitionist, snubbed his hosts by leaving the party when champagne toasts were offered.

[3]Frank Hague, Democratic mayor of Jersey City, New Jersey, from 1917 to 1947.

[4]For this and all further references to Al Smith see WA 430:N 3.
Franklin Delano Roosevelt, Democratic governor of New York from 1929 to 1933. Roosevelt and Smith became the leading contenders for the Democratic presidential nomination in 1932. Roosevelt won the nomination and the election and served as president from 1933 until his death in 1945.

442   *TDW*, June 14, 1931

[1]William Henry "Alfalfa Bill" Murray, governor of Oklahoma from 1931 to 1935; agriculturist, attorney, constitutionalist, and Democratic political leader.

[2]For John C. Porter, mayor of Los Angeles, see WA 441:N 2.

[3]James Rolph, Jr., Republican governor of California from 1931 until his death in 1934. A wealthy shipowner and merchant, Rolph served as mayor of San Francisco for twenty-one years before his election as governor.

443   *TDW*, June 21, 1931

[1]Newton Booth Tarkington, American novelist who won Pulitzer prizes for his novels *The Magnificent Ambersons* (1918) and *Alice Adams* (1921).
Rogers was filming *Business and Pleasure,* which was adapted from Arthur Goodrich's play *The Plutocrat,* based on a novel of the same title by Booth Tarkington. The motion picture was released in November of 1931.

[2]Sam "Sammy" Baker, former army sergeant and one-time pugilist who was suspended by the New York State Boxing Commission in 1927.

[3]Harry Wills, black American heavyweight prize fighter who, because of his race, was never given a chance at the world title. He retired from the ring in 1932.
William Harrison "Jack" Dempsey, American boxer who held the world heavyweight title from 1919 to 1926.

[4]Lester Albert Johnson and Vic Alexander, unidentified black boxers and motion picture "extras."

[5]The Barrymores comprised one of the most famous performing families in American stage and screen history, with Lionel, Ethel, and John attracting considerable fame during the 1920s and 1930s.

444   *TDW*, June 28, 1931

[1]Warren Gamaliel Harding, Republican president of the United States from 1921 until his death in 1923. His administration was marred by several scandals. Hoover and Coolidge spoke at the dedication of Harding's tomb in Harding's hometown of Marion, Ohio, on June 16, 1931.

[2]Hoover addressed a large crowd in Springfield, Illinois, on June 17, 1931, at the dedication of the reconstructed mausoleum of Abraham Lincoln.

[3]For Alfalfa Bill Murray see WA 442:N 1.

[1]William James "Will" Durant, American educator, writer, and philosopher; author of *The Story of Philosophy* (1926) and other bestselling works.

[2]James Ramsay MacDonald, prime minister of Great Britain from 1929 to 1935; Labour party leader.

David Lloyd George, British politician and statesman who served as prime minister of Great Britain from 1916 to 1922.

Benito Mussolini, founder and leader of the Fascist movement; dictator of Italy from 1922 to 1943.

Guglielmo Marconi, Italian electrical engineer and inventor, celebrated for his development of wireless telegraphy; co-recipient of the Nobel Prize in physics in 1909.

Mohandas Karamchand Gandhi, Indian political and spiritual leader, known as the Mahatma, or Great Soul; principal leader of the Indian struggle for independence from Great Britain.

Josef Stalin, Russian Communist leader who from 1927 until his death in 1953 ruled as a virtual dictator of the Soviet Union.

Leon Trotsky, Russian Communist leader who served in various posts in the Communist party and the Soviet government. Trotsky was expelled from the party in 1927 and banished from Russia two years later. He was assassinated in Mexico City in 1940.

Rabindranath Tagore, Indian author and guru who founded the internationally-attended Visva-Bharati University; Tagore was awarded the Nobel Prize in literature in 1913.

For this and all further references to Albert Einstein see WA 429:N 6.

Thomas Alva Edison, American inventor and scientist, famous for such innovations as the incandescent electric lamp, the phonograph, and the microphone.

Henry Ford, American automotive pioneer and innovator; founder of the Ford Motor Company; leading automobile manufacturer.

Eugene Gladstone O'Neill, celebrated American playwright; awarded the Pulitzer Prize in drama in 1920, 1922, and 1928 and the Nobel Prize in literature in 1936.

George Bernard Shaw, leading British playwright, novelist, and literary critic; recipient of the Nobel Prize in literature in 1925. Among his works are *Pygmalion* and *Saint Joan.*

[3]William Thomas Waggoner, Texas cattle baron and oilman whose W. T. Waggoner Ranch sprawled over six counties in northwestern Texas.

[4]William "Bill" Hanley, Oregon rancher and wit, noted for his homespun philosophy. Hanley was known as the "Sage of Harney County."

[5]Charles Evans Hughes, chief justice of the United States Supreme Court from 1930 to 1941. In addition to holding other high governmental posts, Hughes served as secretary of state from 1921 to 1925.

Nicholas Murray Butler, president of Columbia University from 1902 to 1945; Republican political leader; co-recipient of the Nobel Peace Prize in 1931.

446   *TDW,* July 12, 1931

[1]Hoover proposed on June 20, 1931, a one-year moratorium on World War I reparations and war debts to ease the financial chaos in Europe.

[2]For this and all further references to Scarface Al Capone see WA 436:N 2.

[3]For Andrew W. Mellon see WA 440:N 9; for this and all further references to Henry Ford see WA 445:N 2.

[4]Marshall Field, Chicago mercantile magnate and philanthropist whose household and dry goods business, Marshall Field & Co., dominated the Chicago retail market. His main department store on Adams Street contained more than thirty acres of floor space. He died in 1906.

447   *TDW,* July 19, 1931

[1]Mary Amelia Rogers, only daughter of Will and Betty Rogers, graduated from a Beverly Hills college preparatory school in June of 1931.

[2]For this and further references to Betty Blake Rogers see WA 435:N 1.

[3]Florenz "Flo" Ziegfeld, Jr., American theatrical producer, best known for the

elaborately-staged *Ziegfeld Follies*. First produced in 1907, these musical revues featured a troupe of beautiful chorus girls and many of the leading stage performers of the day. Rogers performed in the *Follies* from 1916 to 1925.

[4]For this and all further references to Theodore Roosevelt see WA 432:N 3.

[5]Wiley Hardeman Post, Oklahoma aviator who won the National Air Race for long-distance flight in 1930 and also set records for around-the-world and stratospheric flights.

Harold Charles Gatty, Australian navigator who began his study of aerial navigation after his arrival in the United States in 1927. In the summer of 1931, Post and Gatty broke the record for an around-the-world flight, setting a mark of eight days, fifteen hours, and fifty-one minutes.

[6]Post and Gatty were financed in their venture by Florence C. Hall, an Oklahoma oilman and aviation enthusiast who had employed Post for several years as an executive pilot.

[7]Jules Verne, French novelist and originator of modern science fiction. Verne wrote a series of romances of extraordinary journeys, including *Twenty Thousand Leagues Under the Sea* (1870) and *The Tour of the World in Eighty Days* (1870).

[8]For Pat Hurley see WA 440:N 9.

448   *TDW*, July 26, 1931

[1]For Wiley H. Post and Harold C. Gatty see WA 447:N 5.

[2]For F. C. Hall see WA 447:N 6.

[3]Mae Laine Post, wife of Wiley H. Post; native of Sweetwater, Texas.

Elsie Louise Gatty, first wife of Harold C. Gatty. The couple was divorced in 1936.

449   *TDW*, August 2, 1931

[1]Sallie Clementine Rogers McSpadden, eldest sister of Will Rogers; wife of John Thomas "Tom" McSpadden, stockman of Chelsea, Oklahoma.

[2]Herbert Thomas "Herb" McSpadden, a son of Sallie and Tom McSpadden. Herb managed the Rogers Ranch after 1919 and moved to the ranch house—the birthplace of Will Rogers—in 1927. He married Madelyn Pope Palmer in 1924.

[3]Carter (see WA 437:N 2) made his Shady Oak Farm on the shores of Lake Worth famous through the gifts of thousands of hats bearing this trademark.

[4]Gas Sextette probably refers to six Fort Worth city councilmen who were at the time contesting a plan for municipal ownership of local natural gas properties.

450   *TDW*, August 9, 1931

[1]Germany received assurances of short-term credits from the representatives attending an international economic conference in London in July of 1931. The loans helped to steady German finances.

[2]For the Federal Farm Board see WA 432:N 6.

451   *TDW*, August 16, 1931

[1]Governor Alfalfa Bill Murray (see WA 442:N 1) called out the Oklahoma National Guard in mid-July of 1931 during a heated controversy with Texas authorities over the operation of a toll bridge across the Red River. Two weeks later, Murray again used the National Guard to shut-down all oil wells in Oklahoma in an effort to stem overproduction and to raise prices.

[2]For George Bernard Shaw see WA 445:N 2.

Nancy Langhorne Astor, American-born English viscountess who was the first woman to sit in the House of Commons, serving from 1919 to 1945. Lady Astor accompanied Shaw on a well-publicized tour of Russia in July of 1931.

[3]Waldorf Astor, British financier, politician, and publisher who served in the House of Lords from 1919 until his death in 1952. He was the husband of Lady Nancy Astor.

452   *TDW*, August 23, 1931

[1]For this and all other references to Benito Mussolini see WA 445:N 4.

[2]For Aimee Semple McPherson see WA 429:N 4.

[3]King Alfonso XIII of Spain (see WA 428:N 1) left that country in April of 1931 to live in exile in France.

[4]For Wiley H. Post and Harold C. Gatty see WA 447:N 5.

[5]Charles Augustus Lindbergh, American aviator who received international acclaim in May of 1927 for completing the first solo, nonstop transatlantic flight.

Anne Morrow Lindbergh, wife of aviator Charles Lindbergh and daughter of Dwight W. Morrow. The Lindberghs began an aerial journey from Washington, D.C., to the Orient on July 28, 1931.

[6]Two American fliers, Hugh Herndon, Jr., and Clyde Pangborn, attempted to break the record for an around-the-world flight in the summer of 1931. They were detained in Tokyo, Japan, on August 6, however, on charges that they had violated Japanese espionage laws when they took photographs of restricted areas.

[7]For George Bernard Shaw see WA 445:N 2; for Nancy Astor see WA 451:N 2.

[8]For the earthquake in Nicaragua see WA 434:N 2.

[9]For Smedley D. Butler see WA 429:N 3.

[10]James John "Jimmy" Walker, Democratic mayor of New York City from 1925 until his resignation in 1932. In 1931 the popular and debonair mayor became the subject of a state investigation of corruption in his administration.

454   *TDW,* September 6, 1931

[1]MacDonald (see WA 445:N 2) and other members of the Labour ministry resigned on Ausust 24, 1931, because of their inability to meet a budgetary crisis. Several Labourites then joined in a coalition government with MacDonald at its head.

[2]For David Lloyd George see WA 445:N 2.

[3]For Frank Hawks see WA 434:N 3.

455   McN; published: *TDW,* September 13, 1931

[1]Rogers wrote this column during the filming of *Ambassador Bill,* a motion picture released in October of 1931.

[2]Alexander Pollock Moore, American editor and diplomat; editor-in-chief of the *Pittsburgh Leader* from 1904 until his death in 1930; ambassador to Spain from 1923 to 1925.

[3]For George Bernard Shaw see WA 445:N 2.

[4]Prajadhipok, king of Siam (Thailand) from 1925 to 1935. Accompanied by Queen Rambai Barni, Prajadhipok traveled to the United States in early 1931 to undergo eye surgery.

Svasti, Siamese prince and father-in-law of Prajadhipok. He and his family joined the king on his trip to the United States.

[5]Arthur Brisbane, American newspaper editor and syndicated writer whose column, "Today," appeared in more than 1,400 newspapers.

[6]Sam Taylor, American motion picture director and screenwriter of the 1920s and 1930s.

456   *TDW,* September 20, 1931

[1]For J. Ramsay MacDonald see WA 445:N 2 and WA 454:N 1.

[2]For David Lloyd George see WA 445:N 2.

[3]For this and all further references to William E. Borah see WA 432:N 5.

[4]For David S. Ingalls see WA 440:N 11.

[5]For Jimmy Walker see WA 453:N 10.

[6]For Aimee Semple McPherson see WA 429:N 4.

[7]Tammany Hall, a Democratic political organization in New York City that controlled party politics in the city and wielded much influence in municipal affairs.

457   *TDW,* September 27, 1931

[1]McPherson (see WA 429:N 4) married David Hutton, a singer and a member of

her Los Angeles church, on September 13, 1931. Two days later, Hutton was sued by a woman who claimed that he had broken his promise to marry her. McPherson's mother, Minnie Pearce "Ma" Kennedy was also an evangelist. Kennedy's one-month marriage to G. Edward "Whataman" Hudson was annulled in July of 1931 because of bigamy charges against Hudson.

[2]For this and all further references to Mahatma Gandhi see WA 445:N 2.

[3]For Jimmy Walker see WA 453:N 10.

[4]Tristram E. "Tris" Speaker, professional baseball player who starred in the outfield for various clubs, most notably the Cleveland Indians from 1916 to 1926. He was inducted into the Baseball Hall of Fame in 1937.

Walter Perry Johnson, professional baseball player for the Washington Senators. His career as a pitcher and manager lasted from 1907 to 1935. He was inducted into the Baseball Hall of Fame in 1936.

Tyrus Raymond "Ty" Cobb, star outfielder and base stealer for the Detroit Tigers from 1905 to 1926; player-manager of the Tigers from 1921 to 1926. He was named to the Baseball Hall of Fame in 1936.

George Edward "Duffy" Lewis, outfielder for the Boston Red Sox from 1910 to 1917. He also played briefly for the New York Yankees and the Washington Senators before his retirement in 1921.

Harry Bartholomew Hooper, star outfielder for the Boston Red Sox from 1909 to 1920 and the Chicago White Sox from 1921 to 1925. Hooper was inducted into the Baseball Hall of Fame in 1971.

[5]Oscar Joseph "Ossie" Vitt, professional baseball player with the Detroit Tigers from 1912 to 1918 and the Boston Red Sox from 1919 to 1921; manager of the Cleveland Indians from 1938 to 1940.

[6]The "Four Horsemen" of the University of Notre Dame football team in 1924 comprised one of the most famous backfield combinations in collegiate football history. The immortal four included quarterback Harry Stuhldreher (see WA 433:N 2) and running backs Donald Miller, James H. Crowley, and Elmer Francis Layden.

[7]For Arthur Brisbane see WA 455:N 5.

458   TDW, October 4, 1931

[1]Japanese soldiers seized the important Manchurian city of Mukden on September 19, 1931, in an attempt to maintain Japan's commercial interests in northern China. Japanese and Chinese troops clashed repeatedly during the next several months in a bitter struggle for control. Japan completed the occupation of Manchuria in February of 1932 and, soon thereafter, proclaimed the puppet state of Manchukuo.

[2]Huey Pierce Long, Democratic governor of Louisiana from 1928 to 1932; United States senator from 1932 until his assassination in 1935. Angered by oppositon in the Texas legislature to his plan to stem the overproduction of cotton, Long charged on September 15, 1931, that the legislators had been bribed to obstruct the proposal. The indignant solons responded by passing a resolution condemning Long as a "liar."

[3]For Ma Kennedy and Whataman Hudson see WA 457:N 1.

[4]For Aimee Semple McPherson see WA 429:N 4 and WA 457:N 1.

[5]For this and all further references to Franklin D. Roosevelt see WA 441:N 4.

459   McN; published: TDW, October 11, 1931

[1]Zachary Taylor "Zack" Mulhall, Oklahoma rancher and showman whose Mulhall Wild West Show premiered in 1904 at the Louisiana Purchase Exposition in Saint Louis. On April 23, 1905, Rogers made his New York City debut with the Mulhall show. Mulhall died at his Oklahoma ranch on September 18, 1931.

[2]Agnes "Bossie" Mulhall, eldest daughter of Zack Mulhall; noted horsewoman.

Lucille Mulhall, second eldest daughter of Zack Mulhall; star of wild west shows, vaudeville, and rodeo. She retired from the entertainment circuit in 1920.

[3]Charles "Charley" Mulhall, youngest son of Zack Mulhall; Oklahoma rodeo and wild west show performer.

[4]Mary Agnes Locke Mulhall, wife of Zack Mulhall. She died at the Mulhall Ranch on January 19, 1931, at the age of seventy-eight.

[5]For Aimee Semple McPherson see WA 429:N 4.

460   Original Manuscript (OM); published: *TDW*, October 18, 1931

[1]For Flo Ziegfeld see WA 447:N 3.
[2]Billie Burke, American theatrical and motion picture actress. She and Flo Zieg-feld were married in 1914.
[3]Eugene Sandow, German-born strong man of early vaudeville and burlesque who Ziegfeld, his manager and promoter, billed as "Sandow, the Perfect Man." Sandow died in 1925.
[4]Harry Lauder, popular Scottish singer and songwriter who was knighted in 1919 for entertaining troops in World War I.
[5]Elinor Sutherland Glyn, English novelist and script writer whose works included the novel *Three Weeks* (1907), the story of an extra-marital interlude between a Balkan queen and an Englishman. Friends presented her with a tiger skin, because the animal hide was a much publicized feature of the story.

461   *TDW*, October 25, 1931

[1]William Randolph Hearst, American journalist, publisher, and political figure who during a turbulent sixty-year career in journalism fashioned a nationwide news-paper empire based in California. The Hearst-owned Babicora Ranch, headquartered 160 miles south of El Paso, Texas, embraced more than 900,000 acres in northern Mexico.
[2]Robert Moses "Lefty" Grove, professional baseball pitcher who played for the Philadelphia Athletics from 1925 to 1933 and the Boston Red Sox from 1934 to 1941. A winner of 300 games, Grove was enshrined in the Baseball Hall of Fame in 1947.
    George Livingston "Moose" Earnshaw, professional baseball pitcher for several major league teams, most notably the Philadelphia Athletics from 1928 to 1933.
[3]Burleigh Arland Grimes, baseball pitcher who played for several clubs, including the Saint Louis Cardinals from 1930 to 1931 and 1933 to 1934; manager of the Brooklyn Dodgers from 1937 to 1938. Grimes, who won two games in the World Series of 1931, was named to the Baseball Hall of Fame in 1947.
    William Anthony "Bill" Hallahan, professional baseball pitcher who played for the Saint Louis Cardinals from 1925 to 1936. Hallahan's best season was in 1931 when he went 19-9 in the regular season and 2-0 in the World Series.
[4]John Leonard Roosevelt "Pepper" Martin, Oklahoman who played center field for the Saint Louis Cardinals from 1928 to 1944. Martin's aggressive play helped the Cardinals defeat the favored Philadelphia Athletics in the World Series of 1931.
[5]Morrow (see WA 431:N 5) died at his home in Englewood, New Jersey, on October 5, 1931.

462   *TDW*, November 1, 1931

[1]For Pat Hurley see WA 440:N 9.
[2]Henry Lewis Stimson, United States secretary of state from 1929 to 1933; secretary of war from 1911 to 1913 and 1940 to 1945.
[3]For Alfalfa Bill Murray see WA 442:N 1.
[4]George Woodward Wickersham, New York City attorney and chairman of a Hoover-appointed commission that conducted an extensive investigation in 1929 of the federal system of jurisprudence and administration of laws. Its final report, which called for the continuation of prohibition while providing evidence that it could not be enforced, generated much criticism and discussion.
[5]Harry Bartow Hawes, Democratic United States senator from Missouri from 1927 to 1933. Hawes co-authored the Hawes-Cutting bill in 1930, which called for the independence of the Philippines five years after acceptance of a Philippine constitu-tion. He visited the islands in July of 1931 and assured the inhabitants that he would continue to work for independence. The United States granted sovereignty in 1946.
[6]For Reed Smoot see WA 431:N 3.
[7]William McKinley, Republican president of the United States from 1897 until his death in 1901. The United States acquired the Philippine Islands in 1898 as a result of the treaty that ended the Spanish-American War.
[8]Emilio Aguinaldo, Filipino revolutionary leader who led an insurrection against American authority from 1899 to 1901.

[9]William Howard Taft, Republican president of the United States from 1909 to 1913.

[10]Thomas Woodrow Wilson, Democratic president of the United States from 1913 to 1921.

[11]For Warren G. Harding see WA 444:N 1.

[12]Maurice M. Cohen, general manager and president of the Hollywood Palladium.

463   *TDW,* November 8, 1931

[1]Pierre Laval, premier and minister of foreign affairs of France from 1931 to 1932, from 1935 to 1936, and in 1942. Laval's nineteen-year-old daughter, Jose, accompanied him on his state visit to the United States.

[2]For Jimmy Walker see WA 453:N 10.

[3]For George W. Wickersham and the Wickersham Report see WA 462:N 4.

[4]For this and all further references to Woodrow Wilson see WA 462:N 10.

[5]For Augusto C. Sandino see WA 440:N 12.

[6]John Pierpont Morgan, Jr., chairman of the board of J. P. Morgan & Co., one of the most influential banking firms in the world and the major lending house for the Allied nations during World War I.

[7]For Pat Hurley see WA 440:N 9 and WA 462.

[8]Winnie Ruth Judd, so-called Arizona trunk murderer who was convicted in 1931 of the murder of Agnes Anne LeRoi, whose body was dismembered and shipped to Los Angeles in a steamer trunk.

Greta Garbo, Swedish film actress whose sultry sexuality and beautiful features made her one of the foremost star personalities ever to appear on the screen. She arrived in Hollywood in 1926 where she soon became one of the highest paid performers in films; she retired suddenly in 1941 at the age of thirty-six.

464   *TDW,* November 15, 1931

[1]Hal E. Roach, American producer of comedy films, including the profitable serials *Lonesome Luke, Our Gang,* and *Laurel and Hardy.*

Stan Laurel and Oliver Hardy, American comedians who first teamed in 1927 to initiate a highly successful series of short and feature films. Laurel, British, born, played a child-like character who was the antithesis of Hardy's pompous father figure.

Eric Pedley, California stock broker, sportsman, and internationally-acclaimed polo player of the 1920s and 1930s. Rogers and Pedley often played polo together.

[2]James Baker "Jimmy" Dickson, veteran military and private pilot who served in the United States Army Air Service in the 1920s.

[3]For this and all further references to Mary Rogers see WA 447:N 1; for this and all further references to Will Rogers, Jr., see WA 431:N 1.

[4]For William Randolph Hearst and the Babicora Ranch see WA 461:N 1.

[5]For Dwight W. Morrow see WA 431:N 5.

[6]Plutarco Elias Calles, president of Mexico from 1924 to 1928 and the dominant force in Mexican politics during the early 1930s.

[7]For J. Reuben Clark, Jr., see WA 435:N 4.

[8]Stuart Chase, American writer and civil servant; author of *Your Money's Worth, A New Deal,* and other works.

465   *TDW,* November 22, 1931

[1]Charles Curtis, vice president of the United States from 1929 to 1933. A Republican from Kansas, Curtis previously had served in the United States House and Senate.

[2]James Eli Watson, Republican United States senator from Indiana from 1916 to 1933; majority leader from 1929 to 1933.

Byron Patton "Pat" Harrison, Democratic United States senator from Mississippi from 1919 to 1941.

[3]Thaddeus Horatius Caraway, Democratic United States Senator from Arkansas from 1921 until his death in Little Rock on November 6, 1931.

[4]Frederick Huntington Gillett, Republican United States senator from Massachusetts from 1925 to 1931.

[5]John Nance "Jack" Garner, Democratic United States representative from Texas from 1903 to 1933; Speaker of the House from 1931 to 1933; vice president of the United States from 1933 to 1941.

[6]Tully Garner, only son of John Nance Garner; manager of the family property in Uvalde, Texas. He married Ann Fenner of Texas, and they had one daughter, Genevieve.

466   TDW, November 29, 1931

[1]For Knute K. Rockne see WA 433:N 1.
The King Ranch in southern Texas was founded in 1852 by cattleman Richard King. Embracing more than 1,000,000 acres spread over five counties, the ranch supported enormous quantities of livestock and was the birthplace of the Santa Gertrudis breed of cattle.

[2]Adair Bushyhead "Paddy" Mayes, Oklahoman who played briefly with the Philadelphia Phillies in 1911.

[3]Jack H. Lapham, wealthy Texas rancher, oil executive, sportsman, and private pilot. He was married to the former Lucy Jane Thomas.

[4]William "Billy" Post, II, a leading American polo player of the 1930s; member of the national champion Princeton University team of 1930 and the victorious American team in the United States-Argentina matches in 1932.

[5]For Frank Hawks see WA 434:N 3.

[6]Sarah Spohn Kleberg Shelton, eldest daughter of Alice Gertrudis (King) and Robert Justus Kleberg, owners and developers of the King Ranch.
Alice Kleberg East, second daughter of Alice and Robert Kleberg.
Helen Campbell Kleberg, wife of Robert Justus "Bob" Kleberg, Jr.
Robert Justus "Bob" Kleberg, Jr., youngest son of Alice Gertrudis (King) and Robert Justus Kleberg; manager of the King Ranch after his father's death in 1932.

467   TDW, December 6, 1931

[1]John Quillin Tilson, Republican United States representative from Connecticut from 1909 to 1913 and 1915 to 1932; majority leader of the House from 1928 to 1931.

[2]Nicholas Longworth, Republican United States representative from Ohio from 1903 to 1913 and 1915 until his death in 1931. Longworth, who had served as Speaker of the House since 1925, died on April 9, 1931.

[3]For this and all further references to Jack Garner see WA 465:N 5.

[4]For William Randolph Hearst see WA 461:N 1.

468   TDW, December 13, 1931

[1]Kennedy, an unidentified businessman.

[2]Curley Brown, a thoroughbred horse breeder and owner of the Brown-Shasta Ranch near Mount Shasta, California.

469   TDW, December 20, 1931

[1]Harold Clayton Lloyd, American motion picture actor, noted for his comic portrayals of wistful innocents who blunder into and out of "hair-raising" situations. Lloyd raised prize-winning Great Danes as a hobby.

[2]Mildred Davis Lloyd, American motion picture actress and wife of Harold Lloyd. The Lloyds were married in 1923. They had two daughters, Gloria and Marjorie Elizabeth, and one son, Harold, Jr., who was born in January of 1931.

[3]For Hal E. Roach see WA 464:N 1.

[4]For Jimmy Dickson see WA 464:N 2.

[5]Edward "Hoot" Gibson, American cowboy hero of silent films. Winner of the rodeo title "World's Champion Cowboy" in 1912, Gibson became the leading cowboy star at Universal Studios during the 1920s.

[6]Ken Maynard, American cowboy star of more than 300 western films. Once a rodeo rider, he broke into motion pictures as an "extra" and remained active in the industry until his death in 1973.
Wallace Beery, American actor with circus and musical comedy experience. He played villains in early silent films and then developed into a Metro-Goldwyn-Mayer

star and one of the studio's greatest box office attractions during the 1930s and 1940s.

[7]Frank Borzage, American motion picture director and actor, known for soft, sentimental, pictorial films. He won Academy Awards for direction in 1928 and 1933.

[8]Clarence Brown, American film director and former electrical engineer, noted for many spectacular but sensitive motion pictures.

[9]Henry King, veteran American motion picture director with experience in most branches of show business; an exponent of the expensive, family-oriented film.

[10]Mary Warner "Mae" Marsh, American leading lady of the silent screen; later played small character roles in films.

David Lewelyn Wark Griffith, pioneer American motion picture producer, noted for his technical innovations in *Birth of a Nation* (1915) and other films.

[11]Garner was married to the former Ettie Rheiner.

[12]Alice Roosevelt Longworth, daughter of President Theodore Roosevelt, widow of Speaker of the House Nicholas Longworth, and prominent Washington hostess.

[13]For Pat Hurley see WA 440:N 9.

[14]For David S. Ingalls see WA 440:N 11.

[15]Frederick Trubee Davison, United States assistant secretary of war for aeronautics from 1926 to 1932.

[16]Clarence Marshall Young, United States assistant secretary of commerce for aeronautics from 1929 to 1933.

[17]For Chic Sale see WA 434:N 8.

[18]Eddie Cantor, popular American comedian who starred in vaudeville, in motion pictures, and on radio for more than fifty years and who delighted audiences with his rolling eyes, lively movement, and inimitable singing voice.

For Will Durant see WA 445:N 1.

[19]For Amon G. Carter see WA 437:N 2.

[20]Marie Dressler, American comedienne of silent and early "talkies," formerly in opera, vaudeville, and burlesque.

[21]For Bill Hanley see WA 445:N 4.

[22]For Plutarco E. Calles, see WA 464:N 6.

470 *TDW,* December 27, 1931

[1]Rogers was enroute to the Orient to observe and report on war torn Manchuria.

Thomas Donald Campbell, American agriculturalist, inventor, and engineer. His Campbell Farming Corporation, with headquarters at Hardin, Montana, retained 95,000 acres under cultivation. Recognized as an authority on mechanized farming, Campbell was invited by the Soviet Union in 1929 to advise on the development of an agricultural program in Russia's first five-year plan. Campbell was married to the former Bess McBride Bull of North Dakota.

[2]For this and all further references to Josef Stalin see WA 445:N 2.

471 *TDW,* January 3, 1932

[1]Ralph Floyd Phillips Gibbons, American journalist, author, and radio commentator who as an internationally-known roving reporter was recognized as the "premier war correspondent of his generation."

[2]A. J. Hosken, Canadian mariner; ship commander for the Canadian Pacific line for thirty-two years until his death in 1936.

[3]Jesse Woodson James, Missouri outlaw of the western frontier during the post-Civil War era.

The Younger brothers—Thomas Coleman "Cole," John, James, and Robert—Missouri desperadoes who were prominent members of the James gang.

[4]William Sidney Graves, American army officer; commander of an American expeditionary force in Siberia from 1918 to 1920. A major general, he retired from the service in 1928.

472 McN; published: *TDW,* January 10, 1932

[1]For this and all further references to Floyd Gibbons see WA 471:N 1.

[2]Charles B. "Charlie" Irwin, rotund and colorful Wyoming rancher, race horse owner, and showman. At the time of his death in 1934, Irwin weighed more than 500 pounds.

³May Wirth Martin, Australian-born equestrienne. In 1903, at the age of five, May made her debut as a member of the Wirth family circus. Ten years later, the Ringling Brothers Circus showcased her at Madison Square Garden as "May Wirth, the greatest rider who had ever lived."

473   TDW, January 17, 1932

¹For Aimee Semple McPherson see WA 429:N 4.
²For Andrew W. Mellon see WA 440:N 9.
³Newton Diehl Baker, American attorney and statesman; United States secretary of war from 1916 to 1921.

474   TDW, January 24, 1932

¹Lawrence Mervil Tibbett, American operatic baritone who made his debut on the concert stage in 1917. In addition to opera, he also sang on the radio and in motion pictures.
²Ulysses Simpson Grant, president of the United States from 1869 to 1877; commander of the Union armies during the American Civil War.

475   TDW, January 31, 1932

¹Robert Andrews Millikan, American physicist; director of the Norman Bridge Laboratory of Physics at the California Institute of Technology from 1921 until his death in 1953. Credited with being the first to isolate the electron and measure its change, Millikan received the Nobel Prize in physics in 1923.
For Albert Einstein see WA 429:N 7.
²Walton, an unidentified American oilman.
³Riddell, an unidentified American beekeeper.
⁴Maurice Polydore Marie Bernard Maeterlinck, Belgian poet, dramatist and essayist; recipient of the Nobel Prize in literature in 1911. His The Life of the Bee remains one of the most popular treatments of the subject.
⁵Samuel Goldwyn, Polish-born American motion picture producer who formed Goldwyn Pictures Corporation in 1918. It later became a part of the Metro-Goldwyn-Mayer firm.
⁶Vicente Blasco-Ibáñez, Spanish novelist and politician, most famous as author of The Four Horsemen of the Apocalypse. An anti-monarchist, Blasco-Ibáñez died in 1928 in voluntary political exile.
Carl Sandburg, American poet and biographer. Sandburg's most ambitious work was his six-volume biography of Abraham Lincoln (1926-1939), for which he was awarded a Pulitzer Prize.
William Holmes McGuffey, American educator; professor of moral philosophy at the University of Virginia from 1845 to 1873, remembered chiefly as the compiler of the McGuffey Eclectic Readers (1836-1857).
For Jesse James see WA 471:N 3.
The Dalton brothers—Grattan, Robert Rennick, and Emmett—outlaws of the Old West whose gang was wiped out during an infamous raid on Coffeyville, Kansas, in 1892.
Harold Albert Lamb, American author who wrote chiefly about Middle Eastern history. Among his many works are Genghis K han (1927) and Tamarlane (1928).
⁷Henry David Thoreau, nineteenth century American author and naturalist. His most famous book, Walden (1894), is an account of his experiment in near-solitary living in close harmony with nature.
Walter "Walt" Whitman, nineteenth century American poet; considered by many to be the greatest of all American poets.
For Thomas A. Edison see WA 445:N 2.

476   McN; published, TDW, February 7, 1932

477   TDW, February 14, 1932

¹An earthquake in 1923 destroyed much of Tokyo and Yokohama, Japan.

[2]Dwight Filley Davis, United States secretary of war from 1925 to 1929; governor general of the Philippine Islands from 1929 to 1932. Davis was visiting Japan with his eldest daughter, Alice Brooks Davis.

[3]Maurice Auguste Chevalier, French entertainer who gained an international reputation in Paris music halls in the 1920s. He also achieved fame as a star of American films, beginning with his appearance in *The Love Parade* in 1930.

478 *TDW,* February 21, 1932

[1]Robert Tyre "Bobby" Jones, highly-acclaimed Atlanta golfer who won five United States National Amateur championships, four United States Open titles, and three British Open crowns. In 1930 he became the first player to win the national open championships of Great Britain and the United States in the same year.

[2]Ferguson, an unidentified American traveler.

[3]Ma Chan-shan, Chinese general who led military opposition to the Japanese presence in Manchuria and who served as governor of Hejlungkian province in northern Manchuria.

[4]For Pancho Villa see WA 435:N 3.

479 *TDW,* February 28, 1932

[1]Brigham Young, American religious leader who headed the Mormon Church from 1847 until his death in 1877. A polygamist, he was survived by seventeen wives and countless children and grandchildren.

480 *TDW,* March 6, 1932

[1]The University of Southern California football team defeated the Fighting Irish of the University of Notre Dame, 16 to 14, in November of 1931 in the annual renewal of their gridiron rivalry.

[2]For Jimmy Walker see WA 453:N 9.
Thomas Joseph Mooney, American labor agitator who was convicted as a participant in the bomb killings of nine persons in San Francisco and sentenced to death in 1916. His case aroused international interest because of the widely held belief that he was innocent. Jimmy Walker attempted unsuccessfully in November of 1931 to win a pardon for Mooney.

[3]Jesse C. Bushyhead, Claremore physician who served as treasurer and as principal chief of the Cherokee Nation. He and Rogers were first cousins.

[4]Peggy Hopkins Joyce, American vaudeville, stage, and screen actress whose six marriages and countless engagements brought her much publicity.

481 OM; published: *TDW,* March 13, 1932

[1]For David S. Ingalls see WA 440:N 11.

[2]For Newton D. Baker see WA 473:N 3.

[3]For Alfalfa Bill Murray see WA 442:N 1.

[4]William Jennings Bryan, American statesman and orator who ran unsuccessfully as the Democratic nominee for president in 1896, 1900, and 1908. He died in 1925.

[5]Albert Cabell Ritchie, Democratic governor of Maryland from 1920 to 1935.

482 *TDW,* March 20, 1932

[1]William Randolph Hearst, Jr., reporter for the *New York American* and eldest son of publishing tycoon William Randolph Hearst. Young Hearst later served as publisher of the *New York Journal-American* from 1937 to 1956.

[2]Oscar Lawler, Beverly Hills attorney and personal lawyer for Will Rogers.

[3]Betty Rogers was visiting Will's sister, Sallie Rogers McSpadden (see WA 449: N 1).

[4]George Mortimer Pullman, nineteenth century American inventer and manufacturer. Pullman co-designed and built the so-called Pullman sleeping cars for railroad travel.

[5]Charles Augustus Lindbergh, Jr., twenty-month-old son of Charles and Anne

Lindbergh (see WA 453:N 5), was kidnapped from his parents' home at Hopewell, New Jersey, on the night of March 1, 1932. Young Lindbergh's body was found on May 12, 1932, after a $50,000 ransom had been paid.

[6]Shigeru Honjo, Japanese military leader and commander of Japanese forces in Manchuria in 1931.

[7]For Arthur Brisbane see WA 455:N 5.

[8]For Dwight W. Morrow see WA 431:N 5 and WA 461:N 5.

[9]Elizabeth Cutter Morrow, American educator, welfare worker, and poet; widow of Dwight W. Morrow.

483 *TDW*, March 27, 1932

[1]For the Lindbergh kidnapping see WA 482:N 5.

[2]John Cheever Cowdin, American industrialist, financier, and sportsman; member of several leading United States polo and other sports teams; major financer of American aviation companies.

484 (Oklahoma City) *Daily Oklahoman*, April 3, 1932

[1]For the Lindbergh kidnapping see WA 482:N 5.

[2]George Eastman, American inventor, industrialist, and philanthropist who conceived and developed the Kodak camera in 1888; treasurer and general manager of Eastman Kodak Company. Eastman died at Rochester, New York, on March 14, 1932.

[3]Earl Carroll, American theater owner and theatrical and motion picture producer. His *Earl Carroll's Vanities* appeared on Broadway from 1923 to 1925.

[4]Ivar Kreuger, Swedish industrialist, financier, and swindler. Kreuger organized a holding firm, Swedish Match Company, in 1917 and through it developed an international match monopoly. Financial stress beginning in 1929 forced the collapse of his enterprises. He committed suicide in Paris on March 12, 1932.

485 *TDW*, April 10, 1932

[1]John Joseph McGraw, manager of the New York Giants baseball team from 1902 to 1932. McGraw led the Giants to ten league and three world championships.

[2]John Tortes "Chief" Meyers, professional baseball catcher who played for the New York Giants from 1908 to 1915 and later played for the Brooklyn Dodgers and the Boston Braves. A native of California, he was a full-blooded Indian.

[3]John P. "Honus" Wagner, professional baseball star who played for the Pittsburgh Pirates from 1900 to 1913. Many experts rate Wagner as the greatest shortstop in baseball history and one of the finest players of the game. He was named to the Baseball Hall of Fame in 1936.

[4]Charles Albert "Chief" Bender, professional baseball pitcher who played in the major leagues for sixteen years, most notably with the Philadelphia Athletics from 1903 to 1914. He was enshrined in the Baseball Hall of Fame in 1953.

[5]Mordecai Peter Centennial "Three Finger" Brown, professional baseball pitcher who achieved fame with the Chicago Cubs from 1904 to 1912. A winner of 208 games, he was named to the Baseball Hall of Fame in 1949.

John Joseph "Johnny" Evers, professional baseball player for the Chicago Cubs from 1902 to 1913. A shortstop and a member of the Baseball Hall of Fame, Evers was the keystone in the famous "Tinker to Evers to Chance" double-play combination.

For Tris Speaker see WA 457:N 4.

[6]For Walter P. Johnson see WA 457:N 4.

[7]Arthur Joseph "Tillie" Shafer, infielder for the New York Giants from 1909 to 1913.

Fred Carlisle Snodgrass, professional baseball player for the New York Giants from 1908 to 1915 and the Boston Braves from 1915 to 1916.

Stanley Raymond "Bucky" Harris, baseball player with the Washington Senators from 1919 to 1928; manager of the Senators from 1924 to 1928, 1935 to 1942, and 1950 to 1954. Harris was inducted into the Baseball Hall of Fame in 1975.

[8]Bozeman Bulger, American sportswriter and columnist who worked for the *New York Evening World* from 1905 to 1931 and contributed to the *Saturday Evening Post* from 1920 to 1932.

[9]Eddie Mayer, an unidentified Los Angeles sports writer.

[10]William Harold "Bill" Terry, star infielder for the New York Giants from 1923 to 1936 and manager of the Giants from 1932 to 1941. Terry became a member of the Baseball Hall of Fame in 1954.

Fred Charles Lindstrom, professional baseball player who starred for a number of clubs, most notably the New York Giants from 1924 to 1932. Lindstrom was named to the Baseball Hall of Fame in 1976.

486   *TDW,* April 17, 1932

487   McN; published: *TDW,* April 24, 1932

[1]"Amos 'n Andy," popular radio serial which began in 1928 and was aired five times weekly until 1943. The creators and stars were Freeman Fisher Gosden and Charles J. Correll, blackface comedians, who played every male part and wrote every script. The escapades of two Harlem taxi drivers and their friends captivated an enormous and faithful listening audience.

[2]For Chic Sale see WA 434:N 8.

[3]For Billie Burke see WA 460:N 2.

Ignace Jan Paderewski, Polish pianist, composer, and statesman. He made the first of many concert tours of the United States in 1891.

[4]For the Lindbergh kidnapping see WA 482:N 5.

[5]Phar Lap, an Australian thoroughbred, set a new track record in the Agua Caliente Handicap on March 20, 1932. It was the first appearance on a North American track for the six-year-old chestnut gelding, and the victory placed him second among money-winning horses in the world. He died suddenly a few days later at a California ranch.

[6]Herbert Austin Wolfe, racing editor of the *Sidney Daily Telegraph* and the *Sunday Sun* from 1931 to 1933. Wolfe accompanied Phar Lap to the United States as a representative of the Australian press.

488   *TDW,* May 1, 1932

[1]Victor Sassoon, British baronet who headed a vast financial empire in the Far East during the 1920s that included large banking interests and real estate investments in China.

The Rothschild family, European financiers and statesmen who controlled a large part of the European money market in the nineteenth and early twentieth centuries.

[2]The Olympic Games were held in Los Angeles in 1932.

489   McN; published: *TDW,* May 8, 1932

[1]For Pat Harrison see WA 465:N 2.

[2]For Greta Garbo see WA 463:N 8.

[3]For Ivar Kreuger see WA 484:N 4.

490   *TDW,* May 15, 1932

[1]*Grand Hotel,* all-star motion picture of 1932, adapted from the novel by Vicki Baum. Immensely popular, it won an Academy Award in 1933.

[2]Sid Grauman, American showman and motion picture theater owner who built the famous Egyptian and Chinese theaters on Hollywood Boulevard in Los Angeles.

[3]Louis Burt Mayer, Russian-born American film producer who was a cofounder and the first vice president of Metro-Goldwyn-Mayer Corporation.

[4]Garbo (see WA 463:N 8), John and Lionel Barrymore (see WA 443:N 5) and Wallace Beery (see WA 469:N 6) starred in *Grand Hotel.*

Joan Crawford, American leading lady of motion pictures. She made her film debut in *Pretty Ladies* in 1925 and had a major role in *Grand Hotel.*

Jean Hersholt, Danish-born American character actor who first appeared in Hollywood films during the 1920s.

Tully Marshall, American character actor who appeared in motion pictures from 1914 until his death in 1943.

[5]Will Mahoney, American vaudeville entertainer. His "falling-down" dance and his novelty dancing on a xylophone constituted one of the most famous solo acts in the business.

[6]For Earl Carroll see WA 484:N 3.

491   TDW, May 22, 1932

[1]Thomas H. Massie, United States naval lieutenant stationed in Hawaii, was one of four white persons convicted of the murder of a native Hawaiian, Joseph Kahahawai, the alleged assailant of Massie's wife. The prison sentence of the white men were commuted on May 4, after the men had served only one hour in jail.

[2]Clarence Seward Darrow, prominent American defense attorney and civil libertarian whose court cases were almost invariably headline material. Darrow defended Massie and the others accused of the murder of Kahahawai.

[3]James Roosevelt, eldest son of Franklin D. Roosevelt; insurance company executive and political figure. He was married to.the former Betsey Cushing.

[4]Ogden Livingston Mills, United States secretary of the treasury from 1932 to 1933.

[5]For Andrew W. Mellon see WA 440:N 9.

492   TDW, May 29, 1932

[1]Three ground crewmen attempting to moor the United States naval dirigible *Akron* at Camp Kearney, California, on May 11, 1932, were dragged aloft when a trailing line broke. Two of the sailors lost their grip on the rope and plunged to their deaths. The third managed to cling to the line until rescued two hours later.

[2]Charles E. Rosendahl, lieutenant commander in the United States Navy; commander of the dirigible *Akron*.

[3]Marlene Dietrich, German-American film actress and singer. She scored her first success in 1930 as Lola in the German film *The Blue Angel*. She then came to the United States to star in such motion pictures as *Shanghai Express* and *Blonde Venus* in 1932.

[4]For Greta Garbo see WA 463:N 8.

[5]For Douglas Fairbanks, Sr., see WA 434:N 6.

493   TDW, June 5, 1932

[1]For James Rolph, Jr., see WA 442:N 3.

[2]Will Keith Kellogg, American breakfast cereal manufacturer and founder in 1906 of the Kellogg Company of Battle Creek, Michigan. Kellogg donated his Arabian horse ranch at Pomona, California, and an endowment of $600,000 to California State Polytechnic College as a stimulus for teaching and research in animal husbandry. Kellogg was married to Dr. Carrie Staines.

494   TDW, June 12, 1932

[1]Harry Dwight Chamberlain, United States Army officer and internationally known horseman. Chamberlain was a member of the American riding team at the Olympic Games of 1920 and 1928 and captain of the team at the Los Angeles Olympics of 1932.

[2]Thomas Edwin "Tom" Mix, American cowboy motion picture star who was one of the greatest box-office attractions in the history of the screen. His horse, Tony, one of the first of the animal stars of motion pictures, was almost as famous as his master.

Mabel Hubbell Ward, aerial performer with the Sells-Floto Circus. She and Mix were married in early 1932.

[3]Thomasina was Mix's nine-year-old daughter by his third wife, Victoria Forde.

[4]Mix was hospitalized in late 1931 for treatment of an inflammation resulting from a ruptured appendix.

[5]William Gibbs McAdoo, United States secretary of the treasury from 1913 to 1918; leading contender for the Democratic presidential nominations in 1924 and 1928; United States senator from California from 1933 to 1939.

[6]Stephen Grover Cleveland, Democratic governor of New York from 1883 to 1885;

president of the United States from 1885 to 1889 and 1893 to 1897.

[7]Irene Rich, American motion picture actress who appeared in films from 1918 until her retirement in 1948.

[8]Winona Winter, American vaudeville performer and stage actress; ventriloquist, impersonator, and comedienne; close personal friend of Rogers' wife, Betty.

[9]Banks Winter, American minstrel performer whose career as a blackface comedian lasted more than fifty years. He netted almost $500,000 from the song "White Wings," which he wrote in 1884.

[10]James Blake "Jim" Rogers, second son of Will and Betty Rogers. Jim, an excellent polo player and horseman, was a student at New Mexico Military Institute in Roswell. He played number one on the school's polo team.

[11]Stacker Lee "Little Tex" Austin, American polo player and son of John Van "Tex" Austin, American rodeo promoter who was one of the best-known organizers of large-scale shows at Madison Square Garden. Young Austin was number three on the polo team at NMMI.

Charles Wildey "Dick" Waring, a cadet polo player from San Angelo, Texas. He played number two on the NMMI polo team.

Thomas W. "Tommy" Thompson, number four cadet polo player at NMMI. Thompson was from Great Neck, New York, and Wichita Falls, Texas.

E. A. Keyes, polo coach from 1929 to 1932 and professor of military science and tactics from 1926 to 1932 at New Mexico Military Institute.

495   *TDW,* June 19, 1932

[1]For Clara Bow see WA 434:N 5.

[2]Delores Costello Barrymore, actress-wife of John Barrymore (see WA 443:N 5), gave birth to the couple's first child, John Barrymore, Jr., on June 4, 1932.

[3]For Greta Garbo see WA 463:N 8.

[4]Rex Bell, American motion picture cowboy star of the 1930s, husband of Clara Bow, and one-time lieutenant governor of Nevada.

[5]Marguerite Churchill, American leading lady of motion pictures whose first film was the "talkie" *They Had to See Paris* in 1929.

[6]Guinn "Big Boy" Williams, American character actor of films, usually in amiably tough roles. He first appeared in Hollywood in 1919 as an "extra" in motion pictures.

[7]Sam E. Rork, American motion picture maker who produced the film *A Texas Steer* in 1927 in which Rogers starred.

[8]Paul Whiteman, American bandleader who became famous in the 1920s for pioneering the "sweet style" as opposed to the traditional "classical style" jazz music.

Margaret Livingston, American motion picture actress who retired in 1934 after a successful fifteen-year career. She married Paul Whiteman in 1931 and remained with him until his death in 1967.

Water,Water, Everywhere, silent film in 1919 that was adapted from the novel *Billy Fortune* by William and Louis Lighton.

[9]For Irene Rich see WA 494:N 7.

[10]For Chic Sale see WA 434:N 8.

496   OM; published: *TDW,* June 26, 1932

[1]For Amon G. Carter see WA 437:N 2.

[2]Joseph Irvin France, Republican United States senator from Maryland from 1917 to 1923. A physician and businessman, France attempted unsuccessfully to nominate former president Calvin Coolidge at the Republican National Convention in 1932.

[3]Grace Anna Goodhue Coolidge, wife of Calvin Coolidge and popular first lady who was generally considered to be more personable than the president.

[4]Henry Louis Mencken, American editor, author, and publisher; a social and political critic well-known for his acid pen.

James Boswell, Scottish lawyer and biographer. His celebrated *Life of Samuel Johnson* was published in 1791.

[5]Simeon Davison Fess, Republican United States senator from Ohio from 1923 to 1935.

[6]The Bonus Army, a group of more than 15,000 mostly-unemployed veterans who

marched on Washington, D. C., in the spring of 1932 to demand immediate payment of their World War I bonus.

[7]Jouett Shouse, Democratic United States representative from Kansas from 1915 to 1919; assistant secretary of the treasury from 1919 to 1920. An attorney from Kansas City, Missouri, Shouse was active at the Democratic National Conventions in 1920, 1924, and 1932.

[8]The Democratic National Convention was held in Houston, Texas, in 1928.

[9]For Albert C. Ritchie see WA 480:N 8.

497   OM; published: *TDW*, July 3, 1932

[1]*The Good Earth*, Pearl Buck's best-selling novel about life in China. The 1931 work won a Pulitzer Prize.

[2]For William G. McAdoo see WA 494:N 5.

[3]Lewis Edward Lawes, American penologist; warden of Sing Sing Prison in New York from 1920 to 1941; author of works on prisons and penology, including *20,000 Years in Sing Sing* (1932).

[4]Ernest Kinyoun Hutchinson, an unidentified writer.

[5]Elizabeth Berger Nichols, California author whose collection of poetry, *In the Land of Bah*, was published in Los Angeles in 1932.

[6]Harry Micajah Daugherty, United States attorney general from 1921 to 1924. Daugherty was tried for conspiracy in the scandals of the Harding administration but was acquitted. He was coauthor with Thomas Dixon of *The Inside Story of the Harding Tragedy* (1932).

[7]Gaston Bullock Means, American detective and convicted swindler who was a leading witness in the investigation of the Harding administration scandals.

[8]Evalyn Walsh McLean, American gold mining heiress and society hostess; wife of Edward Beale "Ned" McLean, owner and publisher of the *Washington Post*. She paid $100,000 to Gaston Means at the time of the Lindbergh kidnapping (see WA 482:N 5) in hopes that his contacts might lead to the recovery of the child. Excessive publicity and Means' conviction on a grand larceny charge were the only results.

[9]Frederick Lewis Allen, American editor and author; associate editor of *Harper's Magazine* from 1931 to 1941; author of *Only Yesterday* (1931) and *Since Yesterday* (1940).

[10]Ruth Laughlin Barker, American archaeologist and writer. She wrote *Caballeros*, a history and romantic travel guide of New Mexico, as well as articles for the *New York Times* and the *Christian Science Monitor* pertaining to Spanish influences in the Southwest.

[11]George W. Saunders, San Antonio cattleman and livestock commission dealer. An early trail driver, Saunders organized the Trail Drivers Association and served as its president, directing the publication in 1925 of the book *Trail Drivers of Texas*.

498   *TDW*, July 10, 1932

[1]For William McKinley see WA 462:N 7; for William Jennings Bryan see WA 481:N 4.

499   *TDW*, July 17, 1932

[1]Fred Lowry, Oklahoma rancher and steer roping champion. After retiring from the rodeo circuit, Lowry managed a school for steer ropers on his 20,000-acre ranch in Nowata County, Oklahoma.

[2]James Kane Rider, a cowboy from Watova, Indian Territory, who was a familiar figure on the Rogers family ranch during Will's youth.

"Johnnie Blocker," a type of rope throw that was named after its originator, John Rufus Blocker, a Texas cattle rancher.

[3]Robert Anderson "Wild Horse Bob" Crosby, colorful and controversial rodeo performer of the 1920s and 1930s, known as the "King of the Steer Ropers."

500   *TDW*, July 17, 1932

[1]Paavo Nurmi, Finnish long-distance runner; gold medal winner in the Olympic Games of 1920, 1924, and 1928. Nurmi wanted to end his career with a gold medal at

the Los Angeles Olympics of 1932 but was suspended from amateur ranks because of alleged professionalism.

For Greta Garbo see WA 463:N 8.

[2]Luis Angel Firpo, Argentine heavyweight prize fighter, known as "the Wild Bull of the Pampas."

501   *TDW*, July 31, 1932

[1]For this and all further references to James B. Rogers see WA 494:N 10.

[2]Robert Maynard Hutchins, president of the University of Chicago from 1929 to 1945; chancellor from 1945 to 1951. Hutchins did much to change curriculum and teaching methods on the college level.

502   OM; published: *TDW*, August 7, 1932

[1]Mildred "Babe" Didrikson Zaharias, American track and golf star and one of the most accomplished female athletes of all time. In the Olympic Games of 1932 she set world records in the javelin (143' 4") and the eighty-meter hurdles (11.7 seconds).

[2]Helene Madison, Seattle swimmer who was the foremost free-styler of her era. She won all four United States titles in 1930 and 1931 and then bowed out of swimming after the Los Angeles Olympics, in which she won three gold medals and set her twenty-first world record.

[3]Georgia Coleman, Idaho diver and swimmer who won the springboard competition and was second in the highboard event at the Olympics of 1932.

503   McN; published: *TDW*, Ausust 14, 1932

[1]Sebastiao de Frietas de Heredia, Portuguese nobleman, soldier, and athlete.

504   McN; published: *TDW*, August 21, 1932

[1]Patrick "Pat" O'Callaghan, Irish veterinarian and athlete who won gold medals in the hammer throw at the Olympic Games of 1928 and 1932.

[2]Robert M. N. "Bob" Tisdall, Ceylonese-born athlete who competed for the Irish Olympic team in 1932, winning the 400-meter hurdles and finishing eighth in the decathlon.

David Burghley, British lord and track star who competed at the 1928 and 1932 Olympics, winning a gold medal in the 400-meter hurdles in 1928 and finishing fourth in the same event in 1932.

[3]Juan Carlos Zabala, Argentine long-distance runner, won the marathon in 1932 with an Olympic record time of two hours, thirty-one minutes, and thirty-six seconds.

[4]Glen W. Dawson, American track star who finished sixth in the 3,000-meter steeplechase at the 1932 Olympics.

[5]Wilson David Charles, American athlete who finished fourth in the decathlon at the Los Angeles Olympics of 1932.

[6]Members of the Bonus Army (see WA 496:N 6) refused to leave Washington, D.C., after the Senate failed to enact bonus legislation. On July 28, 1932, Hoover ordered the Army to evict the marchers forcibly. Army troops set the veterans' camps on fire and drove them from the city. Hoover was rebuked by the press and the general public for the severity of his actions.

505   *TDW*, August 28, 1932

[1]For "Amos 'n Andy" see WA 487:N 1.

[2]Adolf Hitler, German dictator and founder and leader of the National Socialist (Nazi) party in Germany. Hitler's organization steadily gained support after its birth in 1921, basing its appeal on hatred, anti-Semitism, and German world power.

[3]Paul Ludwig von Hindenburg, president of Germany from 1925 to 1934. Born in 1847, Hindenburg served as German Army Chief of Staff during World War I. He held the presidency during a time of extreme economic distress and political factionalism in Germany.

[4]Edgar Algernon Robert Gascoyne-Cecil, viscount Cecil of Chelwood, a creator of

the League of Nations and a British representative to many post-World War I disarmament conferences; recipient of the Nobel Peace Prize in 1937.

506   TDW, September 4, 1932

[1]Takeichi Nishi, Japanese soldier and equestrian who won the individual title in the *prix des Nations* competition at the Olympic Games of 1932.
[2]For George Higgins Moses see WA 440:N 6.
[3]For James E. Watson see WA 465:N 2.

507   TDW, September 11, 1932

[1]*Lightnin'*, a motion picture which was released in 1930 and starred Rogers, was based on the play by Winchell Smith and Frank Bacon.
[2]For Clara Bow see WA 434:N 5.
[3]*Jubilo*, a silent film released in 1919 and based on the story by Ben Ames Williams. Rogers appeared also in the 1932 remake, *Too Busy to Work*.
[4]Phineas Taylor Barnum, American showman who opened the "Greatest Show on Earth" in 1871 and who was a cofounder in 1881 of the famous Barnum and Bailey Circus.
[5]For Will H. Hays see WA 438:N 2.

508   TDW, September 18, 1932

[1]Joseph "Joe" Gans, American prizefighter known as the "Old Master," held the world lightweight crown from 1902 to 1908.
Oscar "Battling" Nelson, Danish-born boxer who held the world lightweight championship from 1908 to 1910. Nelson and Gans met on September 3, 1906, in a scheduled forty-five round championship bout in Goldfield, Nevada. Gans won the epic battle in the forty-second round when Nelson was disqualified for striking a low blow.
George Lewis "Tex" Rickard, American sports promoter who started in the business by staging the Gans-Nelson bout of 1906.
[2]Walter Scott, "Death Valley Scotty," self-styled prospector and miner who left his native Kentucky in the 1890s to travel through the West. Scott eventually settled in Death Valley, California, where his publicity stunts and moneymaking schemes netted him a small fortune and a legendary reputation. In the 1920s he built a huge, lavish castle on his desert estate.

509   TDW, September 25, 1932

[1]Oscar Odd McIntyre, American syndicated writer whose column, "New York Day by Day," appeared in more than 500 newspapers from 1912 until his death in 1938.
[2]Arthur "Bugs" Baer, popular American newspaper columnist and humorist; wrote for the *New York World* and the *New York American* newspapers.
[3]For Clara Bow see WA 434:N 5.
[4]Winfield R. "Winnie" Sheehan, American motion picture director and producer; vice president of Fox Film Corporation from 1921 to 1935.
[5]For "Amos 'n Andy" see WA 487:N 1.
[6]For William G. McAdoo see WA 494:N 5.
[7]For Greta Garbo see WA 463:N 8.
[8]For Marie Dressler see WA 469:N 20.
[9]Philip Duffield Strong, American newspaperman and author whose first novel, *State Fair* (1932), was made into a highly popular motion picture, starring Rogers.
[10]Dick Powell, American singer and actor who had limited stage experience before signing a Hollywood contract in 1932 and making his film debut in *Blessed Event*. He continued to make motion pictures until his retirement in 1954.
[11]For William Randolph Hearst see WA 461:N 1.
[12]Paul Bern, American actor and motion picture executive whose tragic death in 1932, soon after his marriage to glamorous film star Jean Harlow, remains a subject of controversy.
[13]For Billie Burke Ziegfeld see WA 460:N 2.

[14]*The Stump Farm,* a 1928 non-fiction work by Hilda Rose that chronicled the lives of a pioneer farm family in the Northwest.

510 OM; published: *TDW,* October 2, 1932

511 OM; published: *TDW,* October 9, 1932

[1]For Stan Laurel and Oliver Hardy see WA 464:N 1.
[2]For Samuel Goldwyn see WA 475:N 5.
[3]For Tom Mix see WA 494:N 2; for Hoot Gibson see WA 469:N 5.
[4]For Louis B. Mayer see WA 490:N 3.

512 *TDW,* October 16, 1932

[1]For Ogden L. Mills see WA 491:N 4; for Andrew W. Mellon see WA 440:N 9; for King George V and Queen Mary see WA 440:N 1.
[2]For Aimee Semple McPherson see WA 429:N 4.
[3]Theodore Roosevelt, Jr., eldest son and namesake of the twenty-sixth president. A former assistant secretary of the navy, Roosevelt was a noted writer, explorer, politician, and soldier.
[4]Mills was married to the former Dorothy Randolph Fell of Philadelphia.
[5]For "Amos 'n Andy" see WA 487:N 1.
[6]Robert Pierce "Bob" Shuler, fundamentalist clergyman and lecturer from Los Angeles. Shuler polled more than 560,000 votes for the United States Senate in 1932 while running on the Prohibition party ticket. He was married to the former Nelle Reeves.
[7]For William G. McAdoo see WA 494:N 5.

513 *TDW,* October 23, 1932

[1]Rin-Tin-Tin, German shepherd who between 1922 and 1931 was the most famous canine star in American motion pictures.

514 *TDW,* October 30, 1932

[1]John Edward "Ed" Borein, American western illustrator, etcher, and painter, known as the "Cowpuncher Artist."
[2]For William Randolph Hearst and the Babicora Ranch see WA 461:N 1.
[3]James Harold "Jimmy" Doolittle, American flier noted for his speed marks set in the 1920s and 1930s, his interest in commercial aviation, and his heroism during World War II.
For Frank Hawks see WA 434:N 3.

515 *TDW,* November 6, 1932

[1]For Pat Hurley see WA 440:N 9.
[2]For Ogden L. Mills see WA 491:N 4.
[3]For David S. Ingalls see WA 440:N 11.
[4]George White, Democratic governor of Ohio from 1931 to 1935. White defeated Ingalls in the gubernatorial election of 1932.
[5]A Republican, Davison (see WA 469:N 15) was defeated in his bid in 1932 for the lieutenant governorship of New York.

516 (Oklahoma City) *Daily Oklahoman,* November 3, 1932

[1]For William Jennings Bryan see WA 481:N 4.
[2]Rogers attended Kemper Military School at Boonville, Missouri, from 1897 to 1898.
[3]Thomas Alexander Johnston, American educator and veteran of the Confederate Army; superintendant and owner of Kemper Military School from 1881 to 1909; president and superintendant from 1909 to 1928; president from 1928 until his death in 1934.

[4]W. A. "Billy" Johnson, rancher and banker of Canadian, Texas.
[5]Frank Ewing, son of Perry Ewing, a Texas rancher at Higgins, Texas, for whom Rogers worked in 1898 after leaving Kemper.
[6]For Andrew J. Volstead see WA 431:N 2.

517   McN; published: *TDW*, November 20, 1932

518   *TDW*, November 27, 1932

[1]Frank Alderman Garbutt, California business executive and sportsman who founded the Los Angeles Athletic Club in 1905 and the California Yacht Club of Los Angeles in 1922.

519   *TDW*, December 4, 1932

[1]For O. O. McIntyre see WA 509:N 1.
[2]For Amon G. Carter see WA 437:N 2.
Miriam Amanda Wallace "Ma" Ferguson, Democratic governor of Texas from 1925 to 1927 and 1933 to 1935. Mrs. Ferguson won the gubernatorial election in 1932 despite the vociferous opposition of Amon Carter.
[3]For Flo Ziegfeld see WA 447:N 3.
[4]Henry VIII, king of England from 1509 to 1547.
For Roy W. Howard see WA 437:N 6.
[5]Vanderbilt, name of a noted American family of industrialists, financiers, philanthropists, and sportsmen.
[6]For Peggy Hopkins Joyce see WA 480:N 4.
[7]McIntyre was married to the former Maybelle Hope Small.

520   *TDW*, December 11, 1932

[1]Pearl Sydenstricker Buck, American author who lived and taught in China during the 1920s. Among her many bestselling and award-winning works is *The Good Earth* (see WA 494:N 1).
[2]Donaldson, unidentified missionary.
[3]Pearl Buck was married to Dr. John Lossing Buck. They both served on the faculty of the University of Nanking.

521   OM; published: *TDW*, December 18, 1932

[1]Walter Lippmann, American editor, columnist, and author who served on the editorial staff of the *New York World* from 1921 to 1931 and later contributed columns to the *New York Herald-Tribune* and the *Washington Post*. In one of his columns, Lippmann had questioned the accuracy of some of Rogers' statements concerning the cancellation or postponement of the war debts.

522   *TDW*, December 25, 1932

[1]For Winnie Sheehan see WA 509:N 4.
[2]Rupert Hughes, American novelist, songwriter, playwright, historian, and screenwriter; best known for his multi-volume biography *George Washington* (1925-1930).
[3]For Samuel Goldwyn see WA 475:N 5.
[4]For Maurice Maeterlinck see WA 475:N 4.
[5]Rex Ellingwood Beach, American novelist and miscellaneous writer, noted for his rough-hewn portrayals of life in Alaska. He was married to the former Edith Crater. Rogers' first motion picture, *Laughing Bill Hyde* (1918), was based on one of Beach's novels.
[6]Fred Niblo, famous Hollywood director of the 1920s who had stage and vaudeville experience. Niblo left Hollywood in the early 1930s.
[7]Conrad Nagel, American stage actor and motion-picture leading man of the 1920s and 1930s.

[8]Janet Gaynor, American film star of the 1920s and 1930s who gained immense popularity in sentimental roles. Gaynor won an Academy Award in 1927 for her performance in *Seventh Heaven.*

[9]Harry Carr, reporter and columnist for the *Los Angeles Times* from 1897 until his death in 1936.

[10]Walter Winchell, syndicated columnist for the *New York Mirror* from 1929 to 1963. Winchell, one of the best-known journalists and radio commentators in the country, specialized in show business gossip and political commentary.

523   OM; published: *TDW,* January 1, 1933

[1]James Edward "Jim" Ferguson, Democratic governor of Texas from 1915 until his impeachment and removal from office in 1917 for misappropriation of state funds and other misdeeds. He remained an important figure in Texas politics, strongly influencing the gubernatorial administrations of his wife, Ma Ferguson (see WA 519:N 2).

[2]For Alfalfa Bill Murray see WA 442:N 1.

[3]For Thomas A. Johnston see WA 516:N 4.

[4]Hattie Wyatt Caraway, Democratic United States senator from Arkansas from 1933 to 1945; widow of Senator Thaddeus H. Caraway (see WA 465:N 3).

[5]The Long family, including Huey P. Long, dominated Louisiana politics for several decades.

[6]Rogers was probably referring to Henry Wadsworth Longfellow's narrative poem "Evangeline," which chronicles the lives of the French-speaking inhabitants of early Louisiana.

[7]For Pat Harrison see WA 465:N 2.

524   *TDW,* January 8, 1933

[1]Alsie Raymond Grant, pastor of Simpson Methodist Church, Minneapolis, Minnesota, from 1931 to 1933; Methodist bishop at Portland, Oregon, from 1952 until his death in 1967.

[2]For William H. McGuffey see WA 475:N 6.

525   *TDW,* January 15, 1933

[1]For Howard H. Jones see WA 433:N 5.

[2]Warren Heller, running back for the University of Pittsburgh football team from 1930 to 1932; All-America player in 1932.

[3]Harold Edward "Red" Grange, star football halfback at the University of Illinois from 1922 to 1925. Grange later played professional football, notably with the Chicago Bears from 1926 to 1934.

[4]Hiram Warren Johnson, United States senator from California from 1917 until his death in 1945. Johnson belonged to the progressive wing of the Republican party.

[5]For Pierre Laval see WA 463:N 1.

[6]Helen Adams Keller, famous American author and lecturer, blind from the age of two. She lectured throughout the United States, Europe, and Asia, raising funds for the training of the blind and promoting other social causes.

[7]Louis Braille, nineteenth century French musician and teacher of the blind. Braille devised a raised-point system of writing for sight-impaired persons.

[8]For William G. McAdoo see WA 494:N 5.

George Edward Creel, American journalist, government administrator, politician, and author. During World War I, Creel headed the Committee on Public Information, the federal government's office of wartime propaganda.

526   *TDW,* January 22, 1933

[1]Coolidge died of a heart attack on January 5, 1933, at the age of sixty.

[2]For Grace Coolidge see WA 496:N 3.

[3]Ralph W. Hemenway, Massachusetts attorney; law partner of Calvin Coolidge at Northampton, Massachusetts.

[4]John C. Coolidge, son of President Coolidge, was married to the former Florence Trumbull, daughter of a former governor of Connecticut.

527   OM; published: *TDW*, January 29, 1933

¹Carter Glass, Democratic United States senator from Virginia from 1920 until his death in 1946; widely recognized as a financial expert. Glass and Long clashed repeatedly in early 1933 over a Glass-sponsored banking bill which came up for debate in the Senate in early January. The Louisiana Democrat led a filibuster that delayed the bill for sixteen days.
²For Pat Hurley see WA 440:N 9.
³For Amon G. Carter see WA 437:N 2.
⁴For Ma Ferguson see WA 519:N 2; for Jim Ferguson see WA 523:N 1.

528   *TDW*, February 5, 1933

¹For George W. Norris see WA 429:N 1.

529   OM; published: *TDW*, February 12, 1933

¹For Hal E. Roach see WA 464:N 1.
²For Jimmy Dickson see WA 464:N 2.
³Arthur Marcus Loew, American motion picture producer and president and chairman of the board of Loew's, Inc., the parent company of Metro-Goldwyn-Mayer. Loew escaped serious injury in the plane crash in Africa.
   Marcus Loew, Austrian-born American theater owner and motion picture producer; cofounder and controller of Metro-Goldwyn-Mayer Corporation; father of Arthur M. Loew. Marcus Loew died in 1927.
⁴For Eric Pedley see WA 464:N 1.

530   *TDW*, February 19, 1933

¹Al Jolson, Russian-born American minstrel, vaudevillian, theatrical performer, motion picture actor, and radio star. His film work began with the *Jazz Singer* in 1927, the first major film with sound.
²Ernest Poole, American author and newspaper correspondent; awarded a Pulitzer Prize in 1917 for the novel *His Family*. Mary Breckenridge, a nurse and a member of a prominent Southern family, was the subject of Poole's *Nurses on Horseback*.
³Mary America Schrimsher Rogers, mother of Will Rogers.

531   OM; published: *TDW*, February 26, 1933

¹For William Randolph Hearst see WA 461:N 1.

532   OM; published: *TDW*, March 5, 1933

¹For Will Durant see WA 445:N 1.
²Chester Harvey Rowell, American newspaper editor and political science lecturer; editor of the *San Francisco Chronicle* from 1932 to 1939.
³Rufus Bernhard von KleinSmid, American educator; president of the University of Arizona from 1914 to 1921; president of the University of Southern California from 1921 to 1946.

INDEX

Acting: 17, 41
Actors and actresses: 11, 41, 69, 72, 158, 183, 188, 216
Ade, George: 15
Advertising: 25, 28, 42, 141; on radio, 23; in newspapers, 23; on billboards, 25; in Latin America, 25; for real estate, 38
Africa: 102, 106, 219, 231, 233
Agriculture: prices in, 59-61; study of, 210-11; *see also* Farmers *and related topics*
Aguinaldo, Emilio: 84
Akron (dirigible): 151
Akron, Ohio: 96
Alabama: 185
Alaska: 104
Alberta, Canada: 113
Albuquerque, N. M.: 16
Aleutian Islands: 105, 108-109
Alexander, Vic: 40
Alfonso XIII, king of Spain: 1, 32, 62
Algiers, Algeria: 39
Allen, Frederick Lewis: 163
Allied nations: 47
Amarillo, Texas: 51
American Civil War: 55
Americanism: 234
American Legion: 74
"Amos 'n Andy" (radio show): 140, 179, 188, 194
Anarchists: 5
Andes: 232
Ants: 115
Arabia: 66
Arabian horses: 153, 154
Arabs: 39, 66
Argentina: 56, 62, 170, 178, 203
Arizona: 37, 113, 218
Arizona, University of: 218; polo team of, 157
Arkansas: 30, 65, 91, 219-20
Armenians: 66
Armistice Day: 163
Army, U. S. Department of: 100; *see also* United States Army
Art: 11, 24, 134, 171, 191
Artists: 11
Astor, Nancy L.: 58, 62
Astor, Waldorf: 58
Astronomy: 113
As Young as You Feel (film): 15
Athletes: 158, 169, 170-71, 178, 181, 239; women as, 170, 173-74; men as, 174
Atlanta, Ga.: 17
Atlantic Ocean: 105, 207
Atterbury, William W.: 22
Attwell, Walter G.: 32
Austin, John V. (Tex): 156
Austin, Stacker L. (Little Tex): 156

Austin, Texas: 74, 228
Australia: 49, 62, 65, 107, 170, 237-38; race horse from, 142; Rogers in, 142
Austria: 62
Automatic weapons, and crime: 35
Automobiles: 35, 110, 180, 184; importation of, 9; Chevrolet models, 38, 60, 141, 234; Ford models, 38, 45, 60, 88, 119, 126, 135, 146, 147, 159, 169, 234; accidents involving, 48, 63; Americans' reliance on, 82; in Japan, 118-19; Rolls Royce models, 135, 210; tax on, 145
Autosuggestion: 82
Aviation: 15-16, 42, 49, 51, 62, 88, 93, 96-97, 98, 100, 104, 105, 109, 119-20, 130, 152, 156, 185, 199, 231-33; safety in, 15; in Central America, 17; in South America, 17; in Mexico, 18, 19; in Guatemala, 19; in Russia, 50; and radio, 52; military, 69-70, 180; international, 88; in Canada, 104; in Japan, 110-11, 112

Babies: 158, 159, 188, 221
Baer, Arthur (Bugs): 187
Baghdad, Iraq: 145
Baker, Mount: 104
Baker, Newton D.: 109, 128
Baker, Ruth Laughlin: 163
Baker, Sam (Sammy): 40-41
Bakersfield, Calif.: 158
Balboa, Vasco Núñez de: 107
Banking and bankers: 61, 65, 81-82, 102, 121, 127, 136, 206, 227; international, 55, 136, 154, 213
Banquets: 51; food at, 22
Baptists: 108, 212
Barbers, in China: 123
Barnum, Phineas T.: circus of, 183
Barrymore, John: 41, 147, 148; family of, 157, 158
Barrymore, Lionel: 147
Barrymore family: 41
Bartering: 122, 123-24
Baseball: 93, 136-38, 226; night games in, 72; World Series of 1931, 72, 73, 80-81; in Mexico, 81
Baseball teams, owners of: 136-37
Batavia: 113
Bathtubs: 45
Bats: 30
Battle Creek, Mich.: 153
Beach, Edith C. (Mrs. Rex E.): 215
Beach, Rex E.: 215
Beer: 84
Beery, Wallace: 98, 147, 149
Bees: 113-15, 215, 216

266

Behn, Louise: 32
Belengenland, S. S.: 233
Belgium: 47
Bell, Rex: 157-58
Bellingham, Wash.: 104, 109
Bender, Charles A. (Chief): 137
Berlin, Germany: 50
Bern, Paul: 188
Bethlehem, Pa.: 24
Beverly Hills, Calif.: 17, 188
Bible: 16, 71
Bicycles: 119; in Japan, 110
Bigamy: 70
Big Bend (Texas): 224
"Big business": 3, 207, 226
Billy the Kid: *see* Bonney, William H.
Bishop, Calif.: 185
Black Hills, S. D.: 10, 63
Blasco-Ibanez, Vicente: book by, 114
Boles, Thomas (Tom), Jr.: 30
Bolivia: 38, 178
Bolsheviks: 64, 66, 83
Bonney, William H. (Billy the Kid): 35
Bonus Army: 160, 178-79
Books: 162, 217; reviews of, 163
Boonville, Mo.: 202, 219
Boosterism: 44
Bootlegging and bootleggers: 8, 48; *see also*
    Prohibition
Borah, William E.: 12, 69, 85, 91, 115, 120,
    146, 223
Borein, J. Edward (Ed): 196-97
Borzage, Frank: 98
Boston, Mass.: 115
Boswell, James: 160
Boulder Dam: 75, 157, 229-30
Bow, Clara: 16, 157-58, 183; ranch of, 188
Boxer Rebellion: 115
Boxing and boxers: 39-40, 87, 173, 186
Box T Lad: 202-203
Box T Ranch: 202
Braille, Louis: 223-24
Braille language: 223
Brazil: 20, 62, 177-78, 232
Breckenridge, Mary: 234
Brisbane, Arthur: 66, 73, 130
British Columbia, Canada: 12, 107
British Guiana (Guyana): 18
Brown, Clarence: 98
Brown, Curley: 97
Brown, Mordecai P. C. (Three Finger): 137
Brownsville, Texas: 17
Bryan, William Jennings: 128, 165, 202
Buck, John L.: 210, 211
Buck, Pearl S.: 210-12
Buenos Aires, Argentina: 232
Buffalo, N. Y.: 188
Bulgaria: 135
Bulger, Bozeman: 138
Bullfighting: 18, 25
Bullfrog, Nev.: 187
Burghley, David: 177
Burke, Billie: 78, 142, 188-89

Burlesque: 237
Bushyhead, Jesse C.: 126
Business: 203
Butler, Nicholas Murray: 45
Butler, Smedley D.: 5, 62

Caballeros (book): 163
Cafeterias: 145
Cairo, Egypt: 231, 233
Calcutta, India: 233
California: 13, 14, 15-16, 32, 35, 37, 39, 54,
    70, 86, 95, 130, 151, 153, 154, 163,
    187, 191, 194, 197, 219; climate of, 16,
    38; emigration to, 37-39; governor of,
    39; newspapers in, 46; primary elec-
    tions in, 150; political delegation
    from, 159, 160; ranches in, 188
California State Polytechnic College: 153
Calles, Plutarco E.: 88, 90, 100
Campbell, Bess M. B. (Mrs. Thomas D.):
    101
Campbell, Thomas D.: 101, 102-103
Canada: 66, 96, 104, 105, 107, 109, 113,
    130, 170, 173, 179-80; aviation in, 104
Canadian, Texas: 202
Canton, China: 119, 124, 143, 210
Cantor, Eddie: daughters of, 100
Capetown, South Africa: 233
Capone, Alphonse (Scarface Al): 22, 47-48,
    106, 124, 126, 135, 149, 160
Caraguatay, Paraguay: 232
Caraway, Hattie W. (Mrs. Thaddeus H.):
    220
Caraway, Thaddeus H.: death of, 91-92
Carideo, Frank F.: 14
Carlsbad, N. M.: 28
Carlsbad Caverns National Park: 28, 30, 31
Carnegie, Andrew: 24
Carr, Harry: 216
Carter, Amon G.: 23, 100, 159, 161, 207-
    209, 228; Shady Oak Farm of, 55, 159
Cathay Hotel (Shanghai): 144
Cats: 182
Cattlemen: 45, 76, 77, 102, 132, 167; *see also*
    Ranchers
Cecil, Lord: *see* Gascoyne-Cecil
Central America: 19, 197; aviation in, 17
Chamberlain, Harry D.: 155
Chambers of commerce: 33, 56, 97, 219; in
    California, 37; in Oklahoma, 43
Change: 183
Chaplin, Charles S. (Charlie): 11-12, 33,
    188
Character: 69
Charity: 12, 21, 50, 70-71, 74, 192, 233-35,
    236; football games played for, 15
Charles, Wilson D.: 178
Charleston (dance): 62
Charro Club: 93
Chase, Stuart: 90
Chelsea, Okla.: 53, 130
Cherokee Indians: 85, 90, 93
Cherokee Nation: 39, 188

271

272

Outer Mongolia: 239
Overproduction: 199
Over the Hill (film): 98, 100
Oxford University: 8, 51, 66, 219
Ozark Mountains: 48

Pacific Ocean: 105, 106, 107, 108, 111, 232
Paderewski, Ignace Jan: 142
Pageants: 192-93
Palo Alto, Calif.: 174
Panama: 18
Panama Canal: 19
Parades: 192
Paraguay: 1, 232
Parents, and education: 172
Paris, France: 145, 157, 191, 197
Pasadena, Calif.: 101, 113, 223
Peace: 5, 83, 228
"Peanut Vendor Song": 23
Pears: 97-98
Pecans: 92.
Pecos River: 28
Pedley, Eric: 87, 88, 232; wife of, 88
Peking, China: 116, 119, 120, 210
Pennsylvania: 182, 221
Pennsylvania Hotel: 22
Pentathlon: 175-76
Persia: 231
Peru: 1, 178, 232
Phar Lap (race horse): 142
Philadelphia, Pa.: 81
Philadelphia Athletics (baseball): 72, 81
Philadelphia Phillies (baseball): 93
Philippine Islands: 83-85, 118; independence for, 83-85, 86, 150, 227
Philosophy: 44-46, 220-22
Photography: 10
Physicians: 55, 234
Pickford, Mary: 17
Picnics: 37-38
Pimlico, Md.: 91
Pittsburgh, Pa.: 188
Pittsburgh, University of: 222
The Plutocrat (novel): 39
Poetry and poets: 114, 163
Poland: 85, 86, 155; people of, 66, 85, 86
Pole vaulting: 173, 178
Polish Corridor: 85, 86
Political buttons: 75, 165
Political campaigns: 195-96
Political conventions: 153, 165-66, 169; *see also specific conventions*
Political platforms: 156, 200-201
Political science: 171
Politicians: 22, 34, 42, 57, 91, 128, 133, 166, 191, 193, 197, 199, 214, 222, 225, 230; honesty among, 5
Politics: 5, 8, 32, 42, 43, 44, 69, 71, 92, 102, 109, 127, 143, 150, 155, 157, 159, 165-66, 181, 187, 189, 200-201, 212, 214, 219, 220; harmony in, 7; in Japan, 109-10; in China, 119; humor in, 166

Polo: 73, 87, 93, 111, 132, 155, 156-57, 173, 188, 192, 232
Pomona, Calif.: 8, 153
Pomona College: 8
Poole, Ernest: 234
Popocatepétl: 88
Port Arthur, Russia: 144
Porter, John C.: 36, 38
Portland, Ore.: 40, 41, 96
Port of Spain, Trinidad: 20
Portugal: 176; people of, 111
Post, Emily P.: 33
Post, Fred: 93
Post, Mae L. (Mrs. Wiley H.): 52-53
Post, Wiley H.: 49, 51-53, 62
Post, William (Billy), II: 93
Post offices: 203, 230
Potatoes, price of: 59
Potomac River: 160
Poverty: 21, 70, 132, 140, 162; in Russia, 103
Powell, Dick: 188
Prajadhipok, king of Siam: 66
Preparedness, military: 34
Prices: 59-61; of wheat, 102
Prime ministers: 63, 64
Prince of Wales: *see* Edward Albert
Profanity: 27, 184-85
Professors: 44, 172
Progress: 201
Progressives: 8, 64
Prohibition: 6-7, 8, 21, 22, 23, 84, 129, 156; *see also* Eighteenth Amendment *and related topics*
Propaganda: 83, 115-16, 117, 191, 200; in Russia, 85
Prosperity: 73, 226
Pryor Creek, Okla.: 93
Publicity: 86-87, 131, 142
Public opinion: 181-82, 239
Public works projects: 132; in Los Angeles, 6
Puerto Rico: 17, 20
Pullman, George M.: 130

Racketeering and racketeers: 20, 34
Radio: 23, 60, 73, 87, 105, 129, 140-42, 145, 163, 193, 194, 200, 212, 235; and aviation, 16, 52; advertising on, 23; women on, 195
Railroads: 116, 218; in France, 116, 120; in China, 120-21; *see also* Trans-Siberian Railroad
Rambai Barni, queen consort of Siam: 66
Ranchers: 73, 92, 213, 219; wives of, 54; *see also* Cattlemen
Ranching: 157-58, 219
Rapidan River, presidential retreat on: 33
Raskob, John J.: 6, 7
Reading: 114
Real estate: advertisements for, 38; value of, 188; dealers in, 230

Royalty: 1, 2, 21, 32-33, 66, 68-69
Rum: 20, 21, 22
Rumania: 66
Russia: 49-50, 52, 56, 58-59, 66, 68-69, 82, 101, 102-103, 112, 117, 129, 144, 191, 237, 238-39; aviation in, 50; economic system of, 50; czar of, 52, 69; five-year plans of, 58-59, 62; people of, 66, 68-69, 86, 135; propaganda of, 85; White Russians, 111; military aviation in, 144
Russo-Japanese War: 117
Ryolite, Nev.: 187

Sailors: 151, 152
Saint Louis, Mo.: 81; fair at, 75-77
Saint Louis Cardinals (baseball): 72
Saint Louis World's Fair (1904): 75
Saint Thomas, Virgin Islands: 19, 20, 21
Saint Thomas Mail: 19, 20-21
Sale, Charles P. (Chic): 17, 141, 158; family of, 100
Salt Lake City, Utah: 90
San Angelo, Texas: 156
San Antonio, Texas: 92, 93, 163, 224
San Bernardino, Calif.: 15
Sandburg, Carl: biography of Lincoln, 114
San Diego, Calif.: 151
Sandino, Augusto C.: 34, 86
Sandow, Eugene: 79-80
San Fernando Valley, Calif.: 15
San Francisco, Calif.: 39, 79, 96, 104, 130, 192
San Francisco Chronicle: 237
San Geronimo, Mexico: 19
San Simeon, Calif.: 197
Santa Barbara, Calif.: 197
Santa Monica, Calif.: 18, 51, 155
Santiago, Chile: 232
Sassoon, Victor: 144
Saunders, George W.: 163
Savings: 82
Savoldi, Joseph A. (Jumpin' Joe): 13
Sawtelle, Calif.: 5
Scandals: 5, 6, 16, 189
Schemes: 190
Scholars: 38
Schools: 171, 172; *see also* Education
Schwab, Charles M.: 23-24
Science with a Smile (book): 162-63
Scientists: 113; from Japan, 113
Scott, Walter (Death Valley Scotty): castle of, 187
Screenwriters: 27, 183
Scripps, Robert P.: 24
Seattle, Wash.: 96, 104
Sex: 215
Sex appeal: 25
Shafer, Arthur J. (Tillie): 138
Shakespeare, William: 113, 216, 236
Shanghai, China: 116, 119, 143, 144, 145, 181, 210
Shasta, Mount: 97

Shasta (race horse): 97
Shasta Daisy (race horse): 97
Shaw, George Bernard: 44, 58, 62, 66
Sheehan, Winfield R. (Winnie): 188, 215
Shelton, Sarah S. K.: 93
Shen-yang, China: *see* Mukden
Sherman House (Chicago): 159
Shouse, Jouett: 160
Show business: 77
Shriners: 193; convention of, 192
Shuler, Nelle R. (Mrs. Bob): 195
Shuler, Robert P. (Bob): 195
Siam: 66, 68, 86; monarchs of, 66
Siberia: 49, 106, 111, 144, 232
Sierra Nevada: 184
Sightseeing: 28, 185, 187
Silver, mining of: 186
Singapore: 211, 233
Sing Sing Prison: 162
Sioux Indians: 212
Sir Anthony (horse): 176
Skiatook, Okla.: 178
Sleep: 49, 52
Smell, sense of: 154
Smith, Alfred E., Jr.: 6, 7, 36, 75, 106, 128, 150, 152, 155-56, 161, 169; and Empire State Building, 28
Smith College: 156
Smoot, Reed: 9, 84
Smuggling: 224
Snodgrass, Fred C.: 138
Sobriety: 24
Socialists: 11, 33
Society: 32, 33
Sociology: 171
Solomon, Alaska: 52
Sons (novel): 211
Sophistication: 27
South (as region of U. S.): 2, 39, 56, 74, 140, 182, 206
South Africa: 163, 170, 180
South America: 19, 100, 129, 178, 197, 208, 211, 231, 232; aviation in, 17
South Bend, Ind.: 12
Southern California: 158
Southern California, University of: 13-14, 126, 223, 239
South Pole: 230
Southwest (as region of U. S.): 76, 216, 228
Spain: 62, 66, 84, 129, 155; republicans in, 1; people of, 135; colonies of, 235
Spanish-American War: 21
Speakeasies: 109
Speaker, Tristram E. (Tris): 72, 137
Speakers: 195, 236-37; after-dinner, 13, 82, 136
Speeches: 43, 194; *see also* Oratory
Spoilers (novel): 215
Sports: 138, 173
Sportsmanship, in politics: 200
Sportswriters: 138
Stalactites and stalagmites: 30
Stalin, Josef: 44, 102-103
State Fair (film): 188

278